A Right to Sing the Blues

A Right to Sing the Blues

African Americans, Jews,
and American Popular Song

JEFFREY MELNICK

HARVARD UNIVERSITY PRESS
Cambridge, Massachusetts
London, England
1999

For Rachel and Jake, with love and admiration

Library of Congress Cataloging-in-Publication Data

Melnick, Jeffrey Paul.
 A right to sing the blues : African Americans, Jews, and American
popular song / Jeffrey Melnick.
     p.   cm.
 Includes bibliographical references and index.
 ISBN 0-674-76976-7 (alk. paper)
 1. Popular music—United States—History and criticism.
2. Afro-Americans—Music—History and criticism. 3. Jews—United
States—Music—History and criticism. I. Title.
ML3477.M45   1999
781.64′089′924073—dc21   98-33877

Contents

Acknowledgments

Writing a book has its intrinsic rewards, but they are not always right at hand. Getting to the thank-you stage, however, is one of the real treats. From dedicated archivists to scholars and critics who responded to my unsolicited letters, it has been gratifying to discover how many people in and around academia really do believe that scholarship should be a collective process instead of a solitary endeavor. Although I did not always appreciate it at the time, I have been lucky to come in contact with numerous people whose enthusiasm played a major part in getting me through.

I have benefited from the expert assistance of librarians at Harvard's Theatre Collection, as well as throughout the Harvard library system. This book first saw light as a dissertation in the American Civilization program at Harvard, and I am thankful to have found support there to do interdisciplinary work. I am especially grateful to the department's administrator, Christine McFadden, for so much good talk and help over the years.

Catherine Clinton probably will not remember this, but she gave me the initial idea for this book when I was a teaching assistant for her some years ago. Others at Harvard (including some visitors) who have been generous with their time and ideas are Thomas Cripps, Robert Bone, and Emily Miller Budick. Dick Newman at the Du Bois Institute has been especially helpful in many ways. I consider myself very lucky while at Harvard to have been taught by Barbara Rosenkrantz. At Harvard I was also a member of the History and Literature writing group, which was sustaining; I thank Tom Augst and Dan Morris for all their encouragement. Paul Franklin gets my thanks for challenging me to think through some of my conclusions as far as possible. I am also grateful to Dan Miller, a good friend all through graduate school, who managed to make sure I saw the humor in things. Heather Hathaway and Rosemary Crockett, too, made things much more bearable during those years.

More recently, I have been fortunate to come to know my Trinity colleague and good friend Cheryl Greenberg, who also works on Black-Jewish relations, and whose sense of humor and keen insights have added much to the final stages of my work. At Trinity, Barbara Sicherman has also been a great friend and adviser. Among other colleagues at Trinity who have made my time there so wonderful, special thanks are due to Ron Thomas, Michelle Cliff, Jan Cohn, Jerry Watts, Gayle Wald, and Fred Pfeil. I am also truly indebted to Margaret Grasso and Kimberly Janczuk for all their help.

Scholars who have responded kindly to my inquiries deserve my sincere thanks as well: Hasia Diner, Robert Dawidoff, Jerry Hirsch, Eric Lott, and Mark Slobin especially. Jules Chametzky has also gone above and beyond the call of duty to read my work. Lois Rudnick has been a great friend whose enthusiasm is inspiring. Matt Jacobson and Judy Smith read and commented on the manuscript, for which I am grateful; even more so, they, along with Jim Smethurst, have provided me with extraordinary models of how to combine teaching, scholarship, and parenting. In addition, I thank Michael Rogin, Hazel Carby, and the two anonymous readers for Harvard University Press, along with editors Lindsay Waters, Kim Steere, and Amanda Heller for helping me figure out how to get this book done as best it could be.

My parents have been tremendously encouraging, in a variety of ways, all through this long haul. My mother and Len have helped keep me excited about the project; my father and Noreen have been wonderful supporters all along, and I appreciate that they too seem to think it is okay to have piles of books in many places. Memories of my remarkable grandmother, Sara Cohen, have always been with me. I am blessed with great siblings: my sister, Debby, and my brothers, David and Dan, have, for a long time, been my most important teachers and my most reliable support system. "In-law" always struck me as a weird usage: Hillary Kramer and Karen Bernstein have been good friends—much more than "sister-in-law" communicates. And Tasha and Jaden make me laugh and make me proud. Old friends have been an important part of this effort, too, even though we live so far away from one another. I hope that Gary Wilder, Scott Fabozzi, and Audrey Glassman know how much they mean to me. My newer friend Cindy Weisbart brings much good talk and great spirit to my life.

Early in my graduate career I had the rare good luck to take a course, and then read for my orals, with Leo Marx. Anyone who has been a student of his knows that he is one of the great teachers, and I offer a special thank-you here to him. At a point when I was not sure that I wanted to continue with my studies, he helped show me why scholarship might matter, and even more significant yet, reminded me why good teaching is the heart of this whole endeavor. This brings me to Werner Sollors. I doubt that I can communicate just how deeply I appreciate his help over the years, but I want, at least, to try. From line-by-line editing to broad questions, research hints, and professional advice, he has been a model adviser to me; even more, he has been warm and good-natured throughout, for which he deserves a prize.

Finally there are Jacob Rubin, Jessie Rubin, and Rachel Rubin. Jacob is the most lovely boy and the most searching questioner I have ever known. Between the ages of six and seven he refused the logic of a children's book which compared African American enslavement to the experience of biblical Jews, *and* saw links tying the Passover story to the history of the Underground Railroad; this helped remind me of the complicated power of Black-Jewish relations. Jessie appeared during the final stages of this book's evolution and brought her own party: she is my joy and my hope. Rachel Rubin is my best friend and my most important academic role model. While we have collaborated explicitly on a few projects, Rachel's influence saturates all of my teaching and scholarship. It is an understatement to say that I could not have done this without her help as a reader, critic of received wisdom, and storehouse of knowledge. These words on a page could never show how much I love her.

Introduction: The Languages of Black-Jewish Relations

In the winter of 1965 LeRoi Jones, Archie Shepp, Larry Rivers, and Jonas Mekas participated in a panel discussion about Black Power at the Village Vanguard, New York's famed jazz club. Mekas, a filmmaker, and Rivers, a painter—along with many audience members—wanted to know from Jones, the playwright and poet (soon to change his name to Amiri Baraka), and Shepp, the jazz saxophonist, what they could contribute to the Black Power movement. The answer repeatedly given to these white panelists and audience members was that there was no role for them.[1]

Someone in the crowd finally brought up the names of Andrew Goodman and Michael Schwerner, two young Jewish men who had been killed alongside James Chaney, an African American, in Mississippi during the Freedom Summer of 1964. Didn't the ultimate sacrifice made by these two Jews say something about the willingness of white people—and particularly Jews—to put themselves on the line for African Americans? Jones and Shepp still would not relent: while honoring Chaney's martyrdom, Jones refused to grant the same status to Goodman and Schwerner, calling them "artifacts," and paintings on the wall.[2]

I begin with this moment of public conversation between African Americans and Jews because it emphasizes two major truths about what we have come to call "Black-Jewish relations." First of all, this painful encounter reminds us that "Black-Jewish relations" is, above all, a story which is constructed at just those critical moments when conflict between *particular* African Americans and Jews creates the need for a general chronicle which will explain why things have come to this turn. At times such as these (for example, the late 1960s or the early 1990s), a number of explanations are developed which can explain what has gone on between Jewish Americans and African Americans up until that very instant. Idealized versions read current problems as mere blips on the screen of fruitful alliance; darker accounts announce either that Jews should stop feeling guilty and leave African Americans behind already, or start feeling guilty (for instance, about the slave trade) and begin to make reparations. Our best understanding of "Black-Jewish relations" begins when we first acknowledge that the powerful hold this construction has on our imagination comes from its narrative capability; "Black-Jewish relations," in other words, has the potential to organize quite a lot of diffuse material into a coherent story which has a great plot.

For instance, the specific genealogy of Black-Jewish relations which developed in the 1960s is fairly easy to explain when we take a look at the stated agendas of those most responsible for supporting this cultural work. What the participants in these exchanges in the 1960s and early 1970s shared, with important exceptions here and there, was an interventionist stance: these books and conferences were meant to be palliative. But if such projects were going to be able to maintain their own political energy—if they were to continue to make sense as activist enterprises with "reconciliation" as their goal—they required as an adjunct the creation of a history of the tradition to which they made at least implicit reference in present discussions.

In this light it is important to remember that although it seems to have been born in some far-distant past, it is only since the late 1960s or so that the phrase "Black-Jewish" (as in "relations") has carried the awesome adjectival power it now has for journalists, politicians, and academics alike. Before this time, while considerable attention had been paid to various aspects of the relationship between African Americans and Jews, there had been few systematic attempts to understand a unique area of social activity which could be marked off with such a label; previous discussions were ad hoc and circumstantial.

But then a series of events starting in the mid-1960s revealed deep differences and sometimes outright hostility between the two groups: evidence was found everywhere, most of all in the reactions of African Americans to the 1967 Middle East war, the fragmentation of SNCC (Student Nonviolent Coordinating Committee), and the Ocean Hill–Brownsville school crisis. This ostensibly unprecedented rift between African Americans and Jews called forth a flurry of symposia and printed anthologies, articles, and monographs, whose number did not begin to dwindle until the late 1970s.[3] The early 1990s gave rise to a revival of interest in the subject which promised to surpass the first wave in volume and intensity. Interestingly, while contemporary accounts of Black-Jewish relations do tend to take some notice of the early days of intergroup alliance, they also telescope the most significant interaction into the years of the most public civil rights activism (say, roughly 1954–1968). This is as true of right-wing scholars such as Benjamin Ginsberg, who seeks only to encourage Jews to detach themselves from any involvement with African Americans, as it is of Henry Louis Gates, Jr., who has come to personify moderate rationality on this issue.[4]

The Village Vanguard Speak-Out is also paradigmatic because it allowed its participants to process the relative suffering of African Americans and Jews in the confines of a jazz club. The expansive world of popular culture has been a major site for just the kind of discussion which Jones and Shepp took control of in the Village Vanguard. In this book I trace in detail how Jews and African Americans have organized the evidence of their oppression to make public arguments about their relationship to each other and to the American nation at large. I am especially interested in examining how Jews have orchestrated the concept of pain to explain why they are so attracted to, and so good at expressing, recognizably Black cultural forms.

In a fascinating chapter on Black-Jewish relations in his book on Jesse Jackson (1986), the political scientist Adolph Reed, Jr., wisely focuses on "ambiguity" as a key term for discussing the subject, but stumbles when he suggests that recognition "of this ambiguity is limited by a ritualistic pattern of discussion of black/Jewish relations that obscures the dynamics joining the groups." The guiding assumption of *A Right to Sing the Blues* is that more than anything else, "Black-Jewish relations" *is* "a ritualistic pattern of discussion." Whereas Reed notes with distress that Jews have been able to steer "dialogue" on the major issues of Black-Jewish relations from two supposedly different sides (because they have played such major roles in African American civic organizations), the central assumption of this book is that "Black-Jewish relations" needs to be approached—not exclusively, but still significantly—as a story told *by* Jews *about* interracial relations.[5]

In other words, the beginning premise here is that "Black-Jewish relations" is a language spoken by many—but most frequently and most powerfully by Jews. Despite, or maybe because of, this dominance, some of the most interesting moments in its history have come when African Americans were able to insert themselves into this dialogue. The basic plot of "Black-Jewish relations," as I understand it, is about the comparative suffering of Jews and Blacks. Retellings are pervasive, ranging from children's books to advocacy group publicity releases to the frequent discussions of why Don Byron, now generally known as an African American jazz clarinetist, likes to play klezmer, originally a Jewish wedding music. (Some say he relates to the pain of Jews and hears that pain in both jazz and klezmer; *I* say he likes the great clarinet parts and wonder why he is never understood as a klezmer musician who found his way to jazz.)[6]

Scholars too have rehearsed the story of Black-Jewish relations often, mostly with an eye on the "political" alliances of the two groups. A laudable desire to see African Americans and Jews work together on a number of organized political fronts has helped to set the dominant interpretive turn as a fairly standard version of after-the-fall rhetoric: once there was a great alliance of Jews and African Americans, but it has been disturbed. Such tellings of Black-Jewish relations represent an extreme case of what Raymond Williams has called a selective tradi-tion—"an intentionally selective version of a shaping past and a pre-shaped present, which is then powerfully operative in the process of social and cultural definition and identification."[7]

These accounts, from magazine articles to scholarly monographs, have homed in on the "shared oppression" experienced by Jews and African Americans—an analogy revitalized in the wake of the Nazi genocide—which inevitably brought them together to work for social justice. This collective narrative begins with references to the sympathy

African American slaves felt toward Old Testament Jews, makes note of the similar persecution of Jews in Europe and African Americans in the United States, and then moves on to the signing of the "call" in 1909 which led to the founding of the NAACP (National Association for the Advancement of Colored People); it travels through various civil rights and labor struggles of the 1920s, 1930s, and 1940s, culminating in *Brown v. Board of Education* in 1954, and finds its sanctified apotheosis in the killings of Goodman, Chaney, and Schwerner in 1964. The visible suffering of each group was indispensable to the creation of a vocabulary about their relationship, and analogy led to caricature as world history was reduced to a drawing of parallel lines.

This type of mythologizing has major roots in the Leo Frank case of 1913–1915. Frank, a Brooklyn Jew living in Atlanta, was tried and convicted for the murder of Mary Phagan, a young white woman who worked in the National Pencil Company factory he managed. The case pitted Frank against Jim Conley, an African American man who also worked in the factory, and who was the other major suspect in the crime.[8] This case has been invoked as a touchstone in various chronicles of Black-Jewish relations; in fact, the Frank case has become a conventional starting point for studies of organized alliance building between African Americans and Jews. David Levering Lewis offers the most influential claim for beginning inquiries into the subject with Leo Frank. In the Frank case Lewis discovers the moment when aloof and conservative Jewish leaders, shocked by the recognition that "an established Jewish merchant could be more vulnerable than a black janitor," belatedly threw in their lot with fellow-suffering African Americans.[9] Lewis makes a major contribution here to our understanding of how a very specific enterprise (mostly the joint activity of advocacy groups) has come to stand for the entire shared landscape of African Americans and Jews. But if Lewis is correct to note that one legacy of the Frank case was to bring well-placed Jews and African Americans together, he ignores his own hint by leaving the case behind before coming to terms with what is to be found *within* it.

The Leo Frank case demonstrates that surface similarities in the suffering of African Americans and Jews cannot always cover up deep differences. It was only after the death of Frank—and a defusing and reconfiguration of Jewish concerns around the case—that scripts of

Black-Jewish kinship came to prominence. Before this time the case was marked by intense conflict between Jews and African Americans: not quite a zero-sum game of racial partisanship, but not so far off either.[10] Frank and Conley were imagined by many to be in poisonously close contact with each other; they appeared to be involved together in activities which marginalized both. Rather than the utopian possibilities so often presented by "Black-Jewish relations," the Frank case promoted the provocative notion that this specialized interracial association functioned mostly to advance illicit, or at least unhealthy, social behaviors. It was only after the lynching of Frank in the summer of 1915 (inspired by the commutation of his death sentence by Governor John Slaton) that his tribulations could evolve into a text of unity for African Americans and Jews. The commonsense understanding of Black-Jewish relations as being rooted in shared suffering is undone by the Frank case. This case should, in fact, compel us to reconsider whether *any* summary of Black-Jewish relations can maintain a meaningful relationship to the local events, beliefs, and behaviors which it purports to represent. The Leo Frank case supplies an example of how African Americans and Jews have been related, but not simply as allies; it also demonstrates that surface similarities in the suffering of African Americans and Jews cannot always cover up deep differences.

In the first major wave of inquiry (roughly 1965–1984) into Black-Jewish relations, shared suffering was often a given. Even so, much valuable work was done in this era: the list of important contributions would certainly include the major monographs written by Hasia Diner (1977) and Robert Weisbord and Arthur Stein (1970); essays by Philip Foner (1975), Eugene Levy (1974), and David Levering Lewis (1984); collections edited by Nat Hentoff (1969) and Shlomo Katz (1966); and dissertations by Isabel Price (1973) and Steven Bloom (1973). All of these contributed extensively to our understanding of how Jews and African Americans have come together in the United States.[11] Taken together, however, the yield has been a vision of Black-Jewish relations as a logically unfolding story of intergroup contact which ends up where it is supposed to—in the here and now, whatever we take that to be: Black-Jewish relations as a given set of social circumstances, easily stitched together into a meaningful pattern. This is true too of more recent work done in the field, whether in edited collections put together by Jack Salzman and Paul Berman, or monographs by Laurence Thomas and Murray Friedman.[12] The most pernicious academic work—by Benjamin Ginsberg and Tony Martin, among others—sees conspiracy where advocates see alliance.[13]

I ask whether "Black-Jewish relations" can ever be satisfactorily understood through any kind of totalizing rendering of actual events. Instead, what if we begin with the idea that all the talk about the relationship of African Americans and Jews constitutes the primary materials of Black-Jewish relations. What happens when "Black-Jewish relations" is taken to be a figure of speech, a way of talking about many things—including, but not limited to, the relationship of African Americans and Jews? I argue in this book that there is no definite field of activity which *is* Black-Jewish relations. For instance, when Amy Jacques-Garvey complained in the *Negro World* in 1923 about a *kosher* butcher in New York who was overcharging African American customers for *pork chops*, it was not completely clear what aspect of this was "Black-Jewish relations." The actual sale of the underweight "pork chops"? The journalistic accounting of it? The entire field of economic activity linking Jews and African Americans in New York City?

In the last decades of the nineteenth century and the first few of the twentieth, efforts were made on various fronts to describe the relationship of African Americans and Jews. These years were marked by the first extensive contacts between the two groups, as eastern European Jews immigrated to the United States in massive numbers and African Americans began to migrate to urban areas (and northern cities in particular). Before this, of course, a set of rhetorical usages had already linked the experiences of African American slaves to Old Testament Jews. Albert Raboteau has nicely summarized how enslaved African Americans articulated "their sense of historical identity as a people" by "incorporating as part of their mythic past" the story of the Exodus of Jews from Egypt.[14] The biblical parallels had great staying power, as an African American writer from around the turn of the century revealed in comparing biblical Jews to present-day African Americans moving to the North: "Just as the Jews plodded their way over mountains, across rivers, through valleys and burning plains in quest of a better country, so the Negro leaving home wants a better country now."[15]

Exhibit A in the display of symbolic cultural associations was the language of the spirituals, many of which invoked Old Testament characters and stories as they developed the trope of "shared oppression." But it should also be noted, as Lawrence Levine has shown (with no causal relationship implied), that by the time African Americans came into extensive contact with Jews in America, the Old Testament language of the spirituals was beginning to give way to the New Testament orientation of gospel music.[16] This should remind us that figurations of historical sameness signify but are not static: instead of simply celebrating or burying them, we need to begin examining with great care how they evolved and what their consequences have been.

This accessible comparison of African Americans and Jews was only the first of many ways in which the two groups were linked in the United States. Inspired by the biblical analogy, a new rhetorical correlation matured in the 1880s and 1890s (with a major boost from the African American press), which began from the proposition that the two groups had endured similar afflictions in the past. A typical rendering of this insight can be found in Charles Chesnutt's 1899 short story "Her Virginia Mammy." Here a putatively "white" dance instructor ponders her decision to take on African American students: "She knew that several of the more fashionable dancing-schools tabooed all pupils, singly or in classes, who labored under social disabilities—and this included the people of at least one other race who were vastly farther along in the world than the colored people of the community where Miss Hohlfelder lived."[17] Images of corresponding woe have shown exceptional endurance; witness Zora Neale Hurston's mocking essay "What White Publishers Won't Print" (1950). Hurston argues that "romantic stories about Negroes and Jews" are hard to place because publishers "feel that they know the public indifference to such works, unless the story or play involves racial tension. It can then be offered as a study in Sociology with the romantic side subdued."[18] Flipping the analogy sunny-side up, W. E. B. Du Bois noted in *The Nation* in 1926 that the same three women's colleges which had the highest percentages of Jewish students also received African American women with "tolerance and even cordiality."[19] This is hardly to say that nobody noticed the major differences in the status (and safety) of Jews and African Americans in the United States. It might be worth mentioning at this point one effective (if not necessarily intentional) deflation of the "shared oppression" motif which is found at the beginning of Karl Shapiro's poem "University" (1942): "To hurt the Negro and avoid the Jew / Is the curriculum."[20] Pain and loneliness might be equivalent in the poet's universe, but to my mind "hurt" and "avoid" nicely underscore the difference between racial oppression and social discrimination.

From the ground of analogy it was an easy jump to the conclusion that Jews, because of their evident success in the United States, might serve as an example for African Americans. Evidence was located which suggested that even though Jews, like African Americans, suffered from intolerance in the United States, they still managed to improve their social status. Philip Foner has pointed out that by the turn of the century, many African Americans deduced that Jews had been able, to a large extent, to triumph over their persecutors; African American newspapers made it something of a habit to run editorials titled "Let Us Learn from the Jews," or some variant thereof.[21] The Jewish example was generally encouraging to African Americans, hinting as it did that sheer stamina, racial cohesion, and economic assertiveness could lead them also to improve their situation in the United States.

African American papers began drawing this conclusion as early as 1883. David Hellwig writes that by 1890 the *Southern Christian Recorder* was able to codify this wisdom into "seven practices" by which Jews had ameliorated the effects of persecution: "If the Jew has changed his condition by these rules, the Negro can change his."[22] African Americans, Hellwig goes on to note, were particularly impressed by instances when Jews used their economic power to trump anti-Semites, as when they bought hotels in Saratoga, New York, to bypass exclusionary policies which developed there in the late 1870s.[23]

Perhaps the most oft-cited case of an African American pointing to Jews as a positive example comes from a passage in Booker T. Washington's *The Future of the American Negro* (1899):

> We have a very bright and striking example in the history of the Jews in this and other countries. There is, perhaps, no race that has suffered so much, not so much in America as in some of the countries in Europe. But these people have clung together. They have had a certain amount of unity, pride, and love of race; and, as the years go

on, they will be more and more influential in this country,—a country where they were once despised, and looked upon with scorn and derision. It is largely because the Jewish race has had faith in itself. Unless the Negro learns more and more to imitate the Jew in these matters, to have faith in himself, he cannot expect to have any high degree of success.[24]

Rhetorical moments such as this have talismanic force in recent narratives of Black-Jewish relations; oftentimes they are smugly invoked as confirmation that once, in a happier past, African Americans were able to transcend the "dubious" attractions of their racial specificity in order to acknowledge and embrace their likeness to Jews. This overemphasis on historical intergroup similarity has energized one of the most disturbing trends in recent years within the discourse of Black-Jewish relations—the practice whereby Jewish neoconservatives interpret the "failure" of this alliance as a result of a betrayal by African Americans who refuse the terms of the analogy.

As a popular rhetorical formation, "Black-Jewish relations" has privileged racial-historical analogy over class disparity. Embedded within the most available narrative of Black-Jewish relations is a romantic tale about the relative unimportance of class status in melting pot America. This is not to say that class is never spoken in "Black-Jewish relations"; quite to the contrary, "Black-Jewish relations" itself argues for the utopian (post-class or trans-class) possibilities of liberal democracy.

The anthropologist Sherry Ortner has argued in a very different context that for certain people, "talking about Jewishness and non-Jewishness" is one compelling way of talking about class.[25] If "Jewish" codes monetary comfort (if not properly aristocratic behavior) in the United States, "Black" is surely its opposite number, the customary American way of discussing poverty. What the rhetorical figure of "Black-Jewish relations" implies, therefore, is a triumph of racial/ethnic similitude over class differences. This is, perhaps, the most remarkable achievement of the discourse of "Black-Jewish relations": by the 1950s, as economic disparity and their very different levels of cultural power began to drive African Americans and Jews apart—in terms of geography and so much else—"Black-Jewish relations" remained capable of explaining the relationship of these two groups as natural and abiding. Even while a few critics and historians try to reinject class into the discussion—David Levering Lewis and Tom Wolfe come to mind—it has remained nearly impossible to talk about Black-Jewish relations as anything other than a triumph of ethnic pluralism.[26] Like desirable real estate, a primary appeal of "Black-Jewish relations" is its location: the sunniest and most attractive visions of Black-Jewish relations have derived from the activities of political and civic groups positioned in the middle of the left and in the middle class.

If "Black-Jewish relations" has told a story about class in American culture, it has also articulated major concerns about masculinity and sexuality. Women have been relatively absent from the standard chronicles, most likely because their presence would demand that some attention be paid to the potentially deal-breaking areas of miscegenation and domestic labor relations. The conversations which constitute Black-Jewish relations have generally taken place between representatives of male-dominated secular and religious organizations, who, not surprisingly, understood the subject matter to be themselves. These public discussions established that Black-Jewish relations dwelled in public, and they have drawn attention away from the troublesome reality that one important point of contact for Jews and African Americans has been the employment of African American women as domestics in the privacy of Jewish homes, particularly via the notoriously exploitative "Bronx Slave Market" of the 1930s, where African American women were often constrained to accept absurdly low wages for a long day's work. Even broad positive interactions of African Americans and Jews in labor unions could not efface the particularized difficulties which obtained in the context of work.[27]

A common response to such concerns, then, has been to order Black-Jewish relations around a vision of public male affiliation and, definitionally, to exclude private sexual interactions. Yet, in order to enclose and codify all of the complicated intergroup energy flowing between African Americans and Jews without making reference to women and gay men, it has been necessary to develop a masculinized grammar of group relations which is up to the task. Not surprisingly, that construct which we call "Black-Jewish relations" has never been able to contain all the activity it is called upon to arrange, and so the semiofficial chartering and maintenance of this association has been accompanied by an intense sexualization of the relationship between "straight" African American and Jewish men. While most of the architects of the official, safe version of relations between the two groups avoid calling attention to any examples of bodily closeness, except for the sanctioned all-male kind, this approach has never been able to eliminate competing, less comfortable ideas about the relationship.

The major thrust of this book will be to examine how Jews, African Americans, and others have discussed the relationship of the two groups. *A Right to Sing the Blues* asks how African Americans and Jews (frequently through their diverse public images as "Blackness" and "Jewishness") have been paired—as partners or competitors or some blend thereof—within the controlling American racial system of Black and white. This book assumes that some kind of special relationship has linked African Americans and Jews—which implies a type of Jewish exceptionalism with respect to African Americans. Even so, this volume aims to enter wider discussions about the ways in which white racial formation depends on concepts and structures of Black and white racial identity.[28]

Above all, I am interested in tracing how Jewish musicians, with fluctuating levels of confidence, learned to use their access *as Jews* to African Americans and Black music as evidence of their racial health—that is, of their whiteness. What is most stunning about this cultural work is that the musicians in question were able to situate Jewishness as a kind of white identity—a kind that today we would call ethnic—in an age when this was very much in doubt. Leo Frank, for instance, insisted in many ways that he was white, but his audience did not necessarily believe him. Frank's position in the factory seemed dangerous to many, but he never seemed to understand that he was being called on to deny or veil—not flaunt—his power.

His fellow Jews in the music world were much better able to hide their power and thus find more comfortable places in the social order. In a variety of ways, music industry figures such as Irving Berlin, George Gershwin, Harold Arlen, Al Jolson, and the Witmark brothers established Jewish agility at expressing and disseminating Black sounds and themes as a product of Jewish suffering and as a variant of Jewish cultural nationalism. In direct competition with the Black cultural nationalism of Harlem in the 1920s and 1930s, these Jews (and many other lesser lights) organized Broadway and Tin Pan Alley as central sites of Jewish cultural production.

By the 1930s, I will argue, it had come to seem natural to many observers that Jews should have become the "best"—and best-rewarded—makers of "Black" art. This was the result of a loosely organized group of Jews learning how to organize Black-Jewish relations for their own good—and only incidentally for the good of African Americans. Where Leo Frank denied contact with African Americans as he tried to demonstrate his healthy whiteness, the Jews of Tin Pan Alley figured out how to use their seeming closeness to African American people and expressive forms as proof of their racial fitness.

Of central concern here is how blackface minstrelsy was translated into a modern form by Jews in the early decades of this century. An interest in modern adaptations of blackface by Jews also informs the recent work of Michael Rogin, whose book on blackface in the movies is a major innovation in Black-Jewish studies; differing from Rogin in emphasis, I try to investigate not only how Blackness has come to function as cultural capital, but also how Jewishness itself works in a related fashion.[29] More specifically, I ask not only how "Black-Jewish relations" comes to have such effectivity, but also why—once it is established as currency—it gets spent as it does. The pivotal questions here are about agency: Who is authorized to speak "Black-Jewish relations"? And to what ends?

This volume asks how Jews in the era of Leo Frank's lynching came to promote successfully the idea that their special status in the United States was of value. Was it as a race? (In a 1926 article the ethnologist Lothrop Stoddard suggested that because Jews believe "themselves to be a race, [they] have constantly tended to create one.")[30] Or was it, as Hasia Diner has wisely suggested, exactly in their role as advocates of the social advancement of African Americans that Jews would demonstrate their social worth?[31]

Along this line, one goal of the present study is to place Black-Jewish relations into the context of Black-white relations more generally, in order to come to terms with the slippery category of the "white ethnic."[32] In this age, many Jews wondered as they wandered: How could they best convince the mainstream public that their hazy racial status was a strength, a sign of group health, and, most of all, a desirable commodity?[33] My central contention is that Jews in the music business used their privileged positions to make a number of clear arguments about their status as Jews, and did so particularly by situating themselves at the center of what most people understood to be "Black" music.

To make my case, I first explore how Jews established the world of popular music as a proper place to be having these conversations (Chapter 1); next I discuss the institution of racial "mixedness" as a key term for understanding Jewish success in African American music (Chapter 2). Chapter 3 is concerned with the Jewish translation of stage minstrelsy into purely musical forms and into "offstage" modes of behavior; this section examines especially how Jewish men used Black looks and sounds to shore up their own masculinity. Overt masculinity was effaced in another major project of the era (roughly 1890–1935), which I call the sacralization of Jews in Black music. In Chapter 5 I examine this major public relations effort, whose main goal was to naturalize the presence of Jews in Black music by suggesting that they came to it because as Jews they had special access to the music of the oppressed. This chapter follows one on James Weldon Johnson (Chapter 4), the main goal of which is to show how this influential African American leader helped rationalize the place of Jews in Black music.

Although I make no effort within these pages to fix Black-Jewish relations, I am interested in bringing to light the complex flaws written into the linear and theologically inflected account of political alliance into which almost all the other dimensions of intergroup activity have been folded. The flattening-out of the complicated relationship has wrought some bad effects. By positing the alliances forged between Jewish and African American social advocacy groups as the core of this relationship, the available narrative makes things look too simple, for these organizations already have the apparatus (and the will) necessary for negotiating settlements. A narrative which insists that the formation of these semiofficial alliances is organic communicates a degree of "relatedness" between Jews and African Americans which cannot possibly be assimilated into the complicated lived experiences of all who are supposed to be represented by it. This generalizing tendency is augmented by the publication of very personal testimony of certain privileged individuals—as in the dialogue which Michael Lerner and Cornel West have published under the title *Jews and Blacks*—which assumes that Black-Jewish relations can be defined (and fixed) by role models who talk *better* than those Jews and Blacks who are "ruining" the relationship.[34] Insisting too much on likeness, and too much on rationality, contributes to a cycle in which unrealistic expectation gives way to facile despair. This despair is then cynically manipulated by a rogues' gallery of self-aggrandizing ethnic chauvinists who strip-mine it for the sensational sound bites it offers.

Instead, I want to examine the robust ambivalences which characterize the various associated discourses which together make up Black-Jewish relations. Primarily I want to establish that framing those instances of "actual" contact which have constituted traditional narratives of Black-Jewish relations (for example, in civil rights groups and labor unions) is a prevailing belief that African Americans and Jews are somehow "related" through their history, race, and social status.

Let me return to the Village Vanguard in 1965. At a particularly hot moment in the conversation, a Jewish audience member pleaded with the African American panelists to say what a Jew could do for Black Power. LeRoi Jones responded very simply: "Die Baby. All you can do for me is die."[35] What if we stop insisting that this kind of utterance represents a "break" in the proper unfolding of Black-Jewish relations? What if, instead, we begin by taking this as a classic expression of that habit of speech we have come to call "Black-Jewish relations"? Doing so might help us to understand that one dominant (if misleading) conception which supports Black-Jewish relations is that Jews do indeed "die," or at least suffer quite a bit, to make Black art—the "paintings on the wall" of Jones's description.

1

"Yiddle on Your Fiddle": The Culture of Black-Jewish Relations

During the World War I era many American Jews decided that they were in a special relationship with African Americans. With this dawning realization came a more active effort to rationalize the internal dynamics and public image of Black-Jewish relations. Some important African American political and cultural leaders joined this vital, if diffuse, campaign to link the two groups. A crucial site for this activity was the music business.

These years were truly epochal for the music industry, encompassing the rise and fall of pianistic ragtime music; the ascendancy of ragtime song and its almost imperceptible translation into "Tin Pan Alley" as it combined with sentimental balladry and other related forms; a blues craze; and finally the fuller elaboration of instrumental jazz. Each of these categories was, and to some extent remains, ill defined. Additionally, while it is now likely a cliché to describe popular music as a fierce battleground in these years for the working-out of class, race, gender, and sexual identities, it is an understated one all the same.

The musical relationship of African Americans and Jews was most often expressed in metaphoric terms, terms which often obscured actual moments of contact. The initial figurative explanation of the correspondence between African American and Jewish American musical expressions suggested that since Jews and African Americans had parallel histories of suffering, it was natural that their music should demonstrate a marked similarity.

The field of popular music accommodated appeals to a deeply meaningful similarity between the two groups; these apparent similarities helped call attention away from the multiple aspects of difference (especially class difference) which separated the two groups. The metaphor of musical sameness, while shot through with ambivalence, was so often repeated and innovated upon that what began as a comparison of two distinct if related groups developed at times into an emblem of pure identification. While the Leo Frank case of 1913–1915 found Jews unprepared to explain their relationship to African Americans, the music world afforded more relaxed and congenial opportunities to do this work.

Popular music in this era came to serve as one of the sturdiest foundations for a deeply held belief among Jews—described succinctly in a different context by Cynthia Ozick—that "there are Jews everywhere, and some of them are black."[1] Ozick's point here is to note that a very fragile conceptual base undergirds a relationship which has often been seen as inevitable and natural. She is also aware that the rhetoric of fusion has been most often promoted by Jews unaware of, or unwilling to accept, the significance of the social differences which have separated the two groups, Jews who have been shocked to discover that African Americans do not always accept the terms of the construct.

Certainly many people did dissent from the narrative of kinship which dominated these years. But overall there was a remarkable degree of consensus regarding the natural affinity of African Americans and Jews in the sphere of musical production. To understand the unreasonably high expectations Jews and African Americans have had of each other, we will need to explore moments and places of actual contact which advanced the idea that it made sense to consider the two groups (or "representative" members) relationally. David Levering Lewis and others have focused on how "elite" African Americans and Jews created a sense of alliance through personal contacts made in philanthropic and civil rights work.[2] Yet these "actual" physical meetings are only one part of (perhaps even one result of) a dynamic set of rhetorical practices and lived experiences which served to bring African Americans and Jews together. The best place to view the workings of the engine of analogy is in the popular music business of the first three decades of the twentieth century.

No simple narrative of colonial exploitation can possibly do justice to the dynamics of African Americans and Jews in the world of popular music in the age of ragtime and jazz; Jewish involvement in the business of promoting, adapting, and creating music popularly recognized as "Negro" was too multivalent for such a one-dimensional explanation. In large numbers Jewish men and women made careers—as performers, songwriters, music publishers, agents, club owners, critics, publicists, and fiction writers—which depended on African American music.[3] To understand this cultural saturation, it is important to take ragtime, jazz, blues, and show music all together—even if this is jarring to our current musicological grasp of the distinctness of these forms. The word "jazz" did not enter the public consciousness in any significant way until the end of World War I, although it certainly was in the process of development much earlier;[4] "ragtime" was used well into the 1920s and beyond to signify productions which today might be called Tin Pan Alley, musical comedy, show music, or even jazz. Al Jolson appeared as the "jazz" singer in the 1927 movie of that name and sang songs which fit no category of jazz as we now understand it.

The looseness of definition characterizing discussions of popular music helped outsiders rationalize their appropriations of African American music. We can certainly take comfort at this point in making sure to differentiate between "the melting-pot music of the Jazz Age" and the more authentic jazz of King Oliver, Jelly Roll Morton, Duke Ellington, and Fletcher Henderson, but we ought not to ignore that it took a long time for this distinction to have any real force in the marketplace or in critical study.[5]

It is also important to take ragtime and jazz together, since the rise of jazz led to a notable rewriting of ragtime history. As one historian has noted, "memories of ragtime fed upon surreal nostalgia" for the 1890s, which "had not been so gay" as these reconstructions would have it.[6] An approach which admits the relationship of ragtime and jazz without ignoring the real differences between them will facilitate the best appreciation of the complex analogies which grew up around African Americans and Jews.

So This Is Jazz: Sex, Cities, and Music

"I wanna make a lady out of jazz." So speaks Paul Whiteman, the putative "king" of jazz, as he plays himself in the 1945 film biography of George Gershwin, *Rhapsody in Blue*. In this loose, nostalgia-ridden version of Gershwin's life, Whiteman commissions Gershwin to write *Rhapsody in Blue* for one major reason: he has just witnessed an audience give a lukewarm reaction to Gershwin's *Blue Monday*, a "blues mini-op-era"—later called *135th Street*—in *George White's Scandals of 1922*, and he wants to cheer Gershwin up by convincing him that there is indeed a call for such highbrow adaptations of "lower" musical forms.[7] One obvious response begged by Whiteman's expression—which, as we will see, was hardly the first or last time such a sentiment was uttered—is: Who are you calling a whore?[8]

Discussions of African American music often hinge on the idea that it possesses a higher volume of libido than any competing cultural productions. As the story goes, the bold appearance of sex in the music cannot help but fascinate an unprepared white public; while response alternates predictably between attraction and repulsion, the most significant fact about this process of creation and reception is how habitual and self-perpetuating it is. Without fear, then, we might take as given that much of the early attention bestowed upon ragtime, jazz, and related musical forms had its basis in a concern with sex.

But even as the sexual components of ragtime and jazz were variously being celebrated and fretted over, so too were these new genres enshrined as the perfect expression of America's character—its fast-paced, machine-driven, modern face. MacDonald Smith Moore has helpfully pointed out that criticisms of jazz positioned it as at once representative of the "devolutionary forces of sensual Blackness" and "the antimusic of robots and riveting machines, the technology of urban civilization." In his preface to the stage version of *The Jazz Singer* (1925), Samson Raphaelson described the new music as reflecting the "vital chaos of America's soul"; one writer in the highbrow *Etude* magazine called jazz "the characteristic folk music of modernity."[9] Ragtime had been described frequently in very similar terms, usually with disdain.[10]

Criticisms of ragtime and jazz have often articulated a seeming contradiction: How could they suffer from both overt sensuousness and

mechanism? But these are really two sides of the same coin—the catas-
trophe of modern American city life. Modern music was at once redo-
lent of a racialness frequently imaged in sexual terms, while it was also
produced and marketed in urban centers, with the attendant images of
standardization and mechanization. Waldo Frank—one of the minority
party of secular Jews hostile to jazz—was also one of the very few
contemporary commentators able to articulate a link between the seemingly dissimilar themes of sexual license and modernization. In a 1925
essay for *The New Republic,* Frank called jazz the "music of a revolt that
fails" and insisted that it was "the song of our reaction from the dull
throb of the machine . . . This song is not an escape from the Machine
to the limpid depths of the soul. It is the Machine itself!" Frank admits
the sexual motif in jazz, but insists that it represents only "a moment's
gaiety, after which the spirit droops, cheated and unnurtured."[11] This
is not the threatening license usually depicted but a vague evocation of
pathetic and unsatisfying sexuality—defined, it seems, by images of
premature ejaculation and postcoital depression. Daniel Gregory Mason, a Yankee composer and music theorist, drew an even more explicit
cause-and-effect relationship: "Industrialism has provided widespread
fatigue: fatigue craves exaggerated physical stimuli combined with a
minimum appeal to the mind. Jazz provides both of these."[12]

In the welter of issues surrounding ragtime and jazz discourse, what
is least well understood is how the sexualized language which swarmed
about the music did its work. Few have wanted to consider the actual
demographics (particularly of northern urban centers) which led to the
sharing and appropriation of cultural materials. Not surprisingly, images of fusion were central to this universe of talk about music—and
they tell a particular tale about African Americans, Jews, and their
relation to each other.

In a book called *So This Is Jazz* (1926), one of the first extended
meditations on a music slowly coming to be understood as a distinct
genre, Henry Osgood suggested that Paul Whiteman be honored for
his pioneering work. Osgood's idea was to have a plaque installed
which would call attention to Whiteman's role in "*Making an Honest
Woman out of* JAZZ."[13] As with Whiteman's own lines from *Rhapsody in
Blue,* there are a number of contentions and slurs being made, most
notably that "jazz" before Whiteman was illegitimate, in need of

refinement—raw materials in need of proper masculine attention. The conductor Walter Damrosch employed a similar, if slightly more sophisticated, approach in his program notes for the 1925 New York debut of George Gershwin's Concerto in F. Damrosch describes the many "legitimate" composers who feared to become involved with jazz despite its international reputation: "Lady Jazz, adorned with her intriguing rhythms, has danced her way around the world . . . But for all her travels and her sweeping popularity, she has encountered no knight who could lift her to a level that would enable her to be received as a respectable member in the musical circles."[14] Again, the central imagery is of a ripe but unauthorized femininity, evoking the vaguely scandalous confines of the vaudeville theater or the dance hall; but this sexualizing of ragtime and jazz argued most of all that the origin point for these musical forms was the house of ill repute. Of course, the whole inclination to deride music was rooted in a popular belief that music belonged in the domain of women and disreputable men; as Jacques Barzun has written with only a smidgen of hyperbole, even as late as the 1920s music was considered the "occupation of wretched professionals and scheming young ladies."[15] Also important in this equation is the assumption that whatever men were involved with such a sordid business were likely to be racial or sexual outsiders of one sort or another.

Jazz and ragtime, as many people understood them, owed their existence to the sordid environment of the brothel. The music historian Neil Leonard has located this belief system as the primary cause of the hysteria around the rise of jazz, noting that likely "the most damaging association of 'jazz' was its identification with the brothel, usually the Negro brothel."[16] Following this line, Rabbi Stephen Wise suggested that when America regained its lost soul, jazz would "be relegated to the dark and scarlet haunts whence it came."[17]

It is tempting to explain the focus on brothels as a simple case of white people projecting their own sexual impulses onto Black music. Even so, brothels did play some role in the dissemination of African American popular music. Some music historians explain the importance of St. Louis and Sedalia, Missouri, to the development of ragtime piano by pointing to the large number of brothels in those cities offering employment to pianists. Likewise, most accounts of early jazz in New

Orleans make at least some mention of the significance of the artificially created vice district of Storyville for the growth of that style.[18]

The other social space which encouraged ideas about race mixing was the dance hall. Ragtime and jazz dance, not surprisingly, were frequently described in terms of sex.[19] The truly new aspect of these ragtime and jazz dances was the quite public claim of ownership made on them by African Americans in urban settings. Ragtime and jazz, and their dance counterparts, relied on visible African American players. In the dance world, white performers such as the husband and wife team of Vernon and Irene Castle (and later Fred and Adele Astaire) established careers by taking what was perceived as overt sexuality out of the supposedly freer African American dance forms.

The historian Lewis Erenberg has located a central figure for many of the anxieties surrounding the sexualness of the new dances in the person of the "tango pirate" (sometimes tellingly called the social gangster). The tango pirates, according to Erenberg, were lower-class men (often Italians or Jews) who attracted rich women at afternoon dances with their dancing skills. Bending the woman backward in the course of dancing, the tango pirate would enact the sexual domination which was still usually a man's prerogative, while remaining dependent on the monetary favors of his partner.[20] He was feared because he at once threatened women who did not "belong" to him—they were married, above his class, and unmistakably white—while also seducing men into copying his less than masculine ways. Tango pirates were seen to be at once aggressively lustful and effeminized; as Edward Marks noted with some disgust in 1934, these "lounge lizards" would grasp women tightly, push their shoulders down, and then "wriggle about."[21] Here, then, is a conflation—at least on the level of symbol—of dance, ethnicity, and sexual danger.

The idea of racial mixing through dance held utopian possibilities as well. At least as early as 1922, A. Philip Randolph's *Messenger* considered the cabaret (especially the provisionally unsegregated "black and tan") to be a "useful social institution" because it helped to break down the "psychology of caste."[22] The fullest statement of this optimistic approach came with Chandler Owen's article of 1925, "The Black and Tan Cabaret—America's Most Democratic Institution." In this essay Owen goes so far as to suggest that during the Chicago Riot of 1919 peace could be found only in the black and tan.[23] But this hopeful construal of the black and tan had its critics, especially among those who worried that it might function mostly to erase African Americans from the musical equation. The sharpest reproach came in Sterling Brown's poem "Cabaret," published in *Southern Road* (1932); as Sterling Stuckey notes, this poem sets the forced gaiety of a mixed club "against the rural tragedy of a desperate people in the terrible flood of 1927." "Cabaret" also invokes the cheery lyrics of popular Tin Pan Alley "Dixie" songs in order to argue that displays of racial mixing function mainly to deflect attention away from the realities of African American life.[24]

One reason why ragtime, jazz, and blues came to hold so much cultural energy in the early decades of the twentieth century is that they could incorporate these images of mixture. It would not be difficult to plot out a mythology of these forms from standard works which hinge on moments of cross-ethnic or interracial contact. High points might include the introduction of horns into the South by itinerant Mexican musicians; the training of ragtime pioneer Scott Joplin by a German piano teacher; the coercion of New Orleans Creoles, with their European musical backgrounds, to make musical union with "Negroes" by the more stringent racial laws of the 1890s; the diffusion of ragtime through its introduction to white audiences at the Chicago Exposition of 1893; not to mention the incursion of Jews into the music publishing business, which created a favorable climate for Jewish musicians to begin adapting the various urban musical forms surrounding them.[25] These examples bring us to around 1900 and would only multiply if we continued into the succeeding decades.

It was axiomatic to most early twentieth-century observers that popular music could not be understood outside the frame of melting pot ideology. In fact, American music stood as Exhibit A for enthusiasts. But it is important to remember that moments of material contact were able to produce fears and hopes of so much force because they operated within a symbolic system deeply engaged in issues of racial and ethnic mixture. One of the earliest full statements on the hybridity of American culture came in a 1914 afterword which Israel Zangwill attached to his foundational play *The Melting Pot* (1909). Zangwill considers here the increasingly blended condition of American culture without disguising his own racist sentiments: "However scrupulously and justifiably America avoids physical intermarriage with the negro, the comic spirit cannot fail to note the spiritual miscegenation which, while clothing, commercialising, and Christianising the ex-African, has given 'rag-time' and the sex-dances that go to it, first to white America and thence to the whole white world." Zangwill goes on to note that the "Jew may be Americanised and the American Judaised without any gamic interaction" but gives away his motive when he notes that the Jew is a "recessive" type whose characteristics tend to "disappear in the blended offspring."[26] What is clear from this is the belief that while the African American would never literally disappear into the larger population as the Jew might, the cultural productions of the "ex-Africans" were coming to define Americanness itself. But Zangwill's serene formulation of a comic "spiritual miscegenation" could not cancel out persistent apprehension over the tangible implications of racial and ethnic mixture.

Miscegenation was the primary yield of a discourse whose generative metaphor was libido. Whereas Zangwill could placidly point to the international influence of African American music, others were hardly so serene.[27] One contemporary letter writer worried about America "falling prey to the collective soul of the negro" through ragtime, a fate that held particular danger because among African Americans "sexual restraint is almost unknown and the widest latitude of moral uncertainty is conceded."[28] Even boosters of the new music could not avoid such explicit sexualization; in a now clichéd expression, composer George Gershwin's first biographer described jazz as "a symbol of so many things—of social disruption and realignment, of after-war confusion, of world hysteria, or release from individual and social and sexual repression."[29] It did not take much for this metaphor of sexual impulse to dovetail with concurrent anxieties about the rising visibility of "darker" ethnics in cities.

Images of symbolic mixture have dominated discussions of American popular music from the advent of ragtime to our own time. The most common expressions of the miscegenation theme have focused on the mixed African and European heritage of ragtime and jazz. Terry Waldo, one of the more sober historians of ragtime, has written that although "syncopation is essentially of African origin, its combination with the European musical system accounts for the essential uniqueness of ragtime."[30] Others have called attention to the way in which ragtime and jazz each married folk and classical forms, as Samson Raphaelson did when he noted how jazz consisted of "the rhythm of frenzy staggering against a symphonic background." Still others focus on the rural and urban mixtures which defined these evolving forms.[31]

The mixture at the heart of concerns around jazz and ragtime was that of African Americans and Jews, who were widely held to be responsible—in varying ways—for the new music. As Berndt Ostendorf has shown, Jews and African Americans were imagined by the mainstream public as figures of sexual danger. But joined to this idea, according to MacDonald Smith Moore, was the notion that Jews were opportunistic middlemen.[32] A few points might be added to these insights. First, even insofar as both groups were objectified sexually, fundamental differences marked the depictions: in the Leo Frank case, for instance, the Jewish man was accused of being unmanly and of satisfying his sexual needs in perverse ways, while Jim Conley, the African American janitor in the factory, was predictably stereotyped as a hypersexual (but healthy) young man.[33] Also, African Americans and Jews were not only objects of this discourse; the musical world provided a space where African Americans and Jews could speak to, and about, each other. Jews in the music business, in particular, drew connections between themselves and African Americans in order to create a narrative about the ethnic origins of the music which then became operational as a national mythology.

The explicitly sexualized representations of popular music in this era depended on musicological imprecision. One of the few bits of definitional wisdom to take root was that if African Americans held title to valuable raw musical materials, these resources had worth only insofar as they could be "developed." The usual design for this cultural plotting, as MacDonald Moore makes clear, was to acknowledge that while African American music had a "primitive" sensuality distasteful in its own right, Jews pathologized this apparently natural affect by making it conscious and, worst of all, not instantly recognizable. An early full expression of this position came with two articles in Henry Ford's *Dearborn Independent* printed in the summer of 1921. The hysterical argument made here was that Jewish ingenuity was masking the sexuality of African American music, thus making it easy to smuggle the dangerous stuff into proper homes. The first article introduced the idea that the "monkey talk, jungle squeals, grunts and squeaks and gasps suggestive of cave love" were being "camouflaged by a few feverish notes and admitted to homes where the thing itself, unaided by the piano, would be stamped out in horror." The second part suggested that African American music needed Jewish "cleverness to camouflage the moral filth" and finished off with the reminder that it was Jews, after all, who invented camouflage attire during World War I![34] While the anti-Semitic tone here is predictable and banal, what is most interesting is that the vertical scheme imagined—raw African American materials being "improved" by the attention of Jews—is no different from that depicted by many of the most avid partisans of ragtime and jazz.

Real world dangers inhered in this confusion of sex and music. In the United States this tendency encouraged the conflation of African Americans and Jews and sanctioned Jews to act as public representatives of Black music. The sexualizing habit also had a life outside America, as Michael Kater points out in his study of jazz in Hitler's Germany. Kater demonstrates that the very equation worked out in Henry Ford's rag became an important part of Nazi aesthetic theory. According to Kater, the radical right believed that jazz was innocent until Jews adapted it as "part of their systematic plot to poison the blood of German girls and women by seducing them through acts of 'musical race defilement.'"[35]

These projections all relied heavily on a lack of specificity in naming and defining the various musical styles in question. This vagueness had numerous motivating energies, from the inability and unwillingness on the part of well-situated critics and publicists to develop an appropriate vocabulary for describing the intricacies of popular music, to financial interests: Irving Berlin and George Gershwin certainly helped make sure that words such as "ragtime" and "jazz" could be understood to make direct reference to their music.

One prime indicator of the flexibility of musical categories comes from the information on printed versions of popular songs, particularly those which marked the "blues craze" of the middle to late teens. Edward Berlin calls attention to the significant example of W. C. Handy's "Memphis Blues," which often has been considered the first published blues: the subtitle of this piece was "A Southern Rag."

Handy's "Yellow Dog Blues" was first titled "Yellow Dog Rag" (1914). Gunther Schuller observes that Artie Matthews's standard "Weary Blues" (1915) is actually closer to ragtime than blues. Gerald Bordman agrees that the terms "rag" and "jazz" circulated more quickly than a clear understanding of the forms did, and notes that it is not surprising to find a review of a 1921 musical which refers to the songs as "jazz rags." As a final example, Henry Osgood flippantly suggested that Irving Berlin's "Alexander's Ragtime Band" was ragtime when it first appeared in 1911, but in 1926 it was jazz.[36]

One reason why people had a hard time distinguishing between ragtime and jazz is that they had never been quite sure what ragtime was. The confusion here derives from the various uses of "rag" as verb and noun, along with the imprecision of related categorical terms such as "ragtime," "ragtime song," and "coon song." John Edward Hasse has defined "ragtime" as a "dance-based American vernacular music, featuring a syncopated melody against an even accompaniment." More helpfully, he lays out the four main types of composition or performance which have traditionally been considered forms of ragtime: instrumental rags, ragtime songs, "ragging" of preexisting pieces, and syncopated waltzes.[37]

Ragtime broke on the scene in the mid-1890s (according to Hasse the first "substantiated use of the words 'rag' and 'rag-time'" came in August 1896), rose to prominence as a pianistic music along with the simultaneous popularity of "coon songs" through the early years of the new century, and was transformed into "ragtime song" in the wake of "Alexander's Ragtime Band" (1911).[38] This last grouping was particularly problematic, as it came to refer to "virtually any Negro dialect song with medium to lively tempo, or a syncopated rhythm."[39] At issue amid all the vagueness and contestation was whether ragtime was a genre or a style, or even whether it existed as a distinct entity at all. The influential African American bandleader James Reese Europe, whose Clef Club Orchestra exerted a major influence on the course of American music in the 1910s, claimed that "there never was any such music" as "ragtime"; rather the word was a "fun-name given to Negro rhythm" by white musicians.[40] Such measured attempts to move away from the ragtime label were easily overmatched by efforts to infuse ragtime with mythic properties. One of the key elements in the development of the genre, as Eileen Southern relates, was that its ascent had been heralded by a "legendary rag pianist called John the Baptist who had been active in the '70s and '80s," but whom none had actually heard play.[41]

The musical nomenclature was exceptionally elastic. This suppleness was caused by and was in the service of many extramusical concerns. It is no coincidence, for instance, that the number of pianos sold in the United States and the number of published "piano rags" both peaked in 1909.[42] Musical developments, in short, could never remain untouched by market concerns, racial ideologies, and urban demographics, to name but three shaping influences.

It was clear to most contemporary observers that whatever constituted ragtime, it somehow generated jazz—even if few could describe this relationship with anything like certainty. The apparently inevitable transformation of ragtime into jazz supported the idea that African Americans were no longer wholly (or even primarily) responsible for the musical forms based on their own folk materials. This belief in the ineffable workings of the American crucible only led to an increasing emphasis on the centrality of Jews to the popular music industry.

It is impossible to date with any exactness when the American audience first became widely aware that ragtime had given way to the newer form, but Kathy Ogren's claim that the name "jazz" gained prominence during the First World War is appropriate.[43] One writer for the music periodical *Etude* put it this way: "At the end of the great war, American ragtime simply went wild and that was Jazz." Mark Sullivan, writing in 1932, remembered that it was the agency of the "bunny hug" which transformed ragtime into its "dynastic descendant, jazz."[44] Langston Hughes offered a similar formulation in his 1930 novel *Not Without Laughter*, in which he wrote that the pianist for Rattle Benbow's band had "brought with him an exaggerated rag-time which he called jazz."[45]

Later commentators have debated long and hard about the relationship of ragtime to jazz. Jelly Roll Morton argued that "rag" referred to a very specific formal unit while "jazz" denoted only a style, which was applicable to any tune.[46] LeRoi Jones, no fan of ragtime, identified it as "a music the Negro came to in imitating white imitations of Negro music." Jones does allow that ragtime and jazz were related, calling ragtime "a premature attempt at the socio-cultural merger that later produced jazz."[47] On a different tack, for obvious reasons of self-interest, Paul Whiteman claimed in the publicity materials for his famous 1924 Aeolian Hall concert that jazz had come "into existence about ten years ago from nowhere in particular."[48]

Throughout the 1920s, definitions of ragtime, jazz, and blues remained vague. The long-standing controversy over the origins of the word "jazz" itself—and whether it was the appropriate label for all the music it was taken to describe—derives from battles fought in its early days over what it was and who was responsible for it. (One mid-1920s commentator, fed up with the debates over the terminology, suggested the neologism "unbuttoned" music. No doubt he was referring to men's shirt collars, but the sexual dimension of the name cannot be missed.)[49] The looseness in musical definition was both a consequence and a cause: it was at once a result of the struggles being enacted within the borders of musical production and an instrument which molded the perceptions and behaviors which principal players brought to music-making activity.

"Jazz" did overtake blues and ragtime in the 1920s, and with its prominence came an even more pronounced Jewish presence than there had been in ragtime. The increasing Jewish involvement inspired a general reevaluation of popular music—especially with regard to how honestly and effectively it used "authentic" folk materials. The battle of authentic versus corrupted had already been fought out over ragtime: the publishing company which brought Scott Joplin's compositions to a wide audience beseeched its target audience not to conflate the classic rags it was selling "with the coon songs, or imitations by the *commercial* composer."[50] The whole question of what separated real from fake in this period is a vexed one; MacDonald Moore makes a good case for the position that for many people "Negro" came to equal real and "Jewish" came to signify fake. Moore quotes one critic who outlined this position, bemoaning the "Jewish (Semitic!) direption" of the African American form which on its own "would probably have developed its own independent melody, rather than have become a parasitic mannerism preying upon the classics."[51] This kind of analysis often imagined Jewish "jazz" to be actively dangerous—like a drug or hypnotic sexual force. One proper music writer allowed that good jazz "can be a wholesome tonic" while insisting that "bad Jazz is always a dangerous drug."[52] *The New Republic* made similar reference to the "brutal and aphrodisiac orchestral development of the simple tunes," while admitting that the "germ was latent in the originals."[53]

Alain Locke, one African American intellectual who did not question that Jewish appropriation of African American forms was for ill, described the two different forms of music by utilizing popular psychological terms of the day. Locke described the more "authentic" form of music as "primitively erotic," while deriding the other as "decadently neurotic."[54] But this "decadently neurotic" music represents a crucial, underappreciated episode in the ongoing relations of African Americans and Jews.[55]

Beginning around the turn of the century, as eastern European Jews and southern African Americans came streaming into northern cities, Jews became intimately involved not only with African American music but with African Americans too. For all the talk about alliances between African Americans and Jews, little has been said about the power dynamics and implications of this early expression of intergroup contact, perhaps primarily because it is a less reassuring story than, say, the one about the founding of the NAACP. But still, this musical activity speaks loudly to the willingness of Jews and African Americans, with varying degrees of choice, to be defined in terms of each other. This era was marked by widespread legal and social depredations against African Americans and, to a lesser extent, Jews;[56] the age notably gave rise to a marked degeneration of the actual social and economic conditions of African American people even as their music became more and more crucial to the American cultural scene.[57] These years have also been characterized, though with less unanimity, as a time of social and legal insecurity for Jewish Americans.[58] If the two groups faced some similar expressions of prejudice—college quotas, exclusion from certain hotels, and so on—these points of intersection tell us very little about the overall status of each group. Leo Frank's lynching notwithstanding, Jews were generally safe in America by the turn of the century.

From this position of physical and economic safety, Jews were poised to refine their social status. At the same time, African Americans were involved in a continuing battle for basic human rights. Both groups employed a similar tactic of drawing attention to the centrality of their contributions to what was recognizably "American" culture, but for very different reasons. While leading African Americans seemed most interested in achieving basic civil rights gains through cultural productions, Jews looked to culture as a vehicle to enter the privileged domain of whiteness, American style.[59] We might mark off the two approaches through a shorthand: African Americans hoped their cultural contributions would convince white America that they were *people* who entertained, while Jews hoped their contributions would remind white America that they were *entertaining* people.

No Business Like Show Business

Popular culture went national (and international) at an unprecedented rate in this era. Joined with huge internal migration and immigration to the northern United States were major technological advances which helped the mass entertainment industry, as Michael Rogin puts it, to win the city.[60] A number of new media and institutions were central to this process. The familiar ones—the radio, phonograph, and sound movie, the institution of Hollywood itself—together helped determine the shape of the emerging cultural expressions.[61] Until the onset of the Great Depression the various entertainment industries were steadily growing and were becoming particularly good at nationalizing artists and styles previously bound by region and race.[62]

This rise in mass entertainment cannot be understood without examining the increasingly crucial social activity of Jews and African Americans in northern cities—especially their contact with each other. But if the absence of Jews and African Americans from American popular culture is unthinkable, the two groups were "not moving in the same direction" in this era.[63] This comes particularly clear when we look at how much access members of each group had to positions of real power in the entertainment industries. While African Americans and various representations of "Blackness" (via stereotyped "coon" song lyrics, syncopation, an overall "raciness," and so on) were important commodities, it was Jews who were coming to have most control over these performances, both in the crude sense of owning the means of production, and through the more complex process of gaining status as the best interpreters of African American culture. In early twentieth-century music culture, the success of Jews was inseparable from their management of African American styles, resources, and careers. The discovery of the

African American as a *consumer* dovetailed conveniently with the fact that actual African Americans could be detached from the production of cultural artifacts associated with them.[64]

The privileged place Jews achieved in the business sphere of the culture industry, especially in connection with African American–identified forms, has always been a discomfiting subject. One response, popular with putative alliance builders and Jewish partisans especially, has been to erase the commercial taint. This is most commonly achieved through metaphorical appeals to Black-Jewish sympathy or by claiming that the Jewish presence here made a virtue of oppression, with Jews entering the culture industries as they found their entrance to the more traditional professions blocked.[65] Charges of anti-Semitism have dogged those who call attention to the imbalances in the relationship; the important insights of Harold Cruse with regard to the politics of African American theater, for instance, have been widely discredited because of the anti-Semitism many find in his work.[66] Even so, it cannot be gainsaid that by the mid-1930s Jews had attained positions of shaping influence in virtually every branch of the entertainment complex. In the music business the move toward power began relatively early, even though the cornerstones for the culture industries had been laid well before the mass immigration of Jews to the United States had even taken place.

The first major division of the music business to open up to Jews was music publishing. A recent historian of ragtime reminds us that the publication of sheet music was crucial to the nationwide dissemination of ragtime.[67] In this pre-radio, pre-phonograph age, sheet music was the primary method by which a regional style could be nationalized. The World's Columbian Exposition of 1893 first introduced ragtime to a broad audience (and "broad" should be understood not only as "white," for it was here that many middle-class African Americans first encountered the new music too).[68] By this time music publishing had already come to be dominated by first-and second-generation Jews who centered their activity in New York.[69] These firms developed a complicated system of advertising and marketing which moved well beyond the mere publication of songs: popular singers were paid to associate themselves with a new song, while song pluggers—including the young Irving Berlin—worked their way through the streets, dance halls, and theaters, making sure the public would become quickly familiar with the most recent numbers.[70]

One of the first important Jewish firms was that of M. Witmark & Sons, which was responsible for publishing hit sentimental ballads of the 1890s, as well as some of the most important examples of the new music—whether it was billed as "coon song," "syncopated," or other-wise; the genealogical name was a fiction created because all five of the Witmark brothers were too young to begin their own company. This publishing house played a decisive role in establishing what was to become known as Tin Pan Alley when it moved, in 1893, from New York City's Union Square to West Twenty-eighth Street; the Witmarks also bolstered the increasing importance of Broadway for breaking new songs. In short, they played a shaping role in establishing Broadway and Tin Pan Alley as the two most important physical and symbolic sites of Jewish musical creation during this time.[71] The Witmark brothers (with their affiliate in Chicago, Sol Bloom) had commercial relationships with a variety of the most important African American music figures of the turn of the century including James Weldon Johnson and his brother J. Rosamond Johnson along with their partner Bob Cole, Ernest Hogan, Harry T. Burleigh, and Paul Laurence Dunbar and his partner Will Marion Cook. Sol Bloom was also responsible for publishing a hand-book for playing ragtime which the composer Ben Harney put together. The Witmarks themselves had a "minstrel department," which pro-vided performers not only with music but also with gags, makeup, and costumes. If Jews were becoming important catalysts of change in the music business, then blackface minstrelsy was their medium.[72]

The boundary between publisher and songwriters was not firm. A few of the Witmark brothers were themselves performers—some get-ting their start in blackface minstrel troupes—and they seem to have felt free to interfere in the creative process of others.[73] A notable intervention occurred when Isidore Witmark decided that Ernest Hogan's original melody for "All Coons Look Alike to Me" (1896) was not a good fit with the refrain, and so (Witmark says) he "wrote a new melody, together with some of the words for the second verse."[74] While Hogan is reputed to have suffered all his life for writing a song which was perceived to be an insult to his own race, there is no evidence that Witmark had any similar regret.[75]

Even more chilling than this story is Isidore Witmark's accounting of his dealings with the African American composer Will Marion Cook, who with Paul Laurence Dunbar wrote the important 1898 musical *Clorindy, or the Origin of the Cakewalk.*[76] According to Witmark, Cook belonged to "the short but definite catalogue of men who wronged Isidore Witmark and were never forgiven." Cook's offense was that six months after *Clorindy* opened and was published by the Witmarks, he appeared at the Witmark offices with a white lawyer, and demanded a recalculation of his royalty statement, which he thought was not "commensurate with the success of the play."[77] An affronted Witmark assured Cook that the Witmarks would never again publish one of his songs.

This anecdote points up painfully that African Americans were at the whim of white publishers—first to get their music disseminated, and then to get a fair accounting of their success after publication. The Copyright Act of 1909 gave music publishers and songwriters permission to license their materials for profit, but the American Society of Composers, Authors, and Publishers (ASCAP), a collective which was founded in 1914 to oversee the payment of royalties, did little to protect African Americans. Election to ASCAP (which boasted a large Jewish contingent) was difficult for African Americans notwithstanding an explicit nondiscrimination policy.[78]

The putative protection of law and ASCAP did not stop African American songwriters from being exploited. Writers without steady jobs often sold songs—complete with the rights to them—to well-capitalized publishers who could afford to wait for deferred payments. Fats Waller is perhaps most often cited as having been taken advantage of by unscrupulous publishers; one rumor has it that Waller once sold a song to Irving Berlin for $25.[79] Even more disturbing is the real possibility that African Americans were systematically used to write songs without being given the credit which would lead to future earnings. Sam Wooding, an African American bandleader of the 1920s, insisted that the apparent exclusion of African Americans from Tin Pan Alley was illusory. According to Wooding it was quite common for an Alley songwriter laboring over a difficult number to "go and get one of those spades to come in here" and fix it. Wooding goes on to describe the situation with a thinly veiled reference to the Jewish presence on Tin

Pan Alley: "A lot of those white composers, they were fresh off the boat, they didn't know what America was. They were on the right track, they almost had the idea but it wasn't there yet, so they called in Andy Razaf to straighten out the lyrics and Luckey Roberts or Shelton Brooks to straighten out the music, and they were paid maybe fifty dollars for the whole thing and it got the Negro some beef stew."[80] Here is a valuable complication of "middleman" theories of Black-Jewish relations: Wooding aptly notes that it is impossible to imagine that Jews simply took African American materials and "repackaged" or "interpreted" them for other Americans. Instead it is African Americans who serve as mediators, explaining "America" to immigrant Jews and others.

Rarely did African Americans directly control the final shape or the fruits of their artistic labor. Two African Americans, Porter Grainger and Bob Ricketts, did run Rainbow Music, a song publishing concern, but even this business was in a subsidiary relationship with Irving Berlin's publishing house.[81] When phonograph records took over sheet music's place of prominence in the 1920s, the power differential remained similar: a few important African American firms lasted briefly—Harry Pace's Black Swan records most notably—but African American record companies could never survive for long against the competition of the much larger businesses. As early as 1914 the African American bandleader James Reese Europe was complaining that the music world was "controlled by a trust, and the negro must submit to its demands or fail to have his compositions produced."[82] Europe's complaint reaffirms that the confusion of categories which attended the development of ragtime and jazz was not coincidental, and did not simply grow out of musical ignorance. Instead, ambiguity of definition was highly functional: it allowed interested Jews to create a space for themselves in a musical environment not strictly defined by race.

The regulation of music publishing by Jews was followed and reinforced in the first decades of the twentieth century by a growing Jewish influence in theaters, vaudeville houses, and nightclubs. Since music publishers were partial to songs linked with popular shows, the relationship of theater to publishing house became more than casual.[83] This helped ensure that Jews would play a key part in determining which particular images of Blackness would be disseminated and by whom. Irving Howe, calling attention to the importance of the Klaw and

Erlanger syndicate, the Shuberts, and the Orpheum circuit, writes that
by the early 1900s, "a good portion of the theatrical business in New
York, and some of it beyond, had fallen into Jewish hands."[84] Had he
extended his account into the 1920s, he would have found even more
examples of Jews—and Jewish gangsters especially—controlling entertainment venues, particularly in Harlem. It also bears repeating, as a few
recent commentators have done, that just as Jews were consolidating
their power in the culture industries, African Americans were simultaneously suffering through particularly lean years. Barry Singer notes that
1907–1920 were drought years for African Americans on Broadway,
coming after a spate of productions (*Clorindy*, for instance) around the
turn of the century but before the "vogue" of the 1920s, marked by the
debut in 1921 of the show *Runnin' Wild*. With little adjustment this
same dating might describe the period when Jews came into their full
strength in American popular culture.[85] Of course the two sides were
connected: the rise of Jews in the business of popular music opened up
new opportunities for Jewish performers, many of whom profited by
their real contact with—and imagined closeness to—African Americans.

Whatever metaphors of intergroup likeness ruled the day, Jewish
businesspeople did not, in the world of actual contact, regularly treat
their African American employees as kin. For every actively partisan
Jewish club owner or artist manager who showed honest concern for an
African American performer, we can find an equally corrupt and exploitative one. For instance, the gangster Arnold Rothstein backed a
show featuring Flournoy Miller and Aubrey Lyles in 1927, and became
a good friend and supporter of Fats Waller in the process.[86] By contrast,
we find Dutch Schultz, who, as a backer of the 1929 cabaret revue *Hot
Chocolates*, menaced Waller's songwriting partner Andy Razaf. Razaf's
widow has recalled that while watching a rehearsal, Schultz became
convinced the show lacked something and "asked" Razaf to write a
comic song about a "colored girl" complaining about how tough it is to
be colored. Razaf protested that he did not think he had such a song in
him; Schultz reached for his gun. So, in response, Razaf came up with
"(What Did I Do To Be So) Black and Blue," which has endured as a
song of racial protest. Razaf would later claim that his life depended on
whether or not the opening night audience liked the song: Schultz
would never kill him over a hit.[87]

Although Jews exercised control over many African American performers, this influence did not determine the shape of the main currents
of African American music; that sort of instrumentality simply did not
exist. But Jewish businesspeople—as theater owners, publishers, and
managers—did significantly influence the access African Americans had
to the marketplace. As Lawrence Bergreen has argued, the success of
New York's Tin Pan Alley was due in large part to its ability to collate
many styles into a recognizable musical language which could then be
commodified and distributed nationally; diffuse regional jazz styles had
little hope of competing with this "monolith."[88] One effect of this,
perhaps most striking for our purposes, is that the material leverage of
Jews in popular culture played a decisive role in creating the performance opportunities on which Jewish artists would stake their claim as
extraordinary translators of African American music. In other words,
not only did Jewish productions elbow African Americans out, but also
this same success in the marketplace allowed Jews to begin positioning
themselves as the most accomplished composers of African American
music.

"Cheek to Cheek": Al Jolson and the Jewish Switchboard

Jews did not invent a wholly new place for themselves in American
popular culture but instead made their first major incursion into the
market as blackface performers. Mark Slobin has written that "virtually
every Jewish-American stage personality, from Weber and Fields
through Al Jolson, Sophie Tucker, and Eddie Cantor, first reached out
to American audiences from behind a mask of burnt cork."[89] Jews were
quite successful at selling themselves in blackface: Irving Howe argues
that by 1910 or so, Jews had more or less taken over blackface entertainment. A 1923 article in *Variety* supports this sentiment, suggesting
that "most blackface comedians do an Al Jolson with a touch of [Eddie]
Cantor." American popular culture is drenched in the props, tropes,
and imagery of minstrelsy; it comes as no surprise, then, to find that
Jews made their first major appearance in the national marketplace of
popular culture through their travesties of African Americans.[90]

Al Jolson was especially important because his early stage performances provided a figure around which emerging analogies of Blackness

and Jewishness could begin to take form. Jolson had some of his earliest successes with acts that placed "Jew" and "Black" in close contact, as with his 1906 appearance with Joe Palmer in *The Hebrew and the Coon*. By the time Jolson starred in *The Jazz Singer* in 1927, he was America's biggest vaudeville star, and blackface was central to his act.[91] Still more significant was the widely held perception that one could find in Jolson's personal style, in the tonality and rhythms of his singing, and in his penchant for wearing blackface the natural marriage of "Yiddish schmaltz and blackface sentiment."[92] Isaac Goldberg, George Gershwin's hand-picked biographer, pointed to the person of Al Jolson as he tried to describe the sympathy between "Yiddish" and "Black" elements in Gershwin's song "Funny Face"; in the words of this Harvard professor, Jolson was "the living symbol of the similarity."[93] Samson Raphaelson claimed that his attendance at a Jolson show led him to discover the correlation between cantors and jazz singers which inspired him to write the short story from which the movie of *The Jazz Singer* would later be drawn.[94] Jolson's appearance in this movie would, of course, help ratify the logic of these analogies. Jewish minstrelsy, then, contributed important terms for a comparison of African American and Jew which would have growing power in the 1910s and 1920s.

Stage minstrelsy did not only lead to the creation of metaphors connecting African Americans and Jews. It also served, for a time, as a switchboard connecting a loose network of Jewish businesspeople and artists. Jolson stands as a peerless example of the support Jews in various branches of the entertainment industry could offer one another. Jolson's key career breaks relied equally on his popular representations of Blackness and the backing and promotion he received from Jewish theater owners, managers, and so on—not to mention the songs written for him by Jewish songwriters. With Lew Dockstader's Minstrels (booked by the Shubert brothers), Jolson introduced Irving Berlin's "Alexander's Ragtime Band"; later he received some attention through his work on Orpheum's vaudeville circuit.[95] His first truly major moment came in 1911, when he appeared in *La Belle Paree* at the Winter Garden theater (a building planned by Jewish vaudevillian Lew Fields and brought to completion by the Shuberts). It was with this role that Jolson refined the "Continental effeminacy" of the "colored aristocrat" which would become his blackface trademark.[96] This show also provided an important opportunity for the Jewish composer Jerome Kern, who wrote the music for one of its songs ("Paris Is a Paradise for Coons").[97]

A fuller articulation of Jewish investments in Blackness came with the Jolson show *Sinbad*, which opened at the Winter Garden in 1918 and ran intermittently there and elsewhere until 1921. As was the custom of the time, the content of the show was unfixed, and open to interpolations of appropriate songs (meaning either songs that fit the loose plot of the production, or songs that had hit potential and would improve the visibility of show, performer, and songwriter all). *Sinbad* had room for two numbers in particular, "Swanee" and "My Mammy," which were to become Jolson signature songs. "My Mammy" reached Jolson through the efforts of Saul Bornstein, who was general manager of Irving Berlin Music. Bornstein was able to obtain not only the priceless publicity of a Jolson stage performance but also Jolson's consent to publish the sheet music with his picture on it.[98] The music for "Swanee" was written by George Gershwin, whose career was launched by Jolson's performance. (According to a recent biography, Gershwin maneuvered to get himself invited to a party thrown by Jolson at Bessie Bloodgood's Harlem brothel in order to audition the song for him.)[99] Gershwin never had a bigger commercial success, and in the 1920s and 1930s he would be established as the central figure in formulations of African American–Jewish relatedness.[100]

It is worth pausing to consider the fact that both Irving Berlin ("Alexander's Ragtime Band") and George Gershwin ("Swanee") established their careers with songs which quoted the music of, and made textual reference to, Stephen Foster's "The Old Folks at Home" (better known as "Swanee River").[101] Foster's song narrates a vague, atemporal tale of the longing an African American singer feels for home. In music and text, as William Austin describes it, "The Old Folks at Home" combines the "blackface mask with the tradition of home songs."[102] Austin notes that home songs, codified most significantly in the Irish songs of Thomas Moore, had come to have great popularity in the United States in the middle decades of the nineteenth century; the dialect songs of minstrelsy, of course, rose to prominence at the same time.[103] In this time of rapid industrialization and major population shifts, minstrelsy provided a frame for the articulation of what Eric Lott has called a "rather widespread preoccupation with traumatic parting, distance, temporal and geographic breaks."[104]

In the period under consideration here it was Jewish Americans who most successfully merged Blackness and nostalgia for a mythical homeplace: this homeplace, of course, was situated somewhere in a mythical South—a South which has plenty of local color but no race problems. As members of a newer immigrant group, Jewish composers—however long their own families had been in America—were able to draw on the perception that they personally and perpetually experienced the break from a lost homeland. At the same time, Jews were also quite successful at selling the idea that they bore a special relationship to African Americans which prepared them to interpret the sounds of Blackness. For Berlin and Gershwin to make reference to Foster's song was, among other things, a professional statement of purpose: by incorporating "The Old Folks at Home" into "Alexander's Ragtime Band" and "Swanee," Berlin and Gershwin announced that they were the rightful heirs of the song tradition exemplified by Stephen Foster.[105]

Of course Dixie songs generally, and "Swanee" songs in particular, were not the exclusive trademark of Jewish songwriters. Hazy musical evocations of southern life had been popular since before Foster's time, and at least twelve different "Swanee" songs were written in the first couple of decades of the twentieth century.[106] Even so, the compositions by Berlin and Gershwin deserve special attention because of the way they negotiate a relationship to the traditions of blackface minstrelsy. Berlin's song is particularly important here since, as Robert Dawidoff has argued, it fixed the translation of blackface conventions into nonvisual form.[107]

Berlin went out of his way to call attention to Foster's song. Most obvious is the textual reference which proclaims Berlin's plan to modernize the Foster song: Alexander's band is who you listen to if you want "to hear the 'Swanee River' played in ragtime."[108] In addition, Berlin makes musical reference to "The Old Folks at Home" by quoting nine notes from the Foster tune to set the words "the 'Swanee River' played in ragtime." For these last three words, Berlin uses the four notes which set the words "Swanee River" in Foster's own song. Thus the motive energy of "Alexander's Ragtime Band" builds toward its climax in "The Old Folks at Home." The result, as Austin puts it, is that the Foster tune is "marvelously absorbed into . . . [the] continuity" of "Alexander's Ragtime Band."[109] This is a bold move on Berlin's part, an assertion that, even this early in his career, he was ready to drape himself in Foster's mantle.

Gershwin's song, according to Austin, is much less reverent. Rather than building up to a jubilant climax as "Alexander's Ragtime Band" does, "Swanee" uses Foster's song as one source of cliché among many: "Both text and tune contradict the singer's sentiment; his rush of cliché fragments indicates that he is already farther from Foster's old folks than Berlin and that he is likely to change directions several times before he reaches home . . . The musical quotation [from Foster] is simply the final cliché."[110] By the time Gershwin broke big with "Swanee," Berlin (with the help of Jewish performers such as Fanny Brice and Al Jolson) had already cleared a path for the Jewish composer interested in adapting African American sounds and images for broad popular consumption. As a result, Gershwin and his co-writer Irving Caesar could take the chance of using "The Old Folks at Home" as an object for parody rather than homage. The over-the-top "Mammy" stylizations of "Swanee" not only established Gershwin's career but also helped consolidate Al Jolson's star image.[111]

Berlin and Gershwin (and Jolson and so on) needed African Americans as both source of musical inspiration and object of representation. They summoned the memory of Stephen Foster—whether with veneration or irony—in order to claim their place in the minstrel tradition. The Jewish presence in American popular music has to be plotted along a minstrel continuum: from the Witmark brothers' prop department to the youthful involvement of other Jewish composers (including Jerome Kern and Harold Arlen) with minstrel shows, Jews in the music business participated fully in the American project of making money out of making fun of African Americans.

Any chronicle of Jews making money out of African Americans and representations of Blackness flirts uncomfortably with conventional anti-Semitic stereotypes of Jewish opportunism and parasitism. But Jews did inhabit a place of special power in the culture industries of this time, and they profited from their concrete and symbolic connections with Black America. A proper sensitivity to ethnic typecasting of Jews should not foreclose an investigation of how racist effects issued from the involvement of Jews with African American musical forms. Roger Hewitt has written acutely of white songwriter Hoagy Carmichael's use of "Black" materials: "The 'freeflow' of musical ideas between black and white has been directed and regulated by numerous distinctly unmusical factors—principally the racist ideologies and practices within which musicians, despite their individual proclivities, have lived and worked." Regardless, then, of whether particular Jews in the music business were actively anti-racist (and few seem to have been), their work very often "reproduced the racism written into the culture and it did so precisely at those points where it attempted to draw closest to black culture."[112] My intention here is simply to make clear how extensively Jews were immersed in the manufacture and merchandising of Blackness via the mutually supporting institutions of minstrelsy and Tin Pan Alley. This prepares us for a better understanding of why Jewish interpretations of African American forms could be (and had to be) mystified so intensely in the ensuing decades. The breadth and seeming "naturalness" of these interactions also help us see how the musical relationship could contribute so much energy to a more expansive conception of the relationship of Jews and African Americans.

The connection of blackface minstrelsy to Tin Pan Alley expressions of Blackness was especially crucial for confirming Jewish musical authority. Ronald Sanders has argued that if there were intimations of "a kind of Jewish musical fulfillment in blackface," they appear "even more forcefully when one moves from the realm of performance to that of composition."[113] Although Sanders's description ignores the entrepreneurial base of the cultural activity he is describing, he is correct to call attention to the way the Jews of Tin Pan Alley—writing on African American themes and in (apparently) "Black" styles—imbued metaphors of relatedness with more energy than they previously had in Jewish blackface performances. The frequent interpolation of these Tin Pan Alley musical numbers into the (blackface) Broadway and vaudeville productions of Al Jolson and others shaped a circle of influence which was constantly self-supporting.

The Jewish musical figure most responsible for the translation of blackface from stage performance into song was Irving Berlin; Berlin's most important early hit was "Alexander's Ragtime Band" (1911). I probably do not have to repeat that, as most music historians note, Berlin's songs are not "really" ragtime.[114] This contention is now "true," given that "ragtime" has come to refer mostly to the instrumental piano music of Scott Joplin and his peers and followers. That "Alexander" was considered to be exemplary ragtime reminds us that the musical designation had not come close to achieving its final form. Even more important, insofar as "ragtime" had solidified categorically, it referred to songs (increasingly penned by Jews) in a vaguely "Negro" style whose lyrical content usually helped to reinforce the impression that something Black was going on.

"Alexander's Ragtime Band" did all that. Although the music had very little of ragtime's defining syncopation, it had the up-tempo "raciness" associated with the form. More important yet, as many have noticed, the lyrics speak of ragtime even though the setting is not strictly ragtime.[115] The song participates actively in the nationalization of ragtime, suggesting that hearing the music will make the listener want to "go to war"—thus helping to translate race (in the form of ragtime) into nation. But "Alexander's Ragtime Band" also communicates a sharp racial message, since it derives its title character from the tradition of "coon songs." "Alexander" was, as Laurence Bergreen notes, "supposedly a comically grand name for a black man to possess."[116] With this one song, then, Berlin occupied a number of interesting positions. First, with his evocation of a bandleader named Alexander, Berlin participated in a recognizable minstrel travesty—pointing at the pretensions of a Black man as the basis for a joke. At the same time, in the social world the song lived in, Berlin was—as a purveyor of "ragtime"—at least provisionally and fleetingly in just the same position that Alexander occupies within the song. In the terms of the song, that is, while Alexander might present "Swanee River" in "ragtime," so too does Berlin "rag" familiar tunes (in his case, most famously with a version of Mendelssohn's "Spring Song"). This complex relation of songwriter and song suggests a paradigm of Jewish involvement with African American forms from minstrelsy on: in Berlin's "Alexander," George Gershwin's *Porgy and Bess*, and so many other significant productions, Jews capitalized on their ability to convey both closeness to the cultural stuff of "Blackness" and distance from actual African Americans. Closeness was marked by performance context, general tone ("raciness"), and so on. Distance could be implied in any number of ways: the non-ragtime musical form of "Alexander's Ragtime Band," or the evocation of a temporally and geographically remote folk world in *Porgy and Bess*, for instance.

One of Berlin's first major jobs, beginning in 1904, was as a singing waiter at Mike Salter's bar, the Pelham Cafe, at 12 Pell Street in New York City's Chinatown.[117] Previously Berlin had worked as a busker, as a guide for a blind pianist named Sol, and briefly as a song plugger at Tony Pastor's music hall on Fourteenth Street. At "Nigger" Mike's, Berlin pitched songs in a number of popular styles to an audience made up largely of tourists, come to explore the titillating possibilities of exotic Chinatown, then in vogue much as Harlem would be in the 1920s (though to a lesser extent).[118] So, even while Berlin had only recently been traveling with and learning from Blind Sol and other performers—including the African American pianist at "Nigger" Mike's—he was able to transform himself in short order from "tourist" to "real thing."[119] This is a prime example of a Jewish performer translating nearness to African Americans into a cultural metaphor about the Jewish man's special access to Black forms.

In later years Berlin would "confess" (or insist) that he never really did know what ragtime was anyway, even though a year before "Alexander" he had parodied the idea of a Jew playing ragtime in "Yiddle on Your Fiddle (Play Some Ragtime)."[120] From the evidence of the reception of "Alexander's Ragtime Band," it is clear that Berlin knew enough about what was being sold as ragtime to position himself as its foremost interpreter. Within two years of the release of this song, Berlin was received in England as the "King of Ragtime."[121]

Berlin had unprecedented success in marketing his version of "Black" music as "American" music. Alexander Woollcott, who served as Berlin's first biographer (in 1925), summed up the mainstream opinion on the songwriter when he wrote that Berlin was "the man who took ragtime when it was little more than a mannerism of the pianists in the rathskellers and bordellos and made it into a custom of the country." The composer Jerome Kern concurred, tendering the oft-quoted remark that Berlin had no place in American music because he *was* American music.[122] Gilbert Seldes, summarizing the reception of Irving Berlin in his early career, contended that by the mid-1920s, Berlin could "write nothing wholly divorced from the rhythms of ragtime."[123]

Even as Berlin moved away in his career from explicitly ragtime-inflected music, he returned often to "Black" themes and forms, with his stance ranging from outright mockery to apparent sympathy. In a 1918 show featuring the men of the military camp where Berlin was stationed, the songwriter staged "Mandy," a love song, "as a drag number with a blackface male chorus."[124] By the time of his journalistic 1933 show *As Thousands Cheer*, Berlin was writing songs such as "Harlem on My Mind" and "Supper Time," the second of which had at least some muted racial protest material in it.[125] What was unique about Berlin's talent is that he was able to reconfigure the minstrel stance and defuse its most offensive elements. Berlin thereby disassociated himself from the retrograde aspect of this form which Jolson, for instance, could never lose, all the while maintaining a level of "racialness" which since the early decades of the nineteenth century had been integral to the marketing of so many prominent American popular culture forms. Berlin's "contribution," in essence, was to distill the sights and sounds of minstrelsy into a usable modern musical grammar.

In this way Berlin also functioned as an important forerunner of George Gershwin, whose work stands as the central axis around which any discussion of African American and Jewish musical relatedness must turn. Gershwin's output was much more varied than Berlin's. In addition to individual songs, and scores for Broadway and Hollywood, he also wrote in more consciously highbrow forms. But as with Berlin, Gershwin's career is bound up with his trade in African American styles and images. From the ragtime of his first published song in 1916 to his crowning achievement with *Porgy and Bess* (1935), Gershwin laid claim to having a special access to African American culture and a special talent for interpreting it. Gershwin did this by implication and pronouncement (and with the help of countless advocates) to a much greater extent than Irving Berlin ever had.

In the years following Al Jolson's successful interpolation of "Swanee" in *Sinbad*, Gershwin's adaptation of "Black" themes and styles became more calculated and much more ambitious. The first evidence of Gershwin's aspirations came with the poorly received *Blue Monday Blues* (later known as *135th Street* when Paul Whiteman presented it), a "blues opera" which Gershwin wrote with the lyricist Buddy DeSylva for *George White's Scandals of 1922*.[126] This first attempt to sell a new musical fusion to a Broadway audience did not go over well; DeSylva's libretto was by all accounts subpar, and Gershwin's music has been described as consisting "mainly of feeble popular songs held together by dull, jazz-like recitatives."[127]

But this failure was not without important ramifications. In the first place, the performance piece for which Gershwin wrote the music was done in blackface by white actors, which reminds us again that a very concrete relationship linked the conventional stereotypes of stage minstrelsy with the new music being presented by Jews who purportedly had special access to African Americans and their music.[128] Another important outcome of Gershwin's *Blue Monday* flop was that it set the stage for two of his more resounding successes of the 1920s: his appearance in 1923 at Aeolian Hall as accompanist for a recital by the art singer Eva Gauthier, which included a few popular "jazzy" songs, and the 1924 debut of his *Rhapsody in Blue* at the same venue.

The pairing of Gershwin and Gauthier was arranged by Carl Van Vechten, who later recalled that he and Gershwin developed an interest in the "Negro" at approximately the same time, and together attended many cultural and social events in Harlem. Van Vechten played an important role in fixing Gershwin as the crown prince of the modern attempt to develop African American themes into higher forms; he published a flattering piece on Gershwin for a 1925 issue of *Vanity Fair*, and thought Gershwin's "I'll Build a Stairway to Paradise" was "the most perfect piece of jazz yet written."[129] Van Vechten's influence here serves as an important reminder that the complicated relationship of African Americans and Jews has never existed in the sort of hermetically sealed ethnic laboratories (or, in less optimistic versions, roped-off battle royals) which many accounts imply. Indeed, many of the most important of these cultural moments were brokered, or at least actively encouraged, by the likes of Van Vechten, Flo Ziegfeld, Alexander Woollcott, Gilbert Seldes, and later John Hammond. Whether seen as "white rebels" or exhausted and desperate puritans, these white intermediaries give the lie to models of ethnic discreteness which deny the multiple points of contact in the modern American city, and indeed the multiple elements of identity which always contribute to the constitution of a self in relation to others.[130]

In any case, Gershwin's performance with Eva Gauthier in November 1923 helped to establish him as representing the dawning of "the age of sophisticated jazz."[131] Gauthier included in the "American" section of her recital Berlin's "Alexander's Ragtime Band," a Jerome Kern song, and two by Gershwin: already, with no apparent self-consciousness or need for explanation, three Jewish composers writing "jazz" were being offered up as exemplars of "American" music.[132] The show was a resounding success and led, according to Gauthier, to Paul Whiteman's resolution to commission a longer piece from Gershwin for "an experiment in modern music" he was planning for the following February.[133]

As the oft-repeated anecdote tells it, although Gershwin and Whiteman had generally discussed the proposition, Gershwin only learned of the concrete plans for the now historic Aeolian Hall show to be held on February 12, 1924, through a news release his brother Ira discovered in the *New York Tribune* of January 4. In a little over a month, then, Gershwin composed what Isaac Goldberg would later call the "Declaration of Independence of Jazz."[134]

Whiteman's show, billed as "An Experiment in Modern Music," was a slightly scholarly exercise meant to demonstrate the evolution of jazz and other modern music. According to many contemporary accounts it was a fairly boring hodgepodge of novelty jazz (by Zez Confrey of "Kitten on the Keys" fame among others), a few popular songs, and some other specially written "national" pieces by Victor Herbert, which finally hit a peak with the introduction of Gershwin's *Rhapsody*. Ross Gorman's opening clarinet glissando was received as a thrillingly "jazzy" touch (although listeners today might hear more klezmer than jazz in it), and the audience—which included Willie the Lion Smith, Sergei Rachmaninoff, Jascha Heifetz, John Philip Sousa, and Carl Van Vechten—responded with strong applause.[135] Next-day reviews were mixed, but again, significantly there was little question that what Gershwin had concocted was a logical extension of "jazz." This debut, which not coincidentally had been scheduled to be held on Abraham Lincoln's birthday, has spawned a catalogue of overheated praise along the lines of David Ewen's contention that with the *Rhapsody* Gershwin had "emancipated jazz from the slums."[136] J. Rosamond Johnson, who considered the *Rhapsody* to be the "greatest one-hundred-percent exposition of Negro American idioms and characteristics," recalled turning to Gershwin after watching a performance of it to tell the composer, "George, you've done it—you're the Abraham Lincoln of Negro music."[137]

By the time Gershwin's music for *Porgy and Bess* was heard in 1935, there was little dissent from the dominant idea that Gershwin had a special talent—often attributed to his own racial heritage—for utilizing "Negro American idioms."[138] Before committing to *Porgy*, Gershwin had considered working on an opera derived from S. Ansky's play *The Dybbuk* but concluded that the material was too far from what he knew best, which most commentators agreed was African American music. This is not to say that *Porgy and Bess* garnered very good press; in fact it was criticized fairly roundly for its inability to synthesize disparate materials into a recognizable format. Few quibbled, however, with Gershwin's supposed ability to capture "all the emotional richness of the Negro soul" in his music.[139] Some African Americans did offer protests: choir director Hall Johnson carefully noted that *Porgy and Bess* was "an opera about Negroes rather than a Negro opera." More often a powerfully functional, if usually unremarked, slippage occurred between subject and form, which allowed Jewish representations of Blackness to be offered and received *as* Black music. As such, *Porgy and Bess*, which Harold Cruse has called "surely the most contradictory cultural symbol ever created" in the Western world, most assuredly did not confuse its audience. The opera was easily understood to be a realization of the promise of "Negro" art.[140]

After Berlin and Gershwin, Jerome Kern and Harold Arlen were the two other composers most responsible for repositioning African American music as a province of Jewish art. Kern is less important to this story than Arlen, primarily because he consistently sought to distance himself from the rising tide of jazz in the 1920s. According to his biographer Kern did not feel "at ease with the more blatant, strident side of jazz," and moreover forbade his music from being played in cabarets, on records, or on the radio because of what he perceived as the "distortion" which jazz orchestras wrought on his work.[141]

Kern was cast from quite a different mold than Berlin, Gershwin, or

Arlen. He was third generation, of central European descent, and more influenced by turn-of-the-century sentimental song than the others. But Kern, too, became involved with African American music and attempts at representing Blackness early in his career: by the time he finished high school he had helped to write a senior class minstrel show during which he played ragtime on piano, and had also taken part in a parody of *Uncle Tom's Cabin* which included a character named Svengali Legree. Although a seemingly trivial detail, we might pause over this last. The existence of "Svengali Legree" demonstrates that it was possible to imagine a version of the Jewish involvement in African American music which emphasized force rather than musical sympathy. Indeed, "Svengali Legree" suggests a specific form of hands-off enslavement by which Jews master African Americans; in George Du Maurier's novel *Trilby* (1892), Svengali controls Trilby O'Ferrall (to bid her sing!) with his eyes, not with physical power.[142] A cherished axiom of this time held that since Jews had suffered a history of oppression similar to that endured by African Americans, they were well suited to improvise on materials derived from African American culture and create great art. No competing theories ever developed about what would happen if Jews themselves were to become oppressors of African Americans—except in moments of extreme crisis such as the Leo Frank case.

Kern's most significant contribution for our concerns is the score he wrote for the 1927 *Show Boat*—a Broadway pastiche of spirituals, ragtime, blues, and jazz which was often mistaken for the musical forms it tried to evoke. One critic in Philadelphia was so enthusiastic about this music that he claimed Kern's great achievement had been to catch "the subtle distinction between jazz and the ragtime of twenty or twenty-five years ago."[143] Nonetheless, Kern was widely thought—as was Gershwin in many of his major productions—to have created "authentic" African American music for this epochal stage production. The comedian Phil Silvers developed a routine which demonstrated his appreciation of the ironies embedded in this displacement. In this bit he would impersonate Kern teaching Paul Robeson how to sing "Ol' Man River"—with Robeson interrupting Kern to ask him what "taters" were.[144] By the time of the 1935 rehearsals for *Porgy and Bess*, as many witnesses have recounted, the idea of a Jewish man teaching an African American how to sing authentically "Negro" was no longer a joke: George Gershwin spent time tutoring his mostly northern cast in how to capture the proper southern Black dialect he wanted to match to his music.[145]

Unlike Kern, Harold Arlen happily embraced the possibilities of Jewish expressions of Blackness, and is generally considered to be the Jewish composer of his era with the best feel for the blues. Ethel Waters is purported to have called Arlen the "Negro-ist" white man she had ever known, while a songwriting colleague of Arlen's said of him—as has been said of (and by) Artie Shaw, Mezz Mezzrow, and so many other Jewish "white Negroes"—that he "was really one of them."[146] Born Hyman Arluck in 1905, Arlen fits almost every detail of the paradigm for Jewish identification and participation in African American music set by Jolson and Berlin. Arlen's father was a successful cantor, an immigrant to Louisville who later moved to Buffalo. Cantor Arluck, according to Harold, had a particular affinity for improvisation—a fact which Arlen would make much hay out of later on. (Cantor Arluck's synagogue also is reputed to have hosted a blackface show on one occasion, which should again remind us of the important role played by stage minstrelsy in educating this generation of Jewish performers as to what "Blackness" was, and what could be done with it.)[147]

While much about Arlen's life and career appears as a summary version of this strand of second-generation Jewish life, Arlen also shared much with the generation of Chicago (and Boston and New York) white jazz players who came of age in the mid-1920s after spending years in reverent worship and imitation of the performance styles of Louis Armstrong, King Oliver, and other New Orleans musicians. Jewish players among this group usually refused to accept authenticity as an ethnic birthright (as their Tin Pan Alley contemporaries did) but instead set themselves up as acolytes who might be legitimated by immersing themselves in the culture of Blackness, practicing hard, and maintaining the proper social attitudes. A few of the early Jewish jazz players—most notably Artie Shaw and Mezz Mezzrow—were crucial stylists of the white Negro pose, that brand of self-making which Norman Mailer would memorialize in his famous essay of 1957. After Irving Berlin and company distilled stage minstrelsy into musical codes, Mezzrow, Shaw, and others proposed that from the premise of musical sympathy an entire way of life might be fashioned. While making smaller claims than the Tin Pan Alley group had about their inherited aptitude for interpreting African American music, these Jewish swing musicians declared that they could work themselves *up* to resembling African Americans through acts of will.

But Arlen is better understood as the link between Gershwin and the jazz players than as a full-fledged white Negro in his own right: he was attracted early in his life to ragtime, and as race records became available, he studied and copied them.[148] In fact, as Max Wilk has outlined, Arlen was dedicated to "straight" jazz—playing in a band himself—until hearing the music of Kern and Gershwin. Then he began getting ideas about what could be made out of jazz.[149] Even so, Arlen remained committed to African American jazz players, and seems to have studied particularly the arrangements of Fletcher Henderson.[150]

Arlen was able to put the formula into practice in a long list of successes which began in 1930 with his association with Harlem's Cotton Club. "Get Happy," Arlen's first big success, was introduced here, as were numerous "race" songs he wrote for Cab Calloway. Throughout the next three decades Arlen continued to have great success as he traded on his ability to translate aspects of the blues into his stage and movie songs. The list of Arlen's African American–inspired music is long and impressive: he wrote songs for the 1942 movie version of *Cabin in the Sky*, which included "Happiness Is a Thing Called Joe"; the 1944 stage musical *Bloomer Girl* incorporated parts of *Uncle Tom's Cabin* and included songs with such unlikely titles as "I Never Was Born" and "Liza Crossing the Ice"; with Johnny Mercer he wrote music for the failed 1946 musical *St. Louis Woman*—featuring "Come Rain or Come Shine"—which was based on Arna Bontemps's novel *God Sends Sunday* (1931) and was scripted by Bontemps and the poet Countee Cullen; an extended project which Arlen wrote with Ted Koehler in 1940 called the *Americanegro Suite* was considered by no less an expert than Irving Berlin to be an important contribution to the canon of "American Negro Songs"; another extended piece, originally titled *Blues Opera*, was revised by Arlen in 1959 as *Free and Easy*, and even at this late date was understood by some to be jazz.[151] Arlen made his career out of interpreting African American themes and forms—perhaps more so than any other Jewish composer. This is especially true of his collaborations with southerner Johnny Mercer which replayed the nightmare vision that the pairing of George

Gershwin and DuBose Heyward inspired in Harold Cruse—not only a Jew and an Anglo-Saxon getting together to appropriate African American culture, but a Jew and a southern white man!

"Blues in the Night": Nightlife and Access

From the stage blackface of Al Jolson, Eddie Cantor, and Sophie Tucker to the sounds of Blackness produced by Berlin, Gershwin, Kern, Arlen, and others, Jews seemed to many to be the best-placed interpreters of African American music. By the 1920s this supposed special Jewish ability took on the force of a natural fact. Because Jews had such enormous success with African American music, it became a popular sport to devise and elaborate upon a variety of explanations for this artistic kinship.

What got lost in this shuffle was that the key to this musical relationship was the multitude of urban spaces and activities shared by Jews and African Americans. The "Negro" productions of each of the artists just listed would have been unimaginable without the actual contact these Jews had with African American people and cultural forms. (Which is not, of course, to say that African American culture was the shaping or defining influence for all or any of these Jews; in fact, for some of them—Arlen, for instance—we would have to admit the complex possibility that their greatest influences came from *other* Jews who had been deeply involved with African American music.)[152] Where, then, did these important moments of concrete interaction take place?

As many first- and second-generation Jewish novels and autobiographies have disclosed, the streets of big cities often served as the first and most influential locus of acculturation for Jews—Jewish boys, that is. The streets offered important lessons via sports, gang activities, and the simple yet profound rituals of hanging out. Lewis Erenberg has called attention to how these middle-ground streets served as a first stop as young Jews sped away from the orthodoxy of family, culture, and religion.[153] This intergenerational and intraethnic focus—with an emphasis on what was being left behind—is necessary to our understanding of how Jews ever came to African American music. Just as important is the intragenerational and interethnic perspectives, which force us to think about what these Jews actually found in these streets. The street was a crucial province in popular music's domain.[154]

Opponents of ragtime and jazz frequently noted that the chaos of street activity had inspired these new forms. According to one critic, the evil of ragtime could be traced to "the noise, rush and vulgarity of the street," while folk music remained the product of the "idyllic village" atmosphere.[155] Jews in America were largely urban—"rootless cosmopolitans," as some would have it—and many found education and inspiration in the street. Irving Howe calls the streets "the training ground for Jewish actors, comics, and singers" and offers as a prime example the comedian Joe Sulzer, who admitted that he based his act on those of African American street performers he watched during his Lower East Side childhood in the 1890s: "A colored fellow used to come and dance on our street. It was called buck dancing. He had sand and threw it on the sidewalk and danced. The sound of the sand and the shuffle of his feet fascinated me and I would try to dance like him. It made me feel I wanted to go on the stage . . . When I was fourteen, I met my partner, Dale, on Delancey Street . . . We'd pick up routines from the street."[156] The street was similarly important to young Jewish songwriters and composers—most notably Berlin and Gershwin—who found there the materials which they would combine and interpret in their own productions. In his attempt to explain where Berlin's music came from, Alexander Woollcott pointed to "the polyglot hubbub of the curbs and doorsteps of his own East Side."[157]

George Gershwin, an impressive mythmaker, always insisted that his musical talent was natural, not coached, and came to him randomly through aimless street-kid wanderings. Gershwin claimed, for instance, that he first heard Anton Rubinstein's Melody in F "played on a pianola as he stood barefoot and in overalls outside a penny arcade on One Hundred Twenty-fifth Street in Harlem."[158] Gershwin also remembered first hearing ragtime and jazz as he roller-skated in Harlem and Coney Island.[159] The young Gershwin appears here as equal parts savvy city kid and wide-eyed stranger from the provinces. In either case Gershwin heard professional renditions of various musical creations (and in the case of the player piano, a highly commodified production at that). In the legends of Gershwin's career, however (he sat down at the piano for the first time and just played!), professional African American music was regarded only as raw material for his use.

Once these budding young Jewish musicians were old enough to haunt the city's indoor sites of entertainment (for many this would be in their early teenage years), contacts with African Americans and African American music multiplied significantly. Hasia Diner reports that by the early 1930s, at least one Yiddish paper was trying "to discourage Jewish youths from slumming" in Harlem, but by then a generation of Jewish composers had already translated what they had learned from African American entertainers into broadly successful careers.[160] I have already noted the significance of blackface minstrel shows for this group of Jewish composers and performers; equally important to the development of their art was the access they had to all manner of nightspots—cabarets, clubs, roof gardens, and rathskellers—where they came into contact with African American performers.[161]

These well-placed Jewish musical figures had, so to speak, season passes and reserved tables for the best African American shows around. Jolson, for instance, was proud to be the only white man allowed into Leroy's, an African American cabaret in Harlem, during the early 1910s.[162] Carl Van Vechten, as I have noted, claimed that Gershwin's "interest in the Negro" began in 1924–25 along with his own. Van Vechten's enthusiasm for African American culture certainly inspired Gershwin, and perhaps most significantly helped Gershwin to gain entry to the parties and concerts which functioned at least in part as research trips for the composer. Yet there is abundant evidence that Gershwin was frequenting African American entertainment spots much earlier than this.[163] Gershwin had visited Harlem nightspots from his adolescent days; later on he was known to be a frequent visitor to Barron Wilkins's club on 135th Street and Seventh Avenue.[164] The music historian Charles Hamm has, in passing, suggested that Gershwin's orientation was toward Black bohemia, which marks an important distinction between Gershwin and Irving Berlin.[165] Where Berlin mined a great deal from his early contact with ragtime pianists at Mike Salter's (and, according to Eubie Blake, from watching Blake in Atlantic City as well), Gershwin continually searched out all types of African American music, from the innovative Harlem stride players to the religious music of Gullahs on the South Carolina Sea Islands.[166]

As with Berlin, however, the African Americans who seem to have had the greatest influence on Gershwin's conception of African American culture were, as the critic Paul Rosenfeld pointed out in 1929, "stage Negroes" whose success depended on the pleasure of white audiences. To complicate things further, we need to remember that many of the most influential musical presentations of Blackness—Harold Arlen writing for Cab Calloway at the Cotton Club for one—were partly scripted and largely underwritten by other Jews.[167] Through the medium of African American entertainers, a circle of influence was thus established among Jewish composers and performers. One possible response to Harold Cruse's argument that Gershwin and other Jews "achieved status and recognition in the 1920's for music that they literally stole outright from Harlem nightclubs" is to suggest that if Cruse is going to employ the vocabulary of theft, he could go much further: much of the music Gershwin and his colleagues heard was written by other Jews, and represents the yield of an earlier wave of appropriation.[168]

In addition to expanding his access to African American performers, organized social events in the 1920s provided Gershwin with a forum to show off his own skills and musical ideas. Gershwin's tendency to commandeer the piano at such gatherings is well documented. His confident showmanship allowed him to establish and advertise his privileged position as interpreter of African American music, at least among New York City's elite. Some of these listeners then went on to serve as (presumably) unpaid publicity agents for him.

A Right to Sing the Blues? Behaving and Misbehavin'

The casual social interactions with African American musicians which were so important for Gershwin and others were also sometimes augmented with active searches for material and more formally arranged relationships. This is especially true for Gershwin, who was a pupil of the African American pianist Charles Luckeyth Roberts, and who later made a trip to the South Carolina Sea Islands to collect materials for *Porgy and Bess*.[169]

The extent of contact does raise the question of direct appropriation of African American compositions by Jews. Claims of musical theft have been abundant but often difficult to trace: Eubie Blake believed that Gershwin took a Charles Luckeyth Roberts theme for his own "Swanee Ripples"; Verna Arvey, wife of the African American composer William Grant Still, thought that Gershwin might have nicked part of "I Got Rhythm" from a motif her husband used to play while he was oboist in the hugely popular 1921 show *Shuffle Along;* others have noted the use Gershwin makes of the Charleston rhythm developed by his friend James P. Johnson for his own Concerto in F.[170]

In considering these charges of larceny we must remember that however much piracy actually existed, African American musicians operated in a musical world in which they felt unable to protect the fruits of their labor—especially from the Jewish composers and publishers of Tin Pan Alley. This is nowhere more clear than in the tale of possible theft which links two giants of the era, Scott Joplin and Irving Berlin. In an essay published in 1991, Edward Berlin presented his remarkable findings which show convincingly that Scott Joplin believed that Irving Berlin stole "Alexander's Ragtime Band" from a theme he had been working on for his opera *Treemonisha;* the crucial fact is that Joplin had brought pieces of *Treemonisha* to show to Henry Waterson, a publisher with close ties to Irving Berlin. Tracking a number of different sources, including one which portrays Joplin being reduced to tears upon first hearing Berlin's song, Edward Berlin wisely concludes that it is impossible to ascertain whether Berlin truly ripped Joplin off. More important is that Joplin—not without some grounds—believed this to be true. Perhaps the most chilling piece of evidence in Edward Berlin's account is this snippet, from a gossip column in 1911, the year of "Alexander's Ragtime Band": "Scott Joplin is anxious to meet Irving Berlin. Scott is hot about something."[171]

It is clear that poaching was widespread and mainly benefited those already in positions of cultural power. In the world of Tin Pan Alley this was usually, but not always, Jews. Sometimes things got really complicated: Harry Brooks, who helped Fats Waller and Andy Razaf to arrange "Ain't Misbehavin'" for the 1929 hit show *Hot Chocolates* (featuring Louis Armstrong), confessed that this song was a conscious attempt to copy Gershwin's song "The Man I Love," imitating outright

its opening phrase and part of its bridge.[172] Into this performance of
"Ain't Misbehavin,'" Armstrong playfully incorporates an instantly recognizable bit of Gershwin's *Rhapsody in Blue*. This is a conscious commentary—though not one with an obvious point of view—on the
porous boundaries which existed between African American and Jewish
musicians, and perhaps more critically between those cultural productions which would be identified as "Negro" and "Jewish."

The musical terrain shared by African Americans and Jews was characterized—as the countless assertions of theft and interpersonal friction
attest—by a large amount of antagonism. Even so, it is important to
recognize that the central term for understanding these musical relationships is not antagonism but nearness. There was a good deal of
conscious cooperation and collaboration between Jewish and African
American musicians during this time, as the example of Will Vodery
(1885–1951) makes evident. Vodery "had been Pershing's band director
during the occupation of Germany in 1919" and was tutor to Duke
Ellington, and an early rival of James Reese Europe.[173] From the late
1910s through the 1920s, Vodery was also involved with some of the
most influential Jewish composers and productions of the decade. He
helped Gershwin obtain a (short-lived) piano-playing job at Fox's City
Theater on Fourteenth Street, and went on to orchestrate Gershwin's
Blue Monday; Vodery also did the original vocal arrangements for *Show
Boat*, a Broadway show often thrashed for being a Jewish travesty of
Blackness.[174] Other musical figures also benefited from the largesse of
African Americans. Harold Arlen, for instance, had an important audi-
tion with the Shuberts arranged for him by the African American
composer Will Marion Cook.[175] And many Jewish singers, including
Fanny Brice and Sophie Tucker, leaned heavily on the compositional
skills of African Americans.[176]

Tucker provides a particularly rich example. Her first important
signature song, "Some of These Days," was written by Shelton Brooks,
an African American songwriter. Tucker came to hear this song after
her African American maid, Mollie Elkins, more or less shamed her into
letting Brooks pitch the song to her. Elkins had been a performer
herself, but for reasons Tucker never explains in her autobiography,
earned her living as a maid for various performers. Elkins saw Tucker
through some lean times, lending her money and clothes for an impor-

tant audition. It was after Tucker had become somewhat successful that Elkins had to twist her arm to give Brooks a chance to pitch his song.[177] The career of Fanny Brice provides a similar example. When Brice needed a guaranteed winner for her performance in Ziegfeld's *Follies of 1910*, she went to Will Marion Cook and asked him for a "coon song"; he returned the next day with a completed song, "Lovie Joe," which he wrote with lyricist Joe Jordan. Brice rehearsed the song with a young pianist named George Gershwin.[178]

A wide range of the most influential Jewish and African American composers and musicians of this time were vocationally bound together. My aim in this chapter has been to demonstrate the extent of the concrete interactions of Jews and African Americans and to record the pervasive circulation of cultural and economic assets between them. This core of actual contact was indispensable to the manufacture of the various metaphors and rhetorics I trace out next—superstructural formations which came to brace and naturalize the foundation on which they were erected. The major result of all this concrete and symbolic contact was a general belief that the Jewish elevation (or, for some, exploitation) of African American–derived materials explained American popular music of the early twentieth century.

But even so, it should be noted that the relationship of Jewish and African American musicians along with the associations which lashed their works together was not the only game around. Large systems of African American musical enterprise flourished independent of this nexus, particularly outside the handful of major cities which anchored, but did not circumscribe, the music business. Successful careers, not to mention significant styles—country blues and territory band jazz to name two—remained relatively untouched by the connection of Jews and African Americans. By the mid-1920s, African American neighborhoods in New York and Chicago were being organized as critical sites for the interlocked mechanisms of consumption and production, with a heavy reliance on the so-called development of folk materials into higher forms; at the same time, actual flesh-and-blood "folk" were being "discovered" in the South and authorized to sing and play their own themes. Ralph Peer of Victor Records was particularly important for his recordings of some of the key "race" and "hillbilly" artists in the

South. Still, coming to terms with the musical association of African Americans and Jews which grew during the years in between the nationalization of ragtime and that of jazz helps us to understand how the evolution of American popular music in these years was tied up with the deepening relationship of Jews and African Americans in general.[179]

2

"I Used to Be Color Blind": The Racialness of Jewish Men

Discussions surrounding Jews in American music were, to put it briefly and mildly, overdetermined. The central issue, not surprisingly, had to do with the relationship of Jewish Americans to the melting pot. Were Jews a mixed race or pure? Which answer would indicate better results as Jews integrated into "mainstream" America? Were Jews successful *as* Jews, or was their musical success a sign of their complete Americanization? These questions were also yoked to reflections on the conspicuous uses Jews made of African Americans and "Blackness" in their musical productions and what this had to say about the position of Jews with specific reference to African Americans.

Behind the eastern European Jews who came to dominate American music were the huddled masses who had been immigrating to the United States since the early 1880s. Before this time Jewish immigration to the United States was slight and the presence of Jews in American social life negligible. German Jews such as the Seligman, Schiff, and Warburg families had been immensely successful financially; scattered acts of anti-Semitism—such as the 1877 barring of Joseph Seligman and his family from a hotel in Saratoga Springs—led to a bit of talk about nouveau riche Jews, but little widespread or sustained contemplation of the Jew in America took place before the arrival of the "new" immigrants.[1] This all changed with the wave of immigration initiated in part by the assassination of Czar Alexander II of Russia in 1881: between 1880 and 1930, 2.5 million Jews came to the United States from Russia and eastern Europe.[2] Now Jews were more conspicuous and had to be reckoned with as major factors in the American racial calculus. In particular, the takeover of the American popular music business by Jews who specialized in "Black" music inspired much discussion about their place in American social life.

What messages might be taken from the mixed signals broadcast by the public drama of Jews starring in African American music? Many have noted that musical metaphors have been particularly available as summary figures for America's multicultural life, related to, and perhaps second only to, the melting pot itself; this comes as no surprise given the significance of music in Israel Zangwill's play *The Melting Pot*, which popularized the language of "melting" in the first decade of the century.[3] The visibility of Jews in the entertainment business crossed paths with this handy metaphor and served to establish music as one of the preeminent sources of material for discussions of American Jewish identity in the early twentieth century.

Some of the most fundamental issues of the contemporary secular identity of American Jews were addressed in great detail within these musical discussions.[4] The crux of these ruminations can be put quite simply: What are Jews anyway? How do they relate to Black people? In this discussion "Black" was assumed by many to be a fixed and familiar identity to which the instability of "Jewishness" could be compared. From this root many lines of inquiry developed; all were part of the complementary and interwoven strands of European and American attempts to fix Jews in a racial/religious hierarchy. They also participated in the continuing struggle over the status of African Americans in the American nation.

Tin Pan Alley and Broadway provided congenial places for Jews and their friends to discuss the race of Jews with the confidence that they could successfully promote "Jewishness" as a healthy mixture; Jewishness, in the musical arena, was put on display as a prototype of melting pot success. One accomplishment of the Jews of Tin Pan Alley was to advertise a nonexclusive vision of American nationality rooted not in compulsory and static concepts of race or organic peoplehood but in mobility and union. Even when these Jews did seem to constitute a "race," their racialness was most often explained as a *form* or a *style* of cultural mixing rather than an unchanging essence. In other words, the "race" of Jews was defined mostly by its mutability, its gift for assimilating the racial characteristics of "other" peoples into itself. This came most clear in the productions of composers such as George Gershwin and Irving Berlin, which so many Americans heard as triumphant syntheses of divergent "racial" streams.

Jews in America were not securely fastened into their current identity as "white" ethnics until after World War II. No matter where American commentators stood on the Jewish purity versus mixture issue, near-unanimity existed that there was a Jewish racialness, and that one could perceive it not only in Jewish people but also in the things they made. The matter of debate had to with what constituted their racialness and how it would function in America. In this light I want to advance George Gershwin, Irving Berlin, and their colleagues as major players in what might be called Jewish racial formation. These powerful cultural actors were able, in their musical productions and in their "off-stage" behavior, to wear Jewishness as a kind of magic, a lucky charm which allowed its owner good access to American stuff—especially African American materials.

In this chapter I explore the various ways in which Jewish musicians and those around them co-opted fraught languages of Jewish racialness in order to construct an argument about what we would currently call the "ethnic" (rather than the "racial," or religious) identity of the Jew. The Jewish peoplehood enshrined in this process of ethnic formation was mostly about history—sacred and secular. Less invested in present-day religious practices than in past experiences of oppression, this public fashioning of Jewish identity opened up new ways for American Jews to demonstrate their cultural value. One major benefit of this cultural work is that it allowed Jews—required them, really—to authenticate that they had a natural and productive relationship to both Old World Europe and New World Black America. Jews used the field of music, that is, to establish Black-Jewish relations as a healthy and necessary component of the American melting pot.

What is perhaps most impressive about this achievement is that it allowed these Jews and their fans to revise the race concepts which had done (and would again do) so much to oppress other Jews. The rhetoric around these successful Jews in music made it more possible to imagine that their success owed much to their Jewishness. In short, it represented a move to alter the valence of Jewishness in the cultural arena. Jewishness itself was now being presented as a major social endowment, one which granted its holder amazing powers to blend various American musical vernaculars—most notably the African American—into one triumphant whole. One important message communicated by the success of Irving Berlin's early ragtime hits, George Gershwin's *Rhapsody in Blue*, or Harold Arlen's Cotton Club compositions was that being of Jewish descent was the best possible preparation for a career in American music. So, whatever the Jews of Broadway and Tin Pan Alley *actually* did for, or to, African Americans, it is clear that they used their power in the world of popular culture to organize the idiom of Black-Jewish relations as one which emphasized cultural pluralism, cooperation, and patriotism.

"The Poetry of Motion": Varieties of Jewish Experience

For decades before the rise of the Jews on Tin Pan Alley and Broadway, all manner of people—from racist anthropologists to Jewish Marxists and Zionists—had debated the racial status of Jews, both in Europe and in the United States. As eastern European Jews poured into American cities and partisans of various causes tried to describe their prospects for success in America, a central concern was whether Jews were a pure or mixed race. As late as the 1920s it was not clear what the implications of either answer would be—to put it crudely, if Jews were better off mixed or pure. Sander Gilman's attempt to provide an overview of the fluctuating imaging of Jews leads him to suggest that in the modern nation, Jews often serve as a prime Other used for self-definition. When a group of people prides itself on its healthy mixedness, Jews are imaged as overpure; when racial purity is a standard, Jews appear as the worst brand of mongrel.[5]

Proponents of a circumscribed and exclusive Jewish racialness almost definitionally render Jews marginal, destined to live quietly in their self-sustaining bloodline ghettos. The argument that Jews are racially pure has been put forth by anti-Semites who employ it to argue that

Jews marginalize themselves, as well as by Zionists who insist that Jews had better keep themselves separate.

The extensive presence of Jews in the American popular music scene of the early twentieth century made it more and more difficult to imagine that they inhabited an unmixed, culturally pure racial ghetto: success in the American marketplace argued against the proposition. The belief that Jews are a mixed race has always been more popular than its obverse.[6] The "mongrel" blood thesis was easily incorporated into related debates over culture. The conclusions of racial science would become, in fact, a crucial model for discussions of what the presence of Jews in popular music said about the potential of the melting pot in America.[7] There have also been some who have advanced the notion not only that Jews are the most blended of peoples, but also that this is their strength. Martin Buber saw Jews, in their mixedness, as the perfect bridge between East and West.[8] One logical end of this line of thought is to imagine that "Jew" names a form with no definite content: the novelist Nathanael West, for instance, thought that "the original Jewish people had wandered so far and blended so deeply into the blood of the countries they found that it was senseless to identify them as a blood strain."[9] But to speak of Jews as blended has usually led to considerations of what Jews did with their special access to all sorts of racial matter.

To use Walter Benn Michaels's formulation, discussions of Jewish visibility in music in the 1910s and 1920s (and before) helped translate "race" into culture.[10] Michaels argues that the concept of distinct "cultures" which evolved in the World War I era was a dodge: pretending to be nonracial, "culture" never got much past the idea of "race" that it was meant to replace. As a result, Michaels concludes, "the assertion of cultural identity depends upon an identity that cannot be cultural—we are not Jews because we do Jewish things, we do Jewish things because we are Jews."[11] But Michaels draws his interpretation from relatively few literary, anthropological, and sociological texts, and the popular music scene suggests that some major revision might be in order.

The principal lesson taught by the success of Jews in the music business is that "Jewish things" are, quite simply, all things. These Jews constructed their public image as "omni-Americans": they bypassed the frightening question of what is lost by assimilation into mainstream culture by suggesting that "assimilation" is something that Jews did to other people and their cultural materials—and this while they intermarried, hit the big time, and practiced no religious Judaism. The work of the Jews of Tin Pan Alley and Broadway instructed numerous sympathetic observers to understand the culture of the Jewish "race" to be defined by fusion.[12] These Jewish productions positioned their makers at the heart of modern city life.

The promise of these musical Jews in American life is that they would gladly contribute cultural capital to the American scene without making demands for political power. Irving Berlin put some of this into "Let Me Sing and I'm Happy," which Al Jolson sang as he played the minstrel Mr. Bones in the 1930 movie *Mammy*: "What care I who makes the laws of the nation? . . . As long as I can sing its popular songs?"[13] Berlin was not the only one to be so confident about the Jewish attraction to what so many people heard as Black music; the real master of this was George Gershwin. But here Berlin is able to promote the Jewish performer as a happy white ethnic, content with his portion in the cultural marketplace. What these Jewish composers suggested with such popular productions, in fact, was an influential—if now little-noticed—form of Jewish American cultural nationalism.[14]

Leading a group sing of that old "E Pluribus Unum," Jewish composers and performers were able *as Jews* to justify their place at the center of American popular culture. Moreover, they provided an example of how Jews—in their mixedness and social agility—might operate as an emblem of the healthy nation. The historian Lewis Erenberg argues that Jews were "consummate all around performers because they themselves were rootless"; the mobility of these particular cosmopolitans did not have to be feared (except by Henry Ford and a few other extremists) because it was so obviously being deployed in the service of the cultural well-being of the nation.[15]

The rhetoric which accompanied the career of George Gershwin, for instance, lent credibility to the notion that Jews were healthy cosmopolitans with the special ability to organize the discrete tributaries of American music into a mainstream. Unlike Gershwin, Irving Berlin did not find it so easy to wear his Jewishness as if it were synonymous with Americanness; his overt crowd pleasing (e.g., *This Is the Army*, "God

Bless America") betrays a certain anxiety about his authority to speak American.

The rise of Jews in the arts, particularly in music, has frequently generated a corresponding rise in theorizing about the more general place of the Jew in relation to the modern nation. Various cultural and sociological categories—"middleman" and "stranger" to name two— have been created or adapted to explain the Jew's position in the nation.[16] The prior assumption of most of these speculations is that however blended and flexible Jews might be, they are not organically of the nation. (Race, of course, is not always antithetical to nation; some- times it is constitutive. But the *racialness* of the Jew has never defined any nation, except in the negative.)

So even while the notion of "mixed blood" is itself a metaphor meant to explain the race of the Jew, it has spawned even more elaborate metaphors about the Jew's cultural place. These cultural metaphors have often circled around the flexibility and adaptability of the Jew. The Harlem stride pianist Willie the Lion Smith, for one, insisted that his own mixture of blood (Jewish, Spanish, Mohawk Indian, French, and African) explained his ability to excel at so many musical forms—includ- ing "cantoring."[17] Smith is an interesting case study because he does not try to hide (much) how the move from "blood" (or "race") to "culture" gets executed. Smith's account of his Jewish origins cannot be taken too literally. Very early on in his written autobiography Smith hints that he is Jewish by way of his light-skinned father, whose last name is Ber- tholoff, not through his mother. But Smith's father drops out of the picture quickly, and it is through his mother that Smith finds the source for the most significant aspects of his character—his musicality and Jewish spirituality above all.

For Smith, blood is a metaphor which connects a vague genealogy to a significant body of sentiment. In short, "blood" equals "spirit" for Smith. It follows that as Smith limns his strong attractions to Jews and Judaism, he subtly shifts focus and puts an accent on a symbolic gene- alogy of "Jewishness" inspired by his mother rather than the positivistic demonstration of patrilinear descent implied initially. Once past his early ruminations on an inherited Jewishness, Smith next focuses on a "natural" interest in Hebrew prayer which he picks up at a Jewish home where he is dropping off laundry. For the bulk of his memoirs, however,

Smith leaves behind the explicitly religious allure of Jewishness. Instead, he calls attention to a Jewishness defined by such nebulous
concepts as "soul" or to his own skills at the languages of Jewishness,
described variously as Hebrew, Yiddish, or Jewish, but at times revealed
to be simply the language of commerce. Smith's looseness in defining
the boundaries of Hebrew and Yiddish (or "Jewish," as he and many
others often termed it) inserts both into a public sphere which removes
from them, respectively, sacred character and historical specificity. The
effect is to eliminate "chosenness" as a key category for understanding
Jewishness, and to make the boundaries between Jews and others more
porous than previously understood.

Smith was hardly the first commentator to call attention to the
adaptability of Jews and Jewishness. Many nineteenth-century anti-
Semites saw the mixedness of the Jew as an explanation only for the
Jew's ability to imitate well. Through their singular combination of
marginality and privilege, the argument went, Jews become ideal imi-
tators. In his notorious 1850 essay "Jews in Music," Richard Wagner
asserted that even as the Jew can speak any national language, it is
always as an alien. This line was picked up wholesale by, among others,
Adolf Hitler and the *Dearborn Independent.* Henry Ford's paper brought
forward the economic complaint always lurking in this formulation as
it noted that "Jews do not create: they take what others have done, give
it a clever twist, and exploit it." In American culture this old charge
made against Jews becomes complicated by the fact that a similar charge
was often employed to explain African American achievement in the
arts and sciences.[18]

The idea that Jews reaped benefit from their contingent racial/social
status owes much to anti-Semites, but was also picked up on by scores
of Jews and philo-Semites after the turn of the century; it was the
foundation of the belief that Jews were better situated than any other
group to orchestrate the many races and musical forms which made up
America, not to mention other countries. An influential Marxist summary of this approach was devised by Isaac Deutscher, who wrote of a
notable Jewish type—exemplified by Marx, Heine, and Trotsky—which he called the "non-Jewish Jew": living "on the margins or
in the nooks and crannies of their respective nations," these exceptional
figures are "in society yet not in it, of it and yet not of it."[19] The

assumption made here (which travels throughout discussions of Jews in music) is that rather than being driven into cultural ghettos by their religious and racial heritage, Jews are actually the most agile of secular people. Others have worked variations on this theme, alternately emphasizing either the temporal or the spatial aspects of Jewish mobility. Thorstein Veblen, for instance, writing in 1919 of the "intellectual pre-eminence of Jews," struck an anti-Zionist pose as he argued that concretely moving out of the ghetto and becoming one of the "aliens of the uneasy feet" prefigures the success of the Jew.[20] The influential American sociologist Robert Park reached similar conclusions, arguing that out of the ghetto the Jew becomes a cultural hybrid, "the first cosmopolite and citizen of the world."[21]

"For Your Country and My Country": Melting Pots and Orchestras

The increasing number of Jews in America around the turn of the century motivated many people to consider how these immigrants would adapt and what their presence would mean for (and do to) American identity. The "race" of Jews could be discussed as race itself—as the immigration restrictionists did—or as a discrete culture and history, as did most every observer of the Jewish ascendancy in popular music. The American Jewish composers and performers who were so successful in the early twentieth century offered in their art, and in the example of their own lives, a model of Americanization which at least provisionally appeared to avoid the pitfalls, and consolidate the promise, of the two major symbological paradigms which existed at the time—the melting pot and the orchestra.[22]

Werner Sollors has argued that whether a melting pot "actually" existed or not, it was a pervasive ideological structure which drew attacks from both the left and the right; even opponents of melting pot ideology have been dominated by the image it established for the Americanizing process which Sollors calls "universal regeneration." Whereas Henry Pratt Fairchild and his ilk attacked the melting pot for its "mongrelizing" effects, Horace Kallen, Randolph Bourne, and others attacked from the left, abhorring its "homogenizing" implications, and developing in its stead a descriptive/prescriptive idea of "cultural pluralism" which used the orchestra as an emblem.[23] The figure of the orchestra was meant to suggest that even as different peoples might come together peacefully, even productively, they need not and should not forfeit their special racial gifts. More concretely, as Sollors shows, there was nothing coincidental about Kallen's choice of the orchestra image, for it mobilized a familiar optimism that the arts might be a first—and perhaps best—place for the experiments of racial mixing. There were limitations to the figure of the orchestra: it was rooted in a static conception of racial identity and its expressibility, and it was steeped in assumptions of Western music which excluded African and African American contributions.[24] Jules Chametzky has asked a quite sensible question which is a gloss on one posed earlier by Philip Gleason and others: "If this country is like an orchestra, does it follow that there must be a conductor? Who? And a score? Who wrote it?"[25] If we follow MacDonald Moore's example in discussing American music, we might suggest that until the 1910s or so, Yankees enjoyed complete control and spent the next few decades struggling to maintain it. But Moore's purview is mainly highbrow, and this alone limits the applicability of his conclusions. After all, popular musical theater had been an ethnic free-for-all for decades at this point. I want to suggest that the Jewish takeover of popular music (as well as of what we might retrospectively call middlebrow music) in the 1910s and 1920s provided a compelling linkage of orchestra and melting pot into a design which was utopian in form but not in substance.

Most commentators on American ethnicity have discussed the melting pot and the orchestra as representing discrete and indeed competing ideologies: Kallen's 1915 essay "Democracy *versus* the Melting-Pot" is an early expression of this tendency.[26] But the Jewish adaptations of African American music which I am concerned with present a third possibility, that a certain degree of complementarity obtained between the melting pot and orchestra visions. The two models could exist simultaneously as powerful cultural metaphors because each had its own discrete responsibilities. To put it most broadly for now, "melting pot" functioned on a global plane while "orchestra" did more localized work. I mean this first quite concretely, and only secondarily on the level of operative metaphor. On the material plane, jazz and related forms could be exported as typical examples of America's racial progressivism

("melting pot")—thus carrying out an important diplomatic function—even as at home the music would continue to be understood to
have discrete and recognizable components ("orchestra"): James Weldon Johnson notes in his preface to *The Book of American Negro Poetry*
(1922) that ragtime was "the one artistic production by which America
is known the world over. It has been all conquering. Everywhere it is
hailed as 'American music.'"[27]

George Gershwin later applied this same sentiment to jazz. In the
early 1930s he wrote (or contracted someone to write for him) an essay
in which he tried to define jazz. Jazz, said Gershwin, is "a word which
has been used for at least five or six different types of music. It is really
a conglomeration of many things. It has a little bit of ragtime, the blues,
classicism and spiritual." Gershwin concludes with an argument that
was particularly common at the time, holding that whatever goes into
jazz, when it is played "in another nation, it is called American."[28] This
formulation—used by James Weldon Johnson, among many others—is
meant to end debate over the origins of jazz by appealing to the
common sense of Europeans who received it as American because they
escaped the pitfalls of racialized thinking. But taken more cynically,
Gershwin's claim represents a motivated export of melting pot ideology
to (presumably) unwitting Europeans. This is not to deny that from
early on European people—particularly in France and Denmark—have
embraced African American music as high art and African American
musicians in their full humanity. Even so, the marketing of ragtime and
jazz as simply "American" products can be understood to have played a
politically quietistic role by providing a utopian narrative of American
race relations.[29]

An unspoken corollary to this axiom that Europeans can be counted
on to appreciate the "Americanness" of jazz is that actual Americans are
constrained to call attention to the various racial aspects of jazz because
Americans cannot help but hear them. In a different context Edward
Said has summarized the impulse behind such classifying moves in
musicology:

> To focus more narrowly upon what is purely European, or German,
> or French, or Jewish, or Indian, Black, Muslim, etc., is then to accept
> the very principle of a separate essentialization—the separation of the

Jewish essence from the German, or the black from the white, etc.—and along with that to purify the types and to turn them into universals . . . [These] universals stand today as the legacy of the imperializing process by which a dominant culture eliminated the impurities and hybrids that actually make up all cultures.[30]

In American scholarly and popular approaches to music, this denial of hybridity has most often appeared as an acutely felt need to separate the white from the Black. George Pullen Jackson's 1943 work *White and Negro Spirituals* stands as perhaps the signal (dubious) achievement of this desire in the world of scholarship; on the popular side one has only to look at the trouble *Billboard* has gone to in order to separate white and Black music.[31]

To illustrate my argument about the complex cultural work done by the careers and creations of George Gershwin and his peers, let me first turn briefly to the specific example of his *Rhapsody in Blue*. In a suggestive essay Werner Sollors asserts that the "utopian interpretations of the term 'jazz age' always stressed the modernism that comes from bridging opposites: African masks and western traditions led to cubism; black syncopation and the modernization of romantic music combined to create ragtime and jazz." Therefore, Sollors concludes, truly "modern" as well as distinctively "American" art forms could be understood as springing from racial fusion.[32] This is a productive approach to understanding the excitement attending the debut of Gershwin's *Rhapsody in Blue* (which he planned originally to call *American Rhapsody*) at Paul Whiteman's "Experiment in Modern Music" in 1924.

When Paul Whiteman—himself rumored to be a Jew—contracted with George Gershwin to write this piece, Jews were already well established as prime interpreters and translators of African American music.[33] Even Gershwin himself, never very articulate about his own compositions, made some quite subtle claims about his art in describing the evolution of this work. Here is how Gershwin described the moment of inspiration for *Rhapsody in Blue:* "It was on the train, with its steely rhythms, its rattle-ty-bang that is so often stimulating to a composer . . . I frequently hear music in the very heart of noise. And there I suddenly heard—and even saw on paper—the complete construction of [it]."[34] In this era two kinds of composers might have been most likely to claim inspiration from a train: the avant-garde innovator experimenting with industrial noise and the rural blues or country artist, who would not be called "composer" or be riding first class with George Gershwin. Gershwin pulls off an impressive rhetorical feat here: he claims to have had an authoritative and immediate moment of complete inspiration, which grants him the ability to stylize train sounds. He not only incorporates African American "folk" music into his higher work, but also assimilates into his own person the mythologized pose of the African American "folk" performer. So if with the *Rhapsody* Gershwin had written "the Declaration of Independence of Jazz," perhaps the central "liberating" act he facilitated was to loosen jazz from its racial moorings.[35]

The immediate responses to the *Rhapsody* make it clear that Gershwin's work could be heard "globally" as embodying "Americanness" while its many racial strains remained distinctly audible. A reviewer for *The Nation* was particularly invested in tracing out how the piece could be both mixed and uniform at once:

> It was, on the whole, a curious orgy of unrestrained laughter and tears, in which East and West met and merged with strange, half-caste results. There were, for instance, sustained, drawn-out Slavic effects in melodic passages, of pure, Anglo-Saxon bathos. Perverted brasses and winds depicted, in subtle and intoxicating colors, humor of the slap-stick variety. Aphrodisiacal rhythms alternated with those of the ordinary dance. And in "The Rhapsody in Blue," which takes its title from the Negro phase of jazz, one heard a dialogue between American slang and expressions as elemental as the soil . . . With it all one cannot but wonder whether this now Slavic, now Oriental element in jazz is not due to the fact that many of those who write, orchestrate, and play it are of Russian-Jewish extraction; whether, in fact, jazz, with it elements of Russian, the Negro, and the native American is not the first distinctive phase of the melting-pot for which we have been waiting so long and which seems to have such endless possibilities.[36]

As I have suggested, the most important expression of Gershwin's racialness is its flexibility; the "stuff" of Jewishness—the Slavic and Oriental strains—is important, but not nearly so significant as the polyglot stylistic abilities of the Jewish musician which make it possible for him to establish "Jewish" and "American" as mutually energizing points on a creative circle. Thus both "melting pot" and "orchestra" could be in effect simultaneously because musical productions of "Americanness" were widely held to be a featured expression of the plastic racialness of Jews. This belief was expressed clearly by an early Gershwin biographer who suggested that the fact that Gershwin "was a Jew and that many of his musical sources were Negroid confirms his basic Americanism. For this is not a country of race, it is a country of amalgamated races."[37]

Gershwin and his followers consistently proclaimed the composer's racial fitness to do this work. Gershwin, describing *Porgy and Bess*, asserted that he had devised a method of pastiche which he could adapt "to utilize the drama, the humor, the superstition, the religious fervor, the dancing and the irrepressible high spirits of the race."[38] (It is interesting to note that many Jewish entertainers, including Fanny Brice and Mezz Mezzrow, also used "the race" to refer to Jews.)[39] Rouben Mamoulian, the director of *Porgy and Bess*, loved "all the emotional richness of the Negro soul expressed in it"; the vocal coach Alexander Steinert saw it as typically American, capturing "the vibrant gayety of Broadway and Harlem, the nostalgia of the South, as depicted by a composer whose racial background and environment enabled him to understand these things so well."[40]

Racialized terms of analysis were also employed by unfriendly critics of *Rhapsody in Blue* and other Gershwin works. The English musicologist Constant Lambert saw jazz not as "raw material" but rather as half-finished material. As a result Gershwin's jazz-inspired work struck him as "the hybrid child of a hybrid. A rather knowing and unpleasant child too, ashamed of its parents and boasting of its French lessons."[41] Here Lambert uses an easily recognizable rhetoric of the Jew as cultural newcomer, as striver. Now negatively construed, Jewishness is still marked off by its expression in mixed products.

Gershwin's attempt to forge unity from diversity was widely noted and derided by critics of *Porgy and Bess* (1935). Writing about this work, the composer and critic Virgil Thomson lamented that the "material is straight from the melting pot. At best it is a piquant but highly unsavory stirring-up together of Israel, Africa and the Gaelic Isles." (Naming Jews, African Americans, and Irish, Thomson might as well have announced that *Porgy and Bess* held the history of blackface minstrelsy in it.) Thomson goes on to note and assail the diffuse nature of *Porgy and Bess*'s artistic approach as well, calling it "crooked folklore and halfway opera." Ralph Matthews, the regular arts writer for the *Baltimore Afro-American*, agreed, noting that in its hybridity *Porgy and Bess* lacked the "deep sonorous incantations so frequently identified with the racial offerings." African American choral director Hall Johnson was also cautiously critical, utilizing language which was sometimes used by scientific racists to explain the sterility of "hybrids": "When the leaves are gathered by strange hands they soon wither, and when cuttings are transplanted into strange soil, they have but a short and sickly life."[42] Duke Ellington upped the ante by claiming that Gershwin had no method but only a sweeping talent for appropriation: "Mr. Gershwin didn't discriminate—he borrowed from everyone from Lizst to Dickie Wells' kazoo." Edward Morrow, in a critical piece included with an Ellington interview, added that it was time to "debunk Gershwin's lampblack Negroisms"; this final phrase calls attention to Gershwin's tangible roots in minstrelsy.[43] Morrow, writing in the left-wing magazine *New Theatre*, was virtually alone in suggesting that rather than pointing forward to a new kind of American art, Gershwin's *Porgy and Bess* was instead a late-model reproduction of one of America's oldest popular cultural forms. Rudi Blesh elaborated on the same point in 1946:

> Gershwin's *Porgy and Bess* is not Negro opera despite a Negro cast, a liberal use of artificial coloration, and the inclusion of some street cries. It is *Negroesque*, and the earlier travesty of minstrelsy is continued in a form more subtle and therefore more insidious. This work and more recent ones, like the operetta *Cabin in the Sky*, betray a more deplorable tendency than mere superficiality and lack of understanding. By enlisting actual Negroes for the public performance of the Tin Pan Alley potpourri, a new stereotype—this time a cultural one—is being fitted to the Negro in which he is set forth as an able entertainer singing a music that the white public finds to be just like *its own*.

I would add that Gershwin was hardly the only "high" art performer to repackage minstrelsy as modernism.[44]

Given Gershwin's interest in assigning to himself solid American status through his racial gift for producing pastiche, it is no surprise that he never carried through on his plans to write an opera based on the S. Ansky (Solomon Rappaport) adaptation of the Yiddish folktale *The Dybbuk*. According to Irving Howe, this story of the supernatural became the "most widely produced and acclaimed of Yiddish plays"; it had a run in 1926 at the Neighborhood Playhouse, a Lower East Side experimental theater. In 1929 Gershwin made some tentative agreements with Otto Kahn of the Metropolitan Opera, and at least one Yiddish paper announced that Gershwin was going to "shelve" jazz in favor of opera. Gershwin even spoke of traveling abroad to study Jewish music and collect folk materials, as he later would travel to South Carolina in preparation for writing *Porgy and Bess*.[45] Interestingly, as David Roskies has explained, Ansky had already done the work which Gershwin planned: *The Dybbuk* represents an act of recuperation by Ansky of a "most compelling version of a life that was about to vanish" for an audience which was mostly secular and non-Jewish.[46] But Gershwin's plans came to naught, purportedly because the composer discovered that an Italian named Lodovico Rocca owned the musical rights to the material. (Rocca did present *Il Dibuc* at La Scala in 1934.)[47] Oscar Levant, a Gershwin crony, remarks in his memoir that it "was a stroke of remarkable good fortune" that Gershwin's "serious consideration of such a play as Ansky's *Dybbuk* for operatic purposes was set aside in favor of *Porgy*, in which his songwriting talent found a natural outlet through his Negroid characters."[48] In a perverse way Levant is right: although Gershwin was not shy about emphasizing the material and historical content of his Jewishness when it was convenient, his career relied on an ability to sell Jewishness as a flexible modality—and one particularly suited for absorbing African American music.

Gershwin's death at a youthful age no doubt contributed to the inflated proclamations made about his agile talents, but the racial claims had currency throughout his productive years, and have been repeated frequently even by recent commentators on Jewish involvement in African American music. Ronald Sanders has offered the most explicit sociohistorical explanation for why Jews excelled at pastiche, and how in doing so they were able to wrap themselves in the mantle of Americanness. According to Sanders, pastiche is the "gift of people who live in culturally ambivalent situations, as white Americans have in general throughout their history—which is ever poised somewhere between a European past and a New World present—and as Jews have been throughout their much longer history. It is therefore not surprising that Jews have always had a special talent for pastiche."[49] The foundation of this argument is that a historically determined prior relationship obtained between Jews and Americans before Jews ever hit these shores. The further implication is that Jews occupy a unique position in American cultural life, and are gifted with the ability to articulate Americanness through their Jewishness. The magic of this synergistic relationship is not only that the two identities are sustainable, but that they are in fact mutually supportive. Of course this approach to understanding Jewish success in America does not come to terms with the reality that "Jewish pastiche" actually brought together materials that represented the yield of earlier fusions, usually with important input from African Americans. This oversight can be explained by making reference to another endowment of Jews in America—their ability to assimilate and repackage Blackness. Here we discover the great ability of this variant of Jewish cultural nationalism to explain the power of Jewishness.

The discourse generated by and about Gershwin was incorporated into a much larger one which included considerations of the special ethnic gifts of Jews and the unique blendedness of African American music. Berndt Ostendorf has written that the "Afro-American aesthetic initiated by ragtime and jazz does not so much represent a specific genre of music, but rather projects a world view, namely a uniquely urban, modernist attitude of improvisation, invention, and 'bricolage.'"[50] The ennobling impulse in Ostendorf's rendering is admirable, but it neglects the flip side of such fluidity: the porous boundaries of ragtime and jazz which allowed for productive cross-cultural exchanges to take place also left them vulnerable to total expropriation. Edward Berlin suggests that a universalizing tendency took hold of ragtime in the second decade of the twentieth century, as stereotyped "coon" songs gave way to titles such as "Eskimo Rag" (1912), "Parisian Rag" (1910), and Irving Berlin's "That International Rag" (1913). On the face of things, this seems to be a wholly positive development.[51] But, first of all, "coon" lyrics did not disappear, as "Alexander's Ragtime Band" demonstrates; instead they were folded into the larger process of racialization at work. Many of Berlin's earliest songs took part in this evolution. "Marie from Sunny Italy," "Alexander's Bag-Pipe Band," and "Yiddle on Your Fiddle Play Some Ragtime" each participated in the decades-old American stage tradition of treating ethnicity and national origin mostly as a joke.[52] "Alexander's Bag-Pipe Band" begins:

> Last week when Alexander McIntosh
> Returned from a trip to Yankee Land,
> He got a half a dozen pipers with their bag pipes
> And organized a band.
> He brought back with him a Yankee tune
> That was written all about a coon.[53]

Taken together with the broad uses which were concurrently made of African American music by white musicians, this tendency makes it harder to see which contributions to American popular music come from African Americans. Not incidentally, Berlin also described his own earlier "Alexander" song as a "Yankee tune," thus underlining the Americanness of his own productions. As early as 1910 Berlin was confident that the Jewish involvement with African American music was recognizable and sturdy enough to bear the weight of parody: "Yiddle on Your Fiddle Play Some Ragtime" depicts a woman named Sadie becoming ecstatic when she hears Yiddle—she calls him "mine choc'late baby"—play ragtime.[54] Even as the democratization of rag-time song had obviously progressive implications, it also contributed to the success enjoyed by Jewish musicians in subsuming Blackness into the ethnic cut-and-paste jobs which they presented and promoted as one yield of their own racial gifts.

The major Jewish composers all contributed to this positioning of Jews as experts of ethnic pastiche, but Gershwin was particularly keen on discussing his ambitious musical plans, most of which were predicated on a belief in his special endowment for bringing diverse forms of music together. This is what Gershwin told his first biographer about his aspiration: "What I'd like to do would be to write an opera of the melting pot, of New York City itself, which is the symbolic and the actual blend of the native and immigrant strains. This would allow for many kinds of music, black and white, Eastern and Western, and would call for a style that should achieve, out of this diversity, an artistic and an aesthetic unity."[55] This plucky declaration reminds us, first of all, that a major difference between Gershwin and, say, the African American composer and pianist James P. Johnson is that, while both desired to write "great" music built on American themes, only Gershwin had the institutional support necessary to certify—and of course remunerate—his work: the relative silence surrounding the 1928 Carnegie Hall debut of Johnson's orchestral suite *Yamekraw* makes for interesting comparison with the debut of *Rhapsody in Blue* at Aeolian Hall.[56] In addition to the arrogance which most biographers treat as a rather charming eccentricity, George Gershwin's familiar-sounding bit of melting pot rhetoric is most notable for the way Gershwin substitutes "New York City" where "America" or "the United States" usually goes; this itself can be read as a moment of hubris, since it was hardly a given that any equivalency obtained between the city and the nation. The southern writer Donald Davidson no doubt expressed the feelings of many when he wrote in 1934 that New York, with its radicalism and its foreigners, had enacted a "spiritual secession" from the Union in the 1920s.[57] Gershwin did work on and off during the mid-1920s on a group of twenty-four preludes he planned to call *The Melting Pot;* he played five of them at a 1926 recital which, according to various critics, included evocations of blues, jazz, Chopin, Charleston rhythms, Spanish melodies, and Debussy.[58]

For a number of reasons, which included his lack of technical musical education and his lower ranking on the "brow" scale of American music, Irving Berlin was territorial and defensive about his art in a way that Gershwin had less need to be. Berlin had particularly strong reasons for writing African Americans out of his musical landscape, and made a point of doing so. He claimed in 1915 that his songs alone "started the ragtime mania,"[59] and later insisted that the most popular songwriters in America were all of "Russian birth and ancestry" and of "pure white blood."[60] Such an absolute erasure of African Americans is rare but not unheard of; the more common practice was to assume that African Americans supplied the raw materials which Jews cultivated.

In either case Berlin is true to predictable form in his assertion that this "sort of musical melting pot" was having its popular expression in the work of "Russian" (a synonym for Jewish) composers. The same confidence is disclosed by Jerome Kern in a famous Tin Pan Alley anecdote. Kern, as the story goes, was asked by a worried Oscar Hammerstein II what kind of music he was going to write for a stage version of Donn Byrne's *Messer Marco Polo*, a story written by an Irishman about an Italian in China. Kern's response: "It'll be good Jewish music."[61] In his novel *I Thought of Daisy*, Edmund Wilson tweaks this trope as he describes a character hearing a song at Coney Island which was in "a nondescript dialect—perhaps the result of Irish actors learning from Jewish comedians how to sing Negro songs."[62] Of course, historically speaking, it was the Jews who learned from the Irish "how to sing Negro"; but Wilson's claim is that in the 1920s, the language of the Jews had become the language of urban America. A fable which provides a similar moral with a final turn of the screw has Cole Porter, an Episcopalian from Indiana, telling Richard Rodgers that he had found the key to making it in American music after having labored unsuccessfully for some time: "I'll write Jewish tunes." The punch line, as Rodgers puts it, is that Porter did in fact go on to write the most enduring "Jewish" music of the time.[63]

That the Jews of Tin Pan Alley hit their peak at just about the same time that the National Origins Act of 1924 was passed (which restricted further immigration of eastern European Jews among others) leads us to a few provisional conclusions.[64] First, we might revisit Walter Benn Michaels's race-into-culture formulation in order to note that just as shifting mores made the concept of "culture" an attractive way to discuss race in the 1920s, so had "race" already been a way to talk about the cultural makeup of the United States.[65] Even as the National Origins Act represents the outcome of years of propaganda about "race," its spirit—a moot desire to protect, justify, and/or reestablish cultural purity—could never be enforced by its letter. The 1924 law was a "triumph" for nativists, but it was also futile. The success of Jews in jazz, to cite just one example, verifies this.

The supple racialness of Jews (maybe white, definitely mixed), as well as their social and historical marginality, made the Jewish relationship to ragtime and jazz—also mixed and marginal—appear to be organic, legitimate, and maybe even predestined.[66] This is not to suggest, of course, that Jewish composers, performers, and so on, received any kind of official sanction for this intervention, but to point out that a wide

road had been paved which led to the naturalization of Jewish involvement with African American music. This cross-cultural encounter was
then absorbed by, and helped to reanimate, the handy cultural metaphors of melting pot and orchestra. Even as the late 1910s and 1920s
were dark years for all manner of racial and ethnic outsiders, the good
fortune of many Jews in popular music continued to suggest that the
national advancement of *some* people might still be a reasonable
goal—especially for those willing to barter political conservatism or
quietism for social gain.

"A Typical Self-Made American": Samuel Ornitz's *Haunch Paunch and Jowl*

Perhaps the most fascinating contemporary elaboration of the idea that
the special gift of Jews was flexibility came with Samuel Ornitz's 1923
novel *Haunch Paunch and Jowl*. This mock-autobiography has received
scant critical attention in the years since its publication, but was hugely
popular at first and was accepted in many quarters as the memoirs of a
judge that it pretended to be. It was serialized in the radical Yiddish
newspaper the *Morning Freiheit*, and later dramatized by the working-
class theater, the Artef.[67]

This picaresque novel was originally published as an anonymous
autobiography, presumably to stimulate interest and sales. Gabriel
Miller suggests in his introduction to a 1986 edition of the book (now
retitled *Allrightniks Row* by publisher Markus Wiener, who thought it
would sell better under this title) that there was probably some concern
on the part of publisher Horace Liveright that the book would be
perceived as anti-Semitic.[68] Numerous publishers, it seems, had already turned the book down for just this reason. Ornitz was indeed
forced to defend himself against charges of anti-Semitism, which he
did by quoting the words of one reader who called it simply "a book of
Americans by an American."[69] This claim activates the image of Jews
as flexible and adaptive *because* of their ethnic/historical past; the sense
that Jews were, in fact, perfectly suited racially to take their place as
Americans infused discussions surrounding Jewish involvement within
African American music.

There is an idealized vision of Americanness in *Haunch Paunch and*

Jowl, but it is a complex image based on a blending of disparate ethnic and racial elements. Although the novel ends with its main character abandoning the hopeful vision of ethnic and racial amalgamation of its middle section, the whole book is filled with images of middle grounds, mixes, and happy compromises. Nowhere is this more obvious than in the "fourth period" of the book, in which ragtime song is posited as the utopian moment in which "African rhythm" and "Semitic coloring" combine to form a joyous American music.

Ragtime, as we know, was itself a hybrid form, with its European-derived emphasis on written-out composition and an African- and African American–inspired rhythmic sense. It had no simple ethnic ownership, and so there was much to recommend it to Ornitz as an artistic petri dish for the experiments of ethnic mixing, much as it was for James Weldon Johnson in *Autobiography of an Ex-Colored Man*. But Ornitz was fascinated by ragtime song, that fairly broad category of popular song which can include the minstrel-derived "coon" songs of the 1890s and the Tin Pan Alley material heralded by Irving Berlin's "Alexander's Ragtime Band"; Johnson, of course, was interested in classic ragtime piano, a form that had more or less had its day by the time he published *Autobiography of an Ex-Colored Man* in 1912. (Eileen Southern draws a direct connection between the rise of "ragtime" song and the demise of pianistic ragtime.)[70] But both men seem to have read the public space of popular culture as a place to negotiate the anxiety which is created when a consciousness of ethnic and racial boundaries develops.[71]

Haunch Paunch and Jowl is the life story of Meyer Hirsch, a Jew who moves. He moves spatially, from the Lower East Side to Riverside Drive, or "Allrightniks Row"; economically from abject poverty to overfed, overindulged wealth; and socially from marginal immigrant Jew to powerful "Professional Jew." The book is structured in seven "periods" which reflect the seven ages of man. For the first four Meyer's real hope is to find a blended identity which will locate him on a symbolic middle ground, somewhere between the pure mystic Davie Solomon and the too-worldly, exploitative sweatshop owner that his Uncle Philip becomes. From the very first section of the first period, images of mixture and combination insinuate themselves into the text.

These glimmers are starkly revealed and explicitly valorized in the fourth period's ruminations on music, but are finally abandoned with Meyer's move into professional politics. It is as if ethnic identity is frozen and depreciated when it comes to stand only for itself, with no other referents.

It is too simple to interpret Meyer's mixing as the typical immigrant (or child of immigrant) tale of the negotiation of tensions between old and new.[72] If some critics seem to think of *Haunch Paunch and Jowl's* Meyer Hirsch as nothing more than a dirty David Levinsky, Gabriel Miller is closer to the mark when he reminds us that Meyer "has no roots in the *shtetl* world of Eastern Europe," and that Ornitz "does not directly consider the Old World experience."[73] Even so—as with his real world contemporaries such as George Gershwin and Irving Berlin—Meyer Hirsch and his compatriots are able, as Jews, to gain access to African American materials because they have at least a tenuous connection to an Old World quasi-religious history; this access to plaintiveness conditions them for the task of producing "Black" music. Whatever history these Jews appeared to carry with them, the real links they had to eastern European culture came mainly through New World innovations or reinventions of it, such as New York's Yiddish theater.[74]

The most important blendings in Meyer's life are variously more concrete and more symbolic than the facile Old/New dichotomy allows. To begin, we learn early on that Meyer's family has nicknamed him "Ziegelle" (little goat) (14). This name is bestowed on Meyer because soon after his birth on the ship to America his mother's milk dried up, and he was saved by a sailor's pet "she-goat" who appeared magically below deck to nurse him. Before Meyer even sets foot on American soil he is well mixed: half-boy, half-kid, saved from certain death by the goat.

The "blended" imagery operates on a number of levels here. First, Meyer is, as I just mentioned, part human and part animal, as the titular nickname his political enemies give him will imply. Also, metaphorically, "goat" summons up a number of images, some contradictory: a lecherous man (the satyr in Greek mythology) and a fall guy, to name just two. The image of Meyer as the satyr—half man/half goat—is particularly apt, as he is torn throughout the novel between carnal and spiritual desires. And, of course, the goat is a notoriously unchoosy eater who finds nourishment from a variety of sources.

The goat plays a number of crucial metaphoric roles in the Hebrew Old Testament. Foremost perhaps are the references in the kosher laws which forbid boiling a kid in its mother's milk (in Exodus 23:19 and 34:26). Another key image comes with Jacob's donning of goat skin (and cooking goat meat but presenting it as wild game) in order to fool his father into believing that he is his brother Esau, the hairy hunter (Genesis 27).[75] According to the anthropologist Howard Eilberg-Schwartz, the underlying message of the biblical goat imagery is either an outright incest ban (in the first case) or a reproach of male children who stay too close to their mothers (in the case of Jacob, the "domestic" child, whom Eilberg-Schwartz calls a "mama's boy").[76] The Jewish musicians most involved with African American music—think of Al Jolson flirting with and befuddling his obviously Old World mother in the first talking scene in *The Jazz Singer*—frequently played on their emotional closeness to but social and physical difference from their hypothetical mothers. The goat, then, is an epitome of mixedness as it refers to a deep Jewish history while also signaling a break from the same toward a new urban identity. The second period of the novel opens with an epigraph from Henry Adams—"Neither to him nor his brothers and sisters was religion real" (25)—which seals the idea that Meyer is asserting a version of Jewishness which has little connection to doctrine.[77]

Ornitz does not keep his ruminations on mixtures either indirect or abstract; he attacks frontally how the issue plays out for Jews *as* Jews. An argument plays itself out across the pages of *Haunch Paunch and Jowl* as to whether Jews are the model amalgamated people or the worst kind of cultural isolates, desperate for an infusion of outside blood. The subject is introduced in the third period of *Haunch Paunch and Jowl*, when the novel's "discussionists" argue the contention, introduced by Barney Finn, that Jews present a united front to the world and are clannish. A few members of this talkers' club say their piece, all dwelling mainly on how Jews are the worst exploiters of Jews. But Ornitz explicitly privileges the speech of Simon Gordin, who appears in no other significant way in the novel, but is allowed to deliver a speech which closes the chapter. It is worth quoting at some length.

Jews are not Jews [Gordin says]. They are Germans, Russians, Britons, Italians, Turks, Africans, and so on . . . They are the composite people of the world. They have all the high and low characteristics of the human race. They have the physical stigma of all the peoples of the world . . . Go back through the ages, see the rush and sweep of conquering armies, Babylonian, Assyrian, Egyptian, Persian, Greek and Roman, bringing rapine's infusion of new blood into the veins of Israel. (92)

In this speech Gordin summarizes the tendency to imagine Jews as the most cosmopolitan people in the world, transforming oppression (in the form of "rapine") into power. "Go out into the Ghetto," Simon Gordin finally urges Barney Finn, the "Irisher" socialist, "and look upon the children of the Jews from all lands—and behold the peoples of the world" (92).

The idea of Jewish flexibility gets its fullest articulation when Meyer and his friends begin to sing African American music. Sam Rakowsky, Hymie Rubin, and Meyer have formed a "secretive clique of girl chasers," who begin to explore various "dives, brothels, resorts and theatres" in search of women (68). One day the boys stumble into a Mulberry Street saloon, which doubles as the "headquarters of a murderous gang" (69), and realize all of a sudden that they are in trouble: "It looked threatening for the sheenies when Sam placed himself in the middle of the room and broke out, strongly, in song, a highly smutty thing he picked up in a black and tan joint in Hell's Kitchen. He brought down the house. We were welcomed as entertainers making the rounds" (69). It is only at this point that Meyer informs us that the boys had spent many summer evenings in "achieving certain blends of harmonious effects of the latest rag tunes" (69). Lucky thing for that! (This moment also represents a neat reversal of the usual process whereby people listening to music find sex; here the boys are looking for sex and they find music.)

Although Ornitz becomes much more particular in his uses of "rag music" in the fourth section of the novel, this introductory mention merits some attention. "Rag music" itself, as used here, lacks specific meaning; as we know, "rags," "rag music," "ragtime" "ragged tunes" all might have been used variously at this time (mid- to late 1890s) to mean a variety of things. Since Ornitz is describing a vocal music, he is certainly not referring to what would ultimately come to be called "classic ragtime." But it would be anachronistic for Ornitz to be using "rag" here to describe the body of vaguely rhythmic Tin Pan Alley songs which followed in the wake of Irving Berlin's "Alexander's Ragtime Band," and this kind of misstep is uncharacteristic (and nearly unimaginable) for a writer as concerned with reportage as is Ornitz.

Most likely Ornitz was thinking of what musicologists now generally refer to, with apology, as "coon songs." These songs derived most directly from minstrel shows, but also showed the influence of comic opera, sentimental balladry, and various plantation musics. Though often blatantly racist, "coon songs" also offered an opening for African Americans to break into the music business. Jews, too, made inroads into American music through "coon" songs: Fanny Brice, Sophie Tucker, and Eddie Cantor as performers, Harry Von Tilzer and Irving Berlin as songwriters, and the Witmark brothers as music publishers are but a few of the many Jews who were closely affiliated with the genre. These songs were also widely disseminated by the type of quartets (such as the Empire City Quartette, which gave George Burns his start) which Ornitz is attempting to evoke here.[78]

The shift from "coon" song to "ragtime" was often effaced by performers: Sophie Tucker, for instance, was first billed as a "coon-shouter" and performed in blackface, and later was billed as "the Mary Garden of Ragtime" (and then later as the "Queen of Jazz").[79] As I argued earlier, at the time Ornitz is writing of (and even at the time he was writing in), "rag" was flexible in its musicological meaning and was particularly available for use as a metaphor. Although Ornitz writes of the pre–Irving Berlin 1890s, he no doubt counted on his readers to fold Berlin's work into the vague mix he is describing; *Haunch Paunch and Jowl* makes many references to Berlin's career.

So if "rag" is somewhat lacking in precise meaning, what does Ornitz fill it with, here in this glancing moment in the third period of *Haunch Paunch and Jowl?* The patrons of this Mulberry Bend saloon are white ethnics, probably Italian. They are displeased by the appearance of Sam, Hymie, and Meyer, "the sheenies." Rather than make a run for it, Sam begins to sing a "smutty thing" he learned in a "black and tan joint." In this structure, then, a young Jewish man sings a song learned from African Americans in a mixed club in order to placate some "other" white ethnics. The construct is complicated by the great possibility that the song was created by African American performers as a form of "defensive humor"—that is, in part, as a sort of "safety valve" to ameliorate the depredations of racial stereotyping—and is now being literalized into an actual protective shield for Jews.[80]

It is important to note here that the boys defuse a touchy cross-ethnic showdown by using their Jewish selves to convert *race* into *pleasure*. Ornitz might be accused of distorting the real issue here, the appropriation of African American forms by white performers. At the same time, he also calls attention to a major route Jews took to reassure themselves that they were safe in America: Jewish people producing entertainment have nothing to fear but hecklers. Significantly, once Sam's song brings down the house, the three boys are "welcomed as entertainers making the rounds" (69). No longer are they "sheenies" in a tight spot; the boys have, through an unspoken association with African American culture (not an alliance with actual African Americans), transcended the dangers of bearing the conspicuous markers of difference. In short, Meyer and his friends have transformed themselves into "good" Jews by acting as agreeable interpreters of African American song.

The music theme is then abandoned for the rest of the third period, only to reappear centrally in the fourth chapter. The focus of this third chapter resolves into a consideration of Meyer's Uncle Philip, and his dream of becoming a capitalist who can compete with the hated German Jews. Philip plans to incorporate the "New World Clothing Company" and utilize cheap immigrant labor to become rich. With a bit of rhetoric that will eventually seize Meyer's imagination, Philip argues that this "is a free country and I can exploit whom I like" (104). Then, after informing Meyer that his father (Meyer's grandfather) was a horse thief, he introduces a theme which makes him sound like Faulkner's Thomas Sutpen: "Meyer," he says to the boy, "we've got nothing to look back to. It's up to us to be ancestors" (105). Here Philip steps away from the popular line on Jewish entertainers—articulated in *The Jazz Singer* and elsewhere—which held that modern-day Jewish creativity was in large part the result of good roots.

It is in the fourth period that Meyer and his friends begin to be ancestors and in the fourth period that Ornitz concretizes the "certain blends" that he has been hinting at up until now (69). In this section

Meyer, Sam Rakowsky, Davie Solomon, and Hymie Rubin form a quartet managed by Al Wolff, who is the master of ceremonies at Miner's Burlesque Theatre (and who is, in some ways, reminiscent of Al Jolson). Sam, soon to become Sid Raleigh, has been working as an usher at Tony Pastor's Variety Theatre on Fourteenth Street, and is "smitten more than ever with the song and dance craze" (115). (Working at Pastor's and having a city for a last name are only a couple of ways that Sid's career will parallel Irving Berlin's; appropriately, Ornitz gives him a southern city, instead of a German one, for his last name.)

Sam introduces a surprising fusion at the boys' audition for Wolff. In a song-and-dance routine he proposes to merge two seemingly disparate strains of music. Sam tells Al that he wants to dance "first an Irish reel, very zippy, see, and when I am good and warmed up in the middle of the Irish jig . . . I wants the music to slip into a Jewish wedding *kazzatzka* (Russian-Jewish lively dance)" (116). Al is intrigued, and the two work out the "desired Irish-Russian-Jewish potpourri" (116). The audition is a success, and Al Wolff agrees to run the four boys through the gauntlet of rathskellers and back rooms in their attempt to make it to Frenchie Lavelle's big Chinatown dance hall. The documentary impulse of Ornitz's work is laid bare here: "Frenchie" Lavelle is actually Scotchy LaVelle, a former gangster who opened a saloon on Doyers Street and once gave Irving Berlin a job as a singing waiter.[81] In Ornitz's version, the boys are renamed (Meyer Hirsch becomes Melville Hart, Sam becomes Sid Raleigh) and begin to rehearse (119). Soon their Irish-Jewish medley—shades of *Abie's Irish Rose!*—will give way to a much more potent brew.[82]

Before their professional engagements begin, the quartet is rehearsed by Al, a cantor's son. Using a technique learned from his father, Al readies the boys for their professional debut at the Dutch Village Rathskeller, which features "roof-reverberating coon shouters and a whiz-bang ragtime band" (129). The boys bring the house down here and move on to Frenchie Lavelle's Chinatown ballroom. Here too Sid Raleigh is following Irving Berlin's story, although Berlin did not start at a Frenchman's Chinatown dance hall; Berlin broke big at a Chinatown establishment run by "Nigger" Mike Salter, a Jew.[83]

It is in section six of the fourth period that ragtime takes center stage. This section begins with a characteristic piece of social history:

Ragtime has the whole country jogging. From the World's Fair in Chicago it sent syncopated waves bounding across the length and breadth of the land. The negroes had given America its music. Soon the white man started stealing the negro's music and making it his own. There was money in the negro's music. Cultured people snickered at it . . . Musicians, who ruled and confined their art with religious dogma, raised their hands and voices in horror and denunciation. The elite, the elect, the polite, the ultra-fashionable, and their aping followers, despised ragtime . . . But ragtime had the vitality of a people's music and the whole country hummed, sang, whistled, two-stepped and cried for more doggerels and maddening tunes. (146)

From this general, and generally accurate, account, Meyer informs us that the "ragtime craze helped to fill Lavelle's every night" (146). Ornitz sets up a caveat here to the utopian construct of merger ("the white man started stealing"), but he quickly introduces a different dichotomy (the cultured elite versus the people) which has more resonance in the context of *Haunch Paunch and Jowl* than his racial politics do. Class trumps race here: since Jews are not safely "white" in *Haunch Paunch and Jowl*, their primary identification is as part of the "people" whose music this is. (Sidney Finkelstein, a later Marxist critic, applied the same concept when he subtitled his book on jazz "a people's music.")[84]

But Al and Sid, the leaders of the group, are not content only to replicate received form; they intend to create their own, with an assist from "Piano" O'Brien, Lavelle's musical director. The mysterious Irish alcoholic, almost wholly blind, gives them the key to the creation of ragtime songs, which of course they have been holding all along: "Semitic coloring." At almost exactly the center of *Haunch Paunch and Jowl* (page 148 of 300), Ornitz finally reveals his utopian vision of racial/ethnic blending: "Al and Sam were busy creating original ragtime songs and dances [Meyer recounts]. O'Brien encouraged them, saying *its flexibility offered infinite possibilities*. He urged them to make use of the negro plantation, levee and spiritual songs with their pulsating African rhythm and ornament them with Semitic colors and figures" (148; emphasis added). There are a number of important things going on here. First, Meyer tells us that Al and Sam want to create original ragtime songs; but in the very next sentence it becomes apparent that the originality will come with a judicious mixing, not with a wholesale new creation. After O'Brien thus charges the songwriters, Davie Solomon, the Whitman-quoting mystic, argues that they "ought to try for originality" (148). In response, "O'Brien said that there was nothing original in music. Man understood only a few sounds" (148). This, then, is an exquisite rationalization for the "borrowing" of African American musical forms by Jewish entertainers. If people can understand only a limited number of sounds, then it is a real service to "ornament them with Semitic colors and figures" to create at least the illusion of newness. Here is Ornitz's articulation of the popular notion that Jews, because of their ability to cross various temporal and spatial borderlines, were best able to manufacture ethnic and racial pastiche. He also gives voice to the idea that Jewish interpretations of African American music transformed collective folk expressions into marketable form.

What is most interesting about O'Brien's approach in *Haunch Paunch and Jowl* is that he sees nothing new or fearful about the lack of originality in modern music: unlike such enemies of jazz as Maxim Gorky and Theodor Adorno, O'Brien thinks the condition of this music has nothing to do with mass production, the diminution of aura, or regressive listeners.[85] Borrowing, admixing, adapting, argues O'Brien, are old hat. To illustrate his point, he cites Palestrina, the sixteenth-century "choirmaster and composer for the Pope" (148). According to O'Brien, Palestrina's "solemn church music was nothing more than lewd tavern songs and troubadour chanties rearranged to meet the Sistine Chapel's needs" (148) When Davie Solomon challenges him by asking if Palestrina could make a cantata out of "Sweet Rosie O'Grady," O'Brien does not reply: "Instead he played Sweet Rosie O'Grady as it is usually played. Then he began to weave its strains until there was left only a remote suggestion, an elusive reminiscence of the hackneyed tune" (148). O'Brien has done exactly what the German musician does in James Weldon Johnson's *Autobiography of an Ex-Colored Man* (1912): instead of "ragging" the classics, he makes classic music out of the building blocks of popular music.

Davie then translates the words to "Sweet Rosie O'Grady" into Latin and Al trains the quartet to sing it; O'Brien compliments Al, telling him that his choir-coaching method is reminiscent of Palestrina. Al responds, appropriately enough, "Palestrina, me eye . . . that's my old man's method. He is a *chazan*. You know what that is, a cantor. He got the method from his father, and his father from his father, and so on. Say, Palestrina must be some four-flusher. The method is as old as the Jews" (149). Here Ornitz ratifies O'Brien's aesthetic of the plasticity of musical form and the benefits of amalgamation. He also introduces the idea that Jews—through a paternal legacy of cantorial music—not only are qualified to produce ragtime and jazz, but are actually previous to it: musical ancestors. A principal component of Ornitz's utopian vision of the promise of Jews in American life is the idea that Jews do not merely donate specific matter to the culture, but contribute the concept of merger itself as an example for all Americans to follow. (It is worth noting that Adorno, with Max Horkheimer, would make a decidedly negative reference to Palestrina in the classic essay "The Culture Industry: Enlightenment as Mass Deception" [1944]. In describing the homogenizing tendencies in jazz, Adorno and Horkheimer write that no Palestrina "could be more of a purist in eliminating every unprepared and unresolved discord than the jazz arranger in suppressing any development which does not conform to the jargon."[86] Here jazz is mistrusted for its ability to hide its hybridity in stereotyped designs: an unmistakable echo can be heard here of the *Dearborn Independent*'s fear—restated by numerous Nazis—that Jews were covertly smuggling degrading Blackness into mainstream culture under the cloak of the smooth exteriors of their tunes.)[87] In any event, when the boys try out this fusion on the crowd, they nearly start a riot. Meyer realizes that "where religion is concerned no one has a sense of humor" (150). The moral of the story, then, is that Ornitz gives sanction only to those ethnic amalgamations which leave religion out of the picture. An exception is made for the capitalization of cantorial style which suggests how easy it was for Ornitz, like so many others, to detach religion from Jewishness—even when discussing sacred music.[88] Jewishness is not Judaism, although sometimes it pretends to be.

Sam and Al become the "richest publishers of popular songs" (150). With Piano O'Brien providing access to the storehouse of the world's melodies, the men weave hit after "ragtime" hit: "And their music became the music of America" (151). Thus "Negro" is translated into "American" through the intervention of Jews. In a final dig Meyer reports that Sam now claims that he can "twist a blareful, stirring Wagnerian fugue into nigger jazzbo stuff" (160). "Ragging" the classics, a cultural intervention with already strong anti-elitist and perhaps anti-hierarchical meaning, takes on an additional resonance in this case: for a Jew to appropriate Wagner using an African rhythmic approach is to draw a mustache on the Mona Lisa.

Of course the use of "nigger" (and "jazzbo" too) should give pause here. The democratic strategy of ethnic/racial mixture is not as jubilant or triumphant as it could have been if the African American contribution had been dignified by a withholding of the racial epithet. If "Negro" had been used instead, it would still be possible to imagine that Ornitz (via his namesake character) was envisioning a meeting of equals. As it stands, this coda undercuts the harmonious image Ornitz has been developing all along.

The utopian moment passes fairly quickly. Meyer puts the music world behind him as he enters politics, a world where the identity formulations of pure pluralism dominate. As he tells it at the beginning of the fifth period, "I became a Professional Jew in emulation of the successful Irish politician whose principal capital is being a Professional Irishman" (183).[89] Following the Irish example, Meyer first makes a name for himself by producing minstrel-type entertainment—which in his case is endorsed as a melting pot utopia. Next, as a Professional Jew, Meyer trades in the false essentialisms of identity politics rather than in the blended constructs which have heretofore dominated the novel. Popular culture has often had more open space for resistance, negotiation, reappropriation, and so on than organized public politics have. Of course the "blendings" were enormously suspect to begin with: while the musical achievement of Meyer and his friends at least makes reference to the reality of fusion in urban American life, it also represents a retailing of Blackness which disempowers, and indeed erases, real-life African Americans. This seizure hints at the possibility that Jews might have the power in cultural life to render African Americans mute. In her reading of Ornitz, Rachel Rubin suggests persuasively that gangsterism and capitalism are linked in this book, and as a result the musical scenes must be understood as part of Ornitz's indictment of economic exploitation.[90]

Meyer's retreat into a "professional" ethnic identity at the novel's end assures that even symbolic mergers have been eliminated. Looking back at what we now call Black-Jewish relations, we see clearly that an overreliance on "professional" delegates has always privileged a circular and inert sort of reasoning whereby official representatives of each group propagate the idea that the "relationship" can be understood as a narrative about themselves.

Before *Haunch Paunch and Jowl* comes to an end, Ornitz completes the conversation that he began through the character of Simon Gordin in the third period. Here, in the somewhat ridiculous guise of "Race Psychopathologist" Lionel Crane, Ornitz argues at last that Jews are Jews, a pure race, and not the ideal fusion of all the world's people. Crane contends that "Jews will create a Jewish Question in America as long as they cling to their bizarre Jewishness" (198). Most responsible for the inability of the Jews to assimilate, Crane avers, is the Professional Jew. The Professional Jew first focuses a spotlight on the Jews, and then demands that the particularities of the Jewish people be "non-discussable" (200). This leads to a neurotic dead end in which Jews at once believe in their racial supremacy and suffer from racial paranoia (201).[91] "There has been too much inbreeding in the fastnesses of the Ghetto," according to Crane, "so there are insanity and feeblemindedness, and [!] diabetes" (201). Jews are not the ideal amalgam of all people, but in truth are suffering from a lack of new blood. Crane says that he will *take the sick ego of my people to the clinic* (201) and looks to intermarriage as the "saving tonic" for Jews (202). He offers, then, both social and genetic solutions to the Jewish problem.

These sentiments have led some observers, Sol Liptzin among them, to conclude that Ornitz was the first of the self-hating, fiction-writing Jews. According to Liptzin, Ornitz "favored the abandonment of all vestiges of Jewish separateness, getting rid of the foul fungus of the ghetto, becoming an integral part of the American nation."[92] This, as I have shown, misstates the case, for Ornitz certainly at least dreamed of a healthy cross-ethnic exchange. It also ignores that Ornitz was participating in a much larger conversation about purity and mixture which was inspired by the huge wave of immigration which had radically changed America in the late nineteenth and early twentieth centuries and which found distinct expression in discussions of the

Jewish mediation of African American music—but which also had roots in racialist science and politics. All manner of commentators, from sober friends of the immigrant to racist anthropologists, debated whether Jews were a pure or mixed race, and which answer would be better. Ornitz comes down on the side of Jews as mixed, showing clearly that the illusion of purity can be maintained only with devastating effects. As a last gasp of sorts he offers up Barney Finn imagining a time when "the workers of America become a racial identity" (224). But the novel peters out in cynicism and self-loathing, with Meyer observing that, Uncle Philip's vision notwithstanding, he and his kind have become ancestors only to the pitiful lapdogs—another result of too much inbreeding and "purity"—favored by Allrightniks Row matrons (288). The utopian possibility of the novel is closed off as the dream and drama of merger is revealed to be mostly a public relations ploy.

Surprisingly little attention has been paid to what has actually been said by and about Jews in music. By the 1920s it was obvious to most interested observers that not only had popular music become the special purview of Jews and African Americans, but also within this sphere members of the two groups came into frequent and significant contact. Because this African American and Jewish influence in the music business was so visible, many felt compelled to develop satisfying explanations which might account for the situation. The rise of Jews and African Americans in the field of popular music provoked careful consideration of their respective racial gifts, and also generated deep questioning about the racial character of the American nation. The angry racist responses to the Jewish–African American nexus in music has been amply documented; what is less well understood is how this musical relationship also animated a competing discourse, one which focused on the positive aspects of racial merger. Many supporters of ragtime and jazz found in these new musical forms the happy yield of a properly functioning American system, one which was being improved every day by the transformation of "raw" Black materials into national styles through the intercession of talented Jews. But these Jews did not constitute a monolith, and their approaches to Black music and Black style differed greatly. Between the deep uneasiness of Irving Berlin and the awesome confidence of George Gershwin, Jews orchestrated public dramas which displayed Black-Jewish relations as a crucial everyday affair. It is to the variety of supervisory and transformative postures adopted by Jews in this cultural sphere—especially by those Jews with an interest in improving the image of Jewish masculinity—that I now turn.

3

"Swanee Ripples":
From Blackface to White Negro

Among the large number of Jews who had enormous success in the music industry during the first few decades of the twentieth century, perhaps none were so successful as those who traded in a Blackness which did not benefit African Americans and often actively worked to exclude them from positions of cultural power. But what was the ideological work which supported the particular success that Jews had at retailing Black looks and sounds? I have been circling around this major issue, and want to turn to it now as a way of breaking down the rather monolithic conception of Jews I have been employing thus far. Different sorts of Jews, with myriad motives and talents, were involved in these cultural phenomena. While most can be loosely identified as "second-generation" Americans (and thus, as Deborah Dash Moore has shown, similarly inspired by a search for "secondary" associations outside religious Judaism, the nuclear family, and so on),[1] it is still useful to trace out a genealogy of Jewish attempts to manufacture Blackness which will underscore the important differences which obtained among the various Jews participating in this broad project. From the blackface antics of Al Jolson and Irving Berlin's early attempts to translate minstrelsy into sound, through George Gershwin's high-art aspirations and the white Negroism of Mezz Mezzrow and Artie Shaw, Jews were holding an intragroup conversation about their status in America, with particular reference to African Americans. At the same time, these Jews were public performers speaking to non-Jews (especially to African Americans) about the place of Jews in American cultural life. The real achievement of Jews in the entertainment business was their fluency in circulating all three key terms—Jewish, Black, and American—in a mutually supporting system which could simultaneously produce numerous positive meanings.

A great deal of talk in the early decades of the twentieth century suggested that the second generation of eastern European Jews represented a decline from the "racial" integrity of their parents' generation. To many it seemed that assimilation threatened to make these Jews—unlike their progenitors—unrecognizable as Jews. In short, they seemed to be losing whatever it was in appearance or behavior that made their parents so instantly recognizable as Jews. One way in which members of this generation of Jews established their legitimacy as a distinct people was by exploiting the racialized notion that their flexibility made them well suited for articulating the music of fusion; the pivot for this contention and its popular reception was a certainty that Jews bore a special relationship to African Americans.

But what was this relationship? Just business? A shared gene pool? Similar pasts of oppression? Above all, did the success of Jews in African American music rely on closeness to or distance from African Americans—or perhaps both consecutively? Was it all, as a character in Ishmael Reed's novel *Reckless Eyeballing* argues in a slightly different context, the conscious route Jews took in their search for deputy whiteness?[2] My aim is to reconstruct the cluster of beliefs—for both producers and consumers—which conspired to situate Jews as prime interpreters (or editors, or even censors) of African American music. There is no single explanation for all this activity. Jewish uses of Blackness ranged from the arrogance of George Gershwin's ethnography to the anxieties raised by Irving Berlin's success in "ragtime" or by any other productions that might lead to the social conflation of Jews with African Americans. In short, moments during which Jewish mediations of African American music appeared as effortless and triumphant syntheses should not blind us to the complex origins and abundant meanings contained in this relationship.

The central focus of this chapter is on the ways in which Jews (mostly men, with one important exception) used Blackness to define their social status. The Jewish men involved in popular culture productions of Blackness projected racial imagery which seems concerned not only with their "ethnic" suitability but also with the confirmation of their gender and sexual legitimacy. The Jews of Tin Pan Alley, in short, were able to figure out some beneficial ways to publicize their relationship to African Americans.

One way to evaluate the relationship of Jews to Blackness in the first few decades of the twentieth century is to explore key moments in the careers of Al Jolson (and the other blackface Jews), Irving Berlin, and George Gershwin. All of these Jewish performers had close connections to actual African Americans, as well as to the popular African American music of their time. But the differences among these Jewish musicians, particularly with respect to how they constructed their relationship to African Americans, are more telling than their similarities. Berlin, for instance, traded on a valuable vernacular credibility early in his career, but found it difficult to throw off the perception that somehow he and his music were racially suspect—that his connections to African Americans were too intimate. Gershwin, by contrast, was more publicity-savvy than Berlin, and quickly established his high-art aspirations and credentials. In so doing, Gershwin at once ennobled his borrowings from African American forms while also cleverly highlighting the distance which separated him from the social spaces these materials occupied.

David Roediger has argued that certain white ethnic groups—Jews among them—have been able to borrow confidently from African American culture without "fearing that they would be cast as 'white niggers' and their jobs as 'nigger work'—an anxiety that the white working poor seldom escaped."[3] What I want to make clear is that as helpful as Roediger's formulation might be, it is necessary to develop a more fluid approach to explain the various stances Jewish musicians adopted with relation to Blackness in the first half of the twentieth century. In the span of a single generation, as we will see, Irving Berlin would strive to dodge the accusation that his compositions were the yield of "nigger work," while at the same time George Gershwin and some of his swing contemporaries worked hard to establish the authenticity of their music by *insisting* upon its organic connection to actual

African Americans. Whereas Berlin apparently lacked the social power
(or the savvy) to control the meanings derived from the racial prove-
nance of his music, Gershwin and others were able to advertise their
Black roots with absolute confidence that they would not personally be
taken for anything but white. Embedded in this chapter, then, is a story
about Jewish racial formation—partial to be sure—from around 1910
to 1950, which emphasizes the connections between the attainment of
suitable racial and gender positions. It does so by tracing the wavering
level of confidence which attended this cultural work, from the anxious
use of the nickname "Nigger" by Jews and the tense drama of the rumor
about Irving Berlin's "little colored boy," through the racial arrogance
of Jews in blackface and the brash confidence of George Gershwin,
Mezz Mezzrow, and Artie Shaw.

The Jewish Nickname "Nigger"

Although it became increasingly clear in the 1930s and 1940s that Jews
were becoming "white" ethnics, their racial status was still undergoing
heavy negotiation in the 1910s and 1920s. It was risky for Jews to be so
deeply involved in blackface and African American music because one
easily available explanation for Jewish successes in representing Blackness was that these performances were essentially autobiographical acts.
While the utopian reading of Jews in African American music focused
on the melting pot promise of American life and the racial agility of
Jews, another story existed—unwelcome for Jews with aspirations to
whiteness—which held that Jews were not just really good at sounding
"Black," but really were Black (or quite close).[4] In America the
conflation of Jew and Black is less common than it has been in Europe.
But this did not stop Jews from displaying great uneasiness about their
relationship to African Americans. One way Jews admitted, addressed,
and perhaps expunged this fear was by calling one another "Nigger."

The nickname "Nigger" (or one of its variants) has been used in
Jewish life and letters to a remarkable extent. In fictional works, for
example, we find in *Jews Without Money* Michael Gold's careful depiction of a "virile boy" named "Nigger," his best boyhood friend.[5] As
with most examples of this slur-as-name, the derivation of "Nigger" is
explained solely as a reference to physiognomy: "His nose had been

squashed at birth, and . . . his black hair and murky face, made inevitable the East Side nickname."[6] Daniel Fuchs gives the same nickname to a gangster in the third volume of his Williamsburg trilogy, *Low Company*.[7]

Real-life gangsters had this name conferred on them as well. The list includes Yoshke Nigger (Joseph Toblinsky), the brains behind a Jewish horse-poisoning gang known as the Yiddish Black Hand. A similar nickname was given to the head of an organization know as the Independent Benevolent Association—really a front for a white slave trade group—who was called "African Jake."[8] Others on this list include "Nigger Benny" Snyder, who worked as muscle for "Joe the Greaser" Rosenzweig, "Nig" Rosen, who operated out of Philadelphia, and, in Newark, "Niggy" Rutman.[9] Women were not exempt either: one prosecution witness during a 1936 Lucky Luciano trial was a brothel madam named "nigger Ruth."[10] Because the nickname "Nigger" was so prevalent among Jewish gangsters, it appears that it might have held some characterological significance in addition to its obvious function as a physical descriptive. But most of all "Nigger" was a name from the street, and gangsters were as "street"-oriented as any Jews.

The American Jewish use of the nickname "Nigger" is hardly without European precedent, as Sander Gilman has shown. But in America it has also long been common to label deviance from a variety of established norms by making reference to darker Others. We might indeed trace this practice back to the nickname "white Indian," used to explain those captured white settlers of the seventeenth century who chose to stay with their abductors.[11] More relevant to our concerns is the process by which other white ethnic groups have been marked as "Black." According to David Roediger, Irish workers in the antebellum era were particularly likely to be slurred as "white niggers" or "white slaves" because of the low-level jobs they held. In this case physiognomy played a smaller role than economy: since they worked at jobs which might otherwise have been filled by African Americans, Irish in the North could be insulted as the mirror image of slaves.[12]

The other immigrants most commonly conflated with African Americans have been southern Italians, as Robert Orsi has demonstrated in "The Religious Boundaries of an Inbetween People." Like the Irish, southern Italians competed for jobs with African Americans, in this case most commonly in the agricultural South rather than the industrial North. Even more pointedly, Southern Italians appeared to many people to bear a physical resemblance—especially in their kinky hair—to African Americans: the slur "guinea" which is applied to Italians is derived, Orsi explains, from a comparison to the Black slaves originally kidnapped from the west coast of Africa.[13] Although the racial status of Jews has corresponded historically to the "inbetween" status of Italian Americans, Jews have less frequently been identified by non-Jews with a "Black" nickname.

So why would Jews apply this nickname to members of their own group? In an important essay on African American–Jewish relations, Leslie Fiedler provides, more or less tangentially, a fascinating narrative about the use of this nickname. Fiedler writes of a neighborhood in Newark which once had been mainly Jewish and now was mostly African American. Here is how he describes the remaining Jews, making particular mention of one local boy:

> The sons of butchers and the few trapped Jewish property owners left in the area seemed to become almost as often as not gangsters (one especially successful one, I recall, ran a free soup kitchen all through the Depression); and a standard way of proving one's toughness was "nigger-smashing." This sport involved cruising at a high rate of speed, catching a lonely Negro, beating the hell out of him and getting back into the car and away before his friends could gather to retaliate. I remember that one of the local figures associated, in kids' legend at least, with "nigger-smashing" was himself called "Niggy" because of his kinky hair and thick lips, features not so uncommon among Jews, after all.[14]

There is a crucial moment of psychological cause and effect which lurks in this anecdote of a Jewish boy who looked like an African American and made a name for himself by battering those who bore "actual" Blackness. This nickname obviously had negative connotations for any Jewish boy, no matter if it was bestowed and borne in a spirit of (heavily masculinized) good humor.[15]

"Nigger-smashing," it seems, became especially compelling for the Jewish boy who had been uncomfortably positioned as a physical link between the two groups. Fiedler's anecdote stands as a vivid individualized expression of what the social psychologists George Devereux and Edwin Loeb have called "antagonistic acculturation": having been forced into too-close contact with the menacing Other, Niggy is compelled to convert his body from being the tie that binds Jews and African Americans into the boundary that separates them.[16] None of this is to deny that the nickname almost certainly bestowed a fair amount of valuable street credibility on the young men so named; embedded within the insult which constitutes "Nigger" is a chance for the Jewish man to capture some of the masculine cachet stereotypically ascribed to the African American male. Unlike the blackface performer, though, the Jewish man named "Nigger" did not gain anything directly through his association with Blackness; nor could he escape the debasement of this affiliation by washing off the greasepaint. Even so, the Jewish "Nigger" most certainly obtained a valuable dividend of masculinity from his nickname.[17]

The nickname was not only popular among Jewish gangsters, as one final, significant example shows. The man who gave Irving Berlin his first major break in show business was called "Nigger Mike" Salter. Salter was a ward heeler who owned and operated the Pelham Cafe—established at 12 Pell Street in New York in 1904—which was, allegedly, the founding place of the fox-trot. Berlin's first biographer, Alexander Woollcott, described Salter as "a Russian Jew of good stock"; yet even in 1922, when Salter died, the *New York Herald* felt constrained to explain that despite "the name by which he was generally known it should be noted that Nigger Mike Salter, although of swarthy complexion, was a white man."[18] This obituary gives us a few key insights into the meanings of the nickname "Nigger." First, for the paper to make special mention of Salter's whiteness (in fact to grant it as a form of respect to the dead) is to admit that the bearer of such a name might indeed be an African American. This possibility communicates that even the most debasing conceptions of Blackness—as delineated by the ugly racist nomenclature—were still being circulated in public forums as late as the 1920s. That the explanation appears in a general-interest daily also suggests that as popular as the nickname had become among Jews, it remained more or less an in-group phenomenon.

Jews communicated mostly to one another with this nickname, but its very prevalence sent messages to non-Jews as well. The clearest point delivered by its use is that many Jews were made anxious by the fact that every now and then (often enough to require comment, that is) a member of their group appeared who displayed physical evidence of closeness to African Americans. The individual racial signs—dark skin, flat nose, curly hair—had disturbing implications for Jews. In social terms, ontogeny was recapitulating phylogeny in a plainly disagreeable manner. The Jew who looked Black was an atavistic reminder that all Jews, as Isaac Goldberg noted in 1930, were "originally much darker than . . . to-day."[19] Most broadly, this promoted the idea that Jews and African Americans had a shared racial heritage. The Jewish "Nigger" offered a public narrative of Jewish history in America, and a cautionary tale for contemporary Jews. The Jew who looked Black reminded Jews, and anyone else watching closely, that specific Jews could be understood as, and treated as, closer to Black than to white. For Jews to call one of their own "Nigger," then, was a preemptive strike, a way to defuse the likelihood of some outsider calling attention to the Blackness of the Jew.[20] Jews who applied this nickname—usually men whose street-life existence brought them into contact with "other" racial or ethnic outsiders—were closing ranks: the particular dissemination of the name among Jews represented a way to sacrifice inconvenient individuals (if only to the certain degree of disrepute and humiliation carried by the nickname) in favor of reinforcing the central postulates of group identity.

Using this slur was also an admission by certain Jews that their relationship to actual African Americans was not of vital importance. Furthermore, in moments when the nickname circulated in a wider forum (as with Mike Salter's *Herald* obituary), it signaled that Jews were willing to participate in a racist discourse which—whatever it said about the status of Jews—actively demeaned African Americans. That an individual Jew could be marginalized as "Nigger" indicates a fairly profound anxiety on the part of the many Jews who came up against a reminder that their identification with African Americans was not always or exclusively voluntary. The domination of blackface performance by Jews helped, in many ways, to defuse this anxiety.

Blackface Jews

"Jazz is Irving Berlin, Al Jolson, George Gershwin, Sophie Tucker." Samson Raphaelson wrote this in his famous preface to the stage version of *The Jazz Singer* in the mid-1920s and in the midst of the development of this influential work from short story to talking picture. Raphaelson was not shy about explaining his claim: "Jews are determining the nature and scope of jazz more than any other race—more than the negroes, from whom they have stolen jazz and given it a new color and meaning."[21] "Color" (as in "Semitic coloring") was particularly functional as a code word in rationalizations of the Jewish involvement with jazz. The conspicuous musicological sense of "color" was that Jews were responsible for developing all of the non-rhythmic characteristics of jazz: the contribution of Jews, whether called "Semitic" or "Hebrew," "European" or "Russian," was usually understood to be the welding of the donated "African" rhythms to those aspects of music—such as harmony and overall unity of composition—most highly valued in the Western high-art tradition. (Jews were also sometimes seen to have a special pipeline to "African" rhythms, as we shall see.)

At the same time "color" could not help but communicate (especially in the hands of Raphaelson) information about the Jews' racial status, with particular reference to their condition relative to African Americans. How might we symbolize the "new color" Jews had given to jazz? "White," to describe the status they might achieve, at least in part, through their popular detachment of jazz from African Americans? "Green," to stand either for the immigrant color these Jews would lose or for the money they made? "Yellow," to evoke the sallow greasepaint which was used as makeup for the stage Jew?[22] A lighter shade of Black? (Certainly not "red," since the generally conservative Jews of the entertainment business offered an antidote to the image of Jews as bomb-throwing radicals which became especially popular in the wake of the Red Summer of 1919.) All three versions of *The Jazz Singer* make a dual claim about the relationship of Jews to African Americans—that Jews share a racial sympathy for African American music while also having (or coming into) a stable enough white identity to make money out of portrayals of Blackness.

In *The Jazz Singer* this social shift is explained in evolutionary

terms, and Jakie Rabinowitz's growth in the story clearly represents
the fortunes of the race. Jakie moves from the overt racialness of his
youth toward American secularized status, which is embodied in his
successes with Broadway jazz, in his triumphant, confident "return"
to the racial/religious site of childhood, and most of all in his courting
of a Christian woman. In the short story which spawned the play
and movie, the beloved is named Amy Prentiss ("A. Prentiss"), which
tells us quite a bit about what kind of a white man Jack Robin has
become.

If the movie version of *The Jazz Singer* was a precariously situated
attempt to bring Jews and Jewish concerns to a broad audience, the
stage version seems to have been more of an in-group affair.[23] According to Robert Carringer the success of the play (starring George Jessel,
later lampooned as Gabe Solomon in Ben Hecht's *A Jew in Love*) was
largely due to "a massive promotional campaign aimed mainly at the
Jewish community." The houses for the show were estimated to be 90
percent Jewish.[24]

Contemporary reviews of the play bear out this assessment. A cautious writer for a New York paper, who criticized the play as being
"morally unsound" for violating the "ethical concept of the greatest
good to the greatest number" (presumably because Jakie disappoints the
theater audiences by returning to the synagogue), noted that the play
did have "a special appeal to a certain class of theatergoers." Other
reviewers were less coy in their descriptions of the audience. The
Herald Tribune reviewer contended that enjoyment of the play depended on a complete "understanding of and sympathy with the Jew
and his faith." This critic went on to complain that many of the lines of
the play were spoken in "wholly unintelligible" dialect which nonetheless went over well with "an audience composed almost entirely of those
of the Jewish race."[25]

Accounts from the 1926 and 1927 Boston performances of the play
confirm the New York reports. The *Boston Transcript* described the
1926 audience for the play as "predominantly of the Hebraic tradition
and temperament" and thus able to comprehend "the words and music
of the Hebrew church music which plays so much a part of the
drama."[26] In short, this dramatization of Jewish themes by a Jewish
author which featured a Jewish vaudevillian in the lead role did much

different cultural work than the movie which followed. As with much stage entertainment, the play version of *The Jazz Singer* afforded Jewish audiences the opportunity to visit a social space which was not blatantly marked as Jewish but which nonetheless provided entertainment with special in-group meaning.[27]

Even without Raphaelson's histrionic preface, the play acts as a conscious summing up of Jewish adaptations of African American forms. *The Jazz Singer* evinces a particular nostalgia for the heyday of Jewish stage minstrelsy which was coming to an end around the mid-1920s.[28] In many ways Raphaelson's play served as a rearguard call to Jews who simulate Blackness to carry on. With its cackling yet still anxious tone, the play introduces a version of Jewish success in African American music which foregrounds appropriation and exploitation and which competes with the more idealistic interpretations of Jewish musical agility then current. The unique aspect of the stage rendition is how playful and unashamed—indeed celebratory—Raphaelson is about characterizing Jewish involvement with African American music as theft.[29]

In his oft-quoted preface to the published play script of *The Jazz Singer*, Raphaelson makes it clear that he accepts, and is interested in advancing, the view that jazz is a "national" translation of the musical grammar of one race by members of another race (and religion). Jazz, for Raphaelson, expresses "the vital chaos of America's soul," and is a form of "prayer" originating with African Americans but brought to its fullest development by Jews with "their roots in the synagogue." Raphaelson continues, "You find the soul of a people in the songs they sing. You find the meaning of the songs in the souls of the minstrels who create and interpret them. In 'The Jazz Singer' I have attempted an exploration of the soul of one of these minstrels."[30] "Minstrel" is a key word here, because Raphaelson uses it in both of its distinct senses—traveling performer of folk materials and professional blackface stage actor—while the context of the preface, not to mention the play itself (and much of the Jews-in-Black-music discourse), argues for a synonymity between the two terms. Whereas a Jewish contemporary of Raphaelson such as Ludwig Lewisohn might focus on the popular reception of Irving Berlin by the second generation as proof of the commercialized debasements inflicted in the name of "Americanization," Raphaelson instead cheerfully endorses the ability of Jews to dress their productions of purloined Blackness in American garb.[31]

Raphaelson was helping to popularize the idea that theft was a characteristically "American" activity, a notion that would gain much currency in American Jewish writing. The American dream of Meyer Hirsch's Uncle Philip was to be able to exploit sweatshop workers; Jerome Weidman takes this theme to the extreme with his Harry Bogen in *I Can Get It for You Wholesale* (1937).[32] Raphaelson explores the thematics of theft most pointedly in the rehearsal scene for Jack Robin's big Broadway debut in the variety show *April Follies*. Jack is to come onstage in blackface as the principal focus for the "Dixie" scene, which is to provide the finale for the first act of the show. The onstage drama has Jack playing Gus (a familiar Jolson role, and a name which brings us back to *Birth of a Nation*), a "colored porter" for the Carruthers family, who has been accused of being a bootlegger and of being disrespectful to Gwendolyn Carruthers, daughter of this southern family. The snippet of the play we are allowed to see is merely a setup to allow Jack to sing his Mammy song. The offstage drama is that Jack is about to upstage Carter, a popular old-time comedian playing the role of Carruthers: Jack's Mammy song at the end of this scene has replaced the "Poppy" song Carter was supposed to sing.[33]

Before he appears onstage, the character Gus is accused of being "none other than Dixie Dan, the Bootlegger." Already Raphaelson prepares us to think about the complicated drama within a drama being played out here. In this play which makes blackface its subject, Raphaelson is still interested in examining the method of blackface as disguise. Gus has, possibly, only been pretending to be a "colored porter" while he might really be a notorious bootlegger—an identity which, whatever his inherited "race," would align him with white ethnic gangsters. The real subject of Raphaelson's inquiry into impersonation is not the character Gus but the actor Jack Robin. Gus is no bootlegger, but Jack is.

After a bit of dialogue between Carruthers and his daughter, Gus is summoned to center stage to defend himself. But at this point there is a break in the rehearsal because Jack Robin misses his cue—he is offstage, absorbed in a card game with a stagehand. About to take his place at center stage in blackface, Jack remains behind for an extra beat. In this suspended moment we realize Jack is poised to cross over from the real play of the backstage card game to playing real as Gus in *April Follies*. To underscore the offstage/onstage drama, Raphaelson has Jack pause before hitting the boards. He turns back to the stagehand to finish their game: "'Spade—spade—spade! You lose!' [*Now he hastens to the center of the scene.*]" The race of the stagehand has not been mentioned before, and of course Jack's line of dialogue refers to his triumph in their card game; still, it is easy to hear Raphaelson sardonically echoing his own prefatory remarks on the theft of jazz from African Americans by Jews as Jack finds success through the travesty of a Black identity. ("Spade" had, by the 1920s, already come into usage as a derogatory reference for African Americans.)[34]

Any question as to whether Raphaelson is making comment (and rather gleeful comment at that) on the Jewish theft of African American looks and sounds is cleared up in the little bit of dialogue which is left in this play within a play. Jack, as Gus, takes center stage and is asked where he has been. He responds: "I've been down to my father's farm where we have a black hen that lays a white egg." Black hens laying white eggs offers a genealogical explanation for the ability of Jack Robin—a white egg instead of the usual blue of the robin—to make white art out of Black materials. That this all takes place on his "father's farm" is not arbitrary either, for Jack has supposedly learned how to sing Mammy songs by listening to his cantor father in synagogue. Even while the father is the source of power in this situation, the son is using his access to that power to honor his mother—who is, in this matrilinear religion, the original source of his Jewishness.

The action stops here because Carter believes he is supposed to sing his specialty number, a Poppy song; the director informs him that not only will Jack do the Poppy song in the second act, but also this first act will climax with Jack doing a Mammy song—also identified in the stage directions as a "Dixie" song and a "Jazz" song—alone onstage. This version of *The Jazz Singer* ends with Jack's unbelievable return to the synagogue to sing the Kol Nidre his dead father cannot perform. So, in the end, Jack gets to sing the Mammy song *and* the Poppy song. His theater friends have faith that he will return to the stage: his rendering of Kol Nidre has the same infusion of emotion which made his Mammy song go over so well.[35]

By the 1910s and 1920s stage blackface was widely understood to have become a special offering of the Jewish entertainment complex. For decades now Jews had enjoyed enormous success as traveling minstrels and, more significant yet, had managed to transplant blackface into the body of Jewish vaudeville. One important function of blackface was as a means for Jewish entertainers to communicate with their audiences and with one another. Such performances might include lessons on American history and on the Jew's social status relative to African Americans and white Americans.

The first crucial message delivered by the unmistakable prosperity of Jews in blackface was quite direct and literal: Jews had taken over a popular cultural form which had originally been the domain of other white Americans (some of whom were also negotiating their particular racial status), and had lately been taken up by African Americans with some success and great ambivalence as well.[36] The Jewish presence in, and indeed domination of, blackface announced that Jews had become actors—on the stage and off—in the urban milieu. This served to mark Jews off from the other recent "darker" immigrants to America and to herald that Jews were going to play dynamic roles in American racial politics. To put this another way, the ubiquity of Jews in blackface disclosed in perhaps the most visible fashion that this group, rather new to the American racial scene, would be defining images. I mean this last phrase in two senses. First, the Jews in blackface (and of course the songwriters, impresarios, theater owners, and so on behind them) represented an early yield of the process whereby self-promotion and public acclaim licensed Jews to take a major role in the manufacture of the racial stereotypes on which American popular culture depended. This accreditation itself spoke to the increasing centrality of Jews as translators of race in America. The second way of understanding Jews as "defining images" derives from the fact that Jews invariably remained visible as Jews even under the greasepaint or burnt cork. This is true in latent terms—because of the performative context of vaudeville—but also in the manifest style and content of these presentations ("plaintive" singing and Yiddish interpolations, to name just two examples).

The subtle performance of Jewishness along with (and/or within) Blackness comes clear in a comment Fanny Brice made in the 1930s about the ragtime and "coon" songs she had specialized in earlier in her career. According to Brice, even as she sang these "Black" songs in the appropriate dialect, she embroidered the vocal exhibition with "grotesque Yiddish steps." As Barbara Grossman explains in her biography of Brice, the entertainer likely meant that she acted out the familiar movements of the stage Jew while she sang her "Black" song; a stylized manner of walking and recognizable gestures would communicate clearly to the audience that Brice was embodying this well-known type. With this single presentation, then, Brice was able to suggest an important shift which had taken place in vaudeville, whereby comic Jews had come to displace the ubiquitous "coon." James Dormon cites a critic for the *New York Telegraph* who registered this transition as early as 1899, in an article which contended that "Hebrews Have Been Chosen to Succeed Coons" in vaudeville. According to this observer, a popularity contest had taken place on the stage with the "chosen people" triumphing over the residents of "Doyers Street."[37] In her performance, Brice made it clear that the real triumph of Jews on the stage was that they permitted audiences to have their cake and eat it too: not having to choose one or the other, spectators could consume Blackness as something which resided inside Jewishness.[38]

The dynamism embodied by Jews in blackface took on many aspects, some of which now seem contradictory. On the one hand, the nostalgia-ridden Jewish productions of blackface, along with the scores of Jewish-penned Dixie songs, appear now as a final stage in the North-South sectional reunion which had been in operation at least since the end of federal Reconstruction—a chapter of Plantation School writing in a sense.[39] On the other hand, Jewish blackface represented a victory for the (northern) city, for the urban entertainment complex which consistently proposed that the South had no current identity but only a history.

Jews in blackface oversaw the demise of the form. In the first two decades of the twentieth century, blackface became only one part of the newer "variety format" which marked Jewish vaudeville productions. While there is no doubt that Al Jolson, Sophie Tucker, and Eddie Cantor—the Holy Trinity of Jews in blackface—owed their popularity to early successes with blackface, they all relied on the apparatus of the Jewish-dominated vaudeville system to provide a supportive frame for their performances. By the time of Jolson's great blackface movie triumphs, *The Jazz Singer* (1927) and *The Singing Fool* (1928), minstrelsy had already been rendered marginal, first by the more polyglot possibilities of vaudeville, and then by cinema itself.[40] Tucker and Cantor had already abandoned the mask by this time, and no major Jewish stars after this made careers in blackface. The 1910s were the high point for Jews in blackface; cinematic representations were nourished by nostalgia and are better understood as a final reckoning with an older cultural moment rather than as a major new entry in the field of Jewish–African American interactions. In other words, filmic blackface needs to be understood as a summary of practices worked out in the theatrical world of Jews in New York City (and on the circuit).

Raphaelson's work represents a relatively late addition to the Jewish blackface tradition, at a time when Jews' anxiety about being conflated with African Americans had eased considerably. In large part this was a result of their conquest of urban mass entertainment, which converted a postulated Jewish closeness to African Americans into a vehicle which carried them closer to a form of white ethnicity. Michael Rogin has wisely differentiated between two opposing ways blackface can function: "As disguise blackface capitalizes on identity as sameness; as expression it creates identity as difference."[41] Rogin's insight comes, we should recall, in a reading of the movie made from Raphaelson's play, and does not take much note of earlier times when the comforts of Jewish whiteness were less secure.[42]

Eric Lott has explained that "the counterfeit" of minstrelsy—its manifest position as a form of racial masquerade—has frequently harbored a strong impulse of identification on the part of the white actor, a combination of desire for and fear of the burlesqued African American subject.[43] It becomes fairly easy to understand why Jews in blackface, with their own racial status a site of struggle and negotiation, would show symptoms of an acute case of desire and fear. Jolson, Tucker, and Cantor all expressed extreme ambivalence about the centrality of blackface to their careers. Of the three, only Jolson relied on blackface during the bulk of his most successful years; Tucker and Cantor both abandoned it as soon as they no longer needed it to put their acts over.

All three developed stock legends about their adoption of blackface which called attention to the personal necessity for adopting the mask while simultaneously disavowing any special racial sympathy for "Black" expression. Jolson claimed to have first blacked up in 1904 because he was nervous about performing a comic role in a burlesque sketch. James Francis Dooley, a minstrel monologuist, told Jolson that the burnt cork would make him feel like a performer. Jolson also circulated a story which had the advice coming from an African American man who worked as his dresser: "Boss, if your skin's black, they always laugh."[44] Tucker maintained that blackface was forced on her after her singing won her a spot at a New York talent night, and the manager of the show told an assistant that "this one's so big and ugly the crowd out front will razz her. Better get some cork and black her up."[45] Finally, Cantor explained that he first wore blackface as a disguise so that he could do more shows with the same jokes.[46]

Significantly, Tucker, Jolson, and Cantor each presented a blackface persona based on an absence of overt (hetero-)sexual appeal. Tucker did not develop her "red-hot mama" routine until she had already abandoned blackface, and Jolson and Cantor both cultivated what Cantor called "the cultured, pansy-like negro"; Cantor described one character he played as "slight and effeminate, with white-rimmed glasses and mincing step." Cantor also made an early blackface appearance in drag (as Salome).[47] The production of effeminacy—which is, in this context, synonymous with homosexuality—as a major modality for these Jewish men in blackface was tied up with their display as children: Cantor did a famous routine in which he played "Sonny" to Bert Williams's "Papsy," and in his first autobiography included a picture of himself hugging Williams with the caption "Sonny and Papsy on the Stage and off." Jolson, of course, leaned heavily on sentimental Mammy songs to carry his act.[48]

To be an "ugly" woman (instead of, say, a dark-eyed Rebecca or lusty "Black" woman) or an effeminate man-child (instead of, say, a white slave trader, hypnotic leading man, or sexually potent "Black" man) was one way that Jews in blackface could address the various deficiencies and threats which lurked in their own and their adopted identities. One of the real selling points for Jews in blackface is that their performances made a case about the safety of African American and Jewish sexuality.

The Jewish minstrel dramatized sexuality as a joke—neutralized it, in fact, as an innocuous affair. Rather than choose among the sexual images most readily available to the Jewish man (e.g., ravenous for Gentile girls, too money-hungry to bother with women, or too weak to do anything with them), Jolson and Cantor instead adapted blackface roles which sidestepped the question of male sexuality via travesty. None of this is meant to suggest that these enactments of effeminacy were sympathetic; as George Chauncey writes of the "pansy craze" of these years, such acts were themselves analogous to blackface, playing gay affect to "the hoots and jeers of an anti-gay audience."[49]

But above all it must be stressed that all three performers demanded that their implementation of blackface be understood as professional decisions, made under duress, within the context of Jewish vaudeville. Unlike George Gershwin, for instance, Cantor and Tucker went so far as to assert that they felt no particular attachment for the "real" Blackness which supposedly stood behind blackface performance; in their explanations, blackface simply represented a necessary apprenticeship in Jewish vaudeville. Key moments in the autobiographies of both Tucker and Cantor revolve around the abandonment of blackface. In her account Tucker describes having to "beg" show producers to let her perform without blackface, and claims that she was first able to do so only because of a baggage mix-up which left her without makeup.[50]

Eddie Cantor was similarly eager to escape the possibility that black-face would limit his career: "I feared the day might come when I could never take it off. I would always be Eddie Cantor the black-face comedian, but if I ever tore the mask off I'd be nobody at all."[51] In his "as-told-to" memoir, Cantor describes his final break with blackface in highly charged terms. During the rehearsals for Ziegfeld's *Follies of 1918* Cantor "made the resolve that old Black-face must die . . . I was not going to be a slave to a piece of burnt cork for the rest of my acting days." Flo Ziegfeld attempted to stop Cantor's "whiteface" debut, but Cantor persisted; as he tells it, "This change meant more than my job to me. It meant my future and freedom from the pale of the black label."[52] Cantor's first symbolic claim in this passage is that to perform in blackface is not merely a representation of Blackness but actually mimics the experience of being an African American: in the hierarchical world of Jewish vaudeville (marked most obviously by how various performers appeared on a given bill), the blackface comedian is low in the cast(e).[53] This sense continued well into the 1920s and 1930s, as witnessed by George Gershwin's demonstrated disdain for the caliber of Al Jolson's entertaining.

We might expect that the escape from blackface, with its connotation of the performer's relatively humble status, would be characterized by a fuller expression and embrace of the vaudevillian's Jewishness. But Cantor's final phrase—"my future and freedom from the pale of the black label"—suggests a different conclusion. "Pale" most obviously refers to the social and psychic landscape of inferiority in which Cantor feels himself quarantined; but "pale" also hints at the limited geographic space allowed to Jews in Russia. Cantor's escape from blackface thus seems to dovetail with a move away from his self-identification as a Jewish performer—and so the justness in Lenny Bruce's later claim that Cantor was *goyish*.[54] But of course "the pale" of the Black label suggests also that a rough synonymity had once obtained, at least between persecuted Russian Jews and enslaved African Americans.

This reading of Cantor's early autobiography is borne out by Henry Jenkins's wonderful work on the national marketing of Cantor as he was transformed from a New York–based vaudeville performer into a Hollywood star. Here is how Cantor announced his intention to leave New York for California: "This is to certify that I am in my right mind, white, free and rearin' to go to Hollywood."[55] While Cantor confidently asserts his whiteness in this press release, it took his studio a few years to come to the realization that his Jewishness would have to be downplayed if he was going to have nationwide success. This is not to say that no references to Cantor's Jewishness were made in his 1930s films, but rather that, depending on the point of reception, as Jenkins writes, "Cantor's screen persona could be at once Jewish and non-Jewish."[56]

Even if these Jewish blackface performers attempted to create distance between themselves and their impersonations, as performers they had a certain level of investment in putting over their racial masquerade: both Sophie Tucker and Al Jolson were reported to have made audiences shriek by taking off their gloves and revealing their whiteness.[57] Jolson claimed, in a ghostwritten story, that he tried consciously to get into the mind of his subject. As he sang "Mammy" in blackface, he tried to imagine a "southern Negro boy who has found life a bitter and terrible tragedy, who has been broken, abused, and who is down and out without a ray of hope left."[58] Additionally, Tucker was quite proud to discover that based on the sound of her voice alone, European audiences expected her to be an African American.[59] Such confidence developed only after years when many Jews felt an itchy nervousness about their racial status. An example of this uneasiness is found in the rumors about a "little colored boy" who supposedly wrote all of Irving Berlin's hits.

A Little Colored Boy in the Closet

Stage blackface represents only an early "generation" of Jewish manipulations of Blackness, which of course was virtually concurrent with the next "generation." The control of stage blackface by Jews helped create a certain confidence—though not a lack of anxiety—about the "natural" connection of Jews to African Americans; George Gershwin's career would offer ample confirmation for the many people looking to construct an account of intergroup sympathy. But between the blackface Jews and Gershwin came the difficult negotiations of Blackness which characterized the early career of Irving Berlin: in the wake of "Alexander's Ragtime Band" Berlin was often forced (by business associates, journalists, and so on) to explain how he came by his inordinate talent for making "Black" music.

Irving Berlin's major biographer recounts that the songwriter was a self-taught pianist who hit only the black keys. Berlin referred to these as "nigger keys," and called his instruments "nigger pianos." (Berlin's lack of skill initially restricted him to the key of F-sharp major. Later he bought a transposing piano which could change keys with the switch of a lever below the keyboard.)[60] The racist language—which biographer Laurence Bergreen says was typical of the heavily Jewish Tin Pan Alley—is not all that surprising coming from a man whose early successes in music were accompanied by the dogged rumor that he kept a "little colored boy" in his closet (or basement) to write his music. The anecdote offers a compelling narrative of Black-Jewish relations in which powerful Jews control hapless African Americans. The rumor also hints at an intimacy between the Jew and the African American which was unsettling for many observers.

In this anecdote, as in the Jewish use of the nickname "Nigger," we find a decidedly anti-utopian rendering of the connections of African Americans and Jews. Rather than the usual melting pot romance of Jewish involvement in African American music, the case of Irving Berlin's "little colored boy" emphasized a bleak vision of group relations in which African American and Jew seem at once unhealthily close yet also estranged. The anecdote interprets Jewish interventions into African American culture as rooted in theft and force rather than in talent and voluntary cultural merger. While the rumor imagined the Jew and the African American as physically intimate—although it did not make clear whether Berlin was in the closet with the "little colored boy"—it also suggested that the terms of the relationship were dictated by Jews, for the benefit of Jews. In the mythology of Berlin's "little colored boy," the Jew emerged as exploitative and paternalistic, and perhaps (most frightening) as sexually interested in the African American. One way to understand this anecdote, then, is as a conflation of Black-Jewish relations with pedophilia (though I should add that "boy" here does not have to be read as child; it certainly could have applied to any African American man at the time as well).[61]

It is also fruitful to read the "little colored boy" rumor in the context of ritual murder charges which have dogged Jews for centuries: Jews are charged with killing Christians—especially Christian children—in order to get their blood, sometimes to use as an ingredient for the baking of Passover matzoh, at other times for its magical qualities. The most famous ritual murder case of the twentieth century, the Mendel Beilis affair, was almost exactly contemporary with Berlin's success with "Alexander's Ragtime Band." (Beilis, a Russian laborer, was charged and tried in 1913 for the murder two years earlier of a thirteen-year-old boy.)[62] The Beilis case received worldwide attention, and was covered in detail by major American newspapers. The literal crux of the blood libel charge—that Jewish creation depends on Christian suffering—was presented metaphorically in the "little colored boy" narrative. Berlin's Jewish wizardry, in short, here relied on his ability to control a weaker African American body.

In the World War I era Jewish men were not commonly characterized as physically strong. Indeed, as Barbara Miller Solomon and others have shown, Jewish men were often considered to be overly intellectual and disinclined to perform manual labor.[63] Abhorrent as the rumor was to Irving Berlin, it certainly endowed him, at least by implication, with a physical strength usually thought unavailable to the Jewish man. But Berlin was not able to manipulate the gossip productively, and it would be left to other Jewish musicians to figure out how to turn an apparent liability (intimacy with African Americans) into a selling point.

The "little colored boy" story inverts the more common stereotypes of the Jewish man as effeminate and the African American man as hypersexual. In this thinly veiled master-slave narrative, the Jew is in command not only of Black sounds but of Black bodies as well. The "little colored boy" story cuts right to the chase: Jewish men and Black men, it suggests, had developed corrupt relationships in the modern city. Additionally, Berlin's "colored boy" can be understood (at least in part) to have helped pave the Jewish songwriter's road to white women, first via Berlin's takeover of a heavily gendered song market, and then more specifically in Berlin's famous marriage (his second) in 1926 to the non-Jewish Ellin MacKay over the objections of her father, the very wealthy Clarence MacKay.[64]

The rumor about the "little colored boy" (sometimes called the "little nigger boy") accompanied the success of "Alexander's Ragtime Band" and was spread in large part by Berlin's closest associates—other Jews. Bergreen writes that because Berlin was "musically illiterate" and had no manuscripts in his own hand, there was a compelling force to the story. The credibility of the story grew as it was repeated by Berlin's publishing house boss (and soon to be partner and rival) Henry Waterson, of Waterson & Snyder. According to one account Waterson told the story at the 1911 party thrown to welcome Berlin as a minority partner into the firm.[65] In this light the accusation leveled against Berlin might have served a regulatory function as it reminded the younger songwriter to mind the power of his elders. It also reminds us that discussions of Black-Jewish relations—however obscure they might be—have often been exclusively intragroup conversations among Jews. There is frequently much more at stake here, in a daily and concrete way, than there is with the interethnic meetings which supposedly define Black-Jewish relations.

The rumor became so pervasive during the 1910s that Berlin could no longer ignore it. In a 1916 article in *Green Book* magazine, Berlin responded to the popular stories with obvious dismay: "If they could produce the negro and he had another hit like 'Alexander' in his system, I would choke it out of him and give him twenty thousand dollars in the bargain."[66] Here Berlin converts a rumor about economic violence into a threat of physical violence (with a reminder of economic inequity in the perfunctory offer of $20,000), thereby making concrete the moral lurking in this story. Berlin's defensiveness can, no doubt, be largely explained by his musical insecurity: he was never comfortable with his technical abilities. At the same time, Berlin could not hide the anxiety he felt whenever he was called upon to discuss the African American roots of his music. Whatever the motivation for these requests, they appear to have struck Berlin as implying his own bodily nearness to actual African Americans. Unlike earlier generations of minstrels who insisted on their closeness to African Americans as a way of authenticating their performances, Berlin consistently attempted to create distance between his "Black" music and African American people. (I want to make clear that what we call Black-Jewish relations still had enormous influence in shaping the contours of Berlin's career. It only needs to be emphasized that in Berlin's case much of this work was done in the negative—with the songwriter frequently defining his status by disavowing his relationship to African American people or their cultural materials.)

Berlin was not the only one called on to respond to the rumor. Lukie Johnson, the African American pianist at the Pelham Cafe during Berlin's tenure there as a singing waiter, was a prime suspect in the quest to name the "little colored boy": Johnson made a point of denying that he wrote Berlin's songs.[67] The lyricist Andy Razaf (longtime partner of Fats Waller) was also rumored to be Berlin's secret weapon, but this made less sense given that the "little colored boy" anecdote gained much of its energy from Berlin's well-known musical inadequacy; no one ever questioned his ability to write lyrics. Nonetheless, Razaf still went on record to clear his name from the roster of possible ghostwriters.[68]

The anecdote had remarkable staying power. During the late 1920s and early 1930s, a period in which Berlin slumped badly, someone asked him if the "little colored boy" was sick; Berlin responded that he had died.[69] Berlin continued to react to the rumor as late as 1954, when he finally seemed to lighten up a little bit. At a fortieth anniversary party for ASCAP (American Society of Composers, Authors, and Publishers) Berlin sang a song parody which revived the old gossip with good humor: in it he thanks the "little colored boy" for his help over the years and bemoans the fact that when the "little colored boy" does not show up for work, Berlin is unable to write.[70] With the distance provided by time, Berlin seems to have conquered his touchiness on the question of the "little colored boy." He also uncovers in his display of mock abjection a homoerotic undercurrent that had always tinged the rumor: in the song Berlin employs images of sexual discontent (or incapacity) to describe what happens to him when his (male) muse disappears.

There was never, of course, any blatant claim that Berlin was sexually interested in or involved with any "little colored boy." I do think, however, that the available nexus which linked Jewishness and homosexuality provided some support for this "queer" story. A number of convincing arguments have appeared recently which argue that Jewish men at the time were widely perceived to be unmanly, overrefined—in short, ripe for homosexual activity.[71] Although the "closet" which Berlin purportedly kept his "little colored boy" in would not have carried the same connotations it does today (the homosexual's hiding place), it certainly did imply secrecy—a hidden relationship between a crafty Jewish man and an innocent African American boy. Another image at work here derives from anti-Semitic literature concerned with the luxurious "secret chambers" of miserly Jews who hide their wealth behind the facade of a shabby front room; in this case the secret wealth of the Jew is his access to Blackness.[72]

The most crucial meaning of the "little colored boy" story is its economic moral. Berlin, whatever his personal relationship to this postulated ghostwriter, had enough distance from him and enough control over him to reap the financial reward of his talents. Extrapolating from this we can easily see that the central social message of this anecdote is that Jews were unfairly exploiting African Americans and their music. As Robert Dawidoff writes, the rumor endorsed the cultural truth of the allegation that "Berlin had taken negro music and put it to his own use."[73] In this particular formulation African Americans are construed to be children unable to protect or develop their own musical materials. But Berlin, uneasy about his own musical capabilities, found that his great early successes with revisions of African American music made it impossible to establish a barrier between himself and Blackness; the anecdote forced Berlin into intimate connection with at least one African American.

Berlin's ambivalence about his relationship to African Americans and Blackness roughly marked the end of one era in the musical relatedness of Jews and African Americans. After him, and in part because of him, it became much easier for Jews involved in African American music to vanquish the anxiety displayed by Berlin. As Jewish endeavors in African American music became even further naturalized, Jews no longer spent much time denying that they shared a profound affiliation with African Americans. In fact, by the 1920s, Jewish musical figures began actively to encourage interpretations of themselves which emphasized their natural sympathy for African American music and their (perhaps now voluntary) closeness to African Americans. The 1920s, in short, set the stage for the appearance of the Jewish white Negro.

George Gershwin Goes Native

The Chicago-born musician Mezz Mezzrow is generally considered to be the first important Jewish white Negro. As Seymour Krim describes him, Mezzrow was "a Jewish man who did everything but paint his face black in his effort to behave and be like a Negro."[74] In his embrace of all things Black, Mezzrow undoubtedly was responsible for codifying the white Negro stance, especially in his 1946 autobiography *Really the Blues*. Mezzrow fixed the essential characteristics of this type more than ten years before Norman Mailer offered up his notorious essay "The White Negro": in this piece, Mailer imagined that the "hipster has absorbed the existentialist synapses of the Negro, and for practical purposes could be considered a white Negro."[75] Mailer's ruminations generated such controversy that later critics of white Negroism have, understandably, found it difficult to emerge from under its shadow. But just as *The Jazz Singer* (1927) was a nostalgic valentine for Jews in blackface, so too must Mailer's essay be understood, in large part, as a summing-up.

Breaking with the conventional wisdom which places the white Negro as the last of a line of avant-garde bohemians, dandies, and so on, Andrew Ross instead offers a history which focuses on "new postwar patterns of affluence, work, and leisure." Ross then situates the white Negro in a similar relationship to cultural capital as that occupied by the alienated intellectual.[76] Of course the vision of Blackness celebrated in the discourse Ross is concerned with has no liberatory potential for actual African Americans. As late as 1961, for instance, Seymour Krim could insist that the "Negro has been and is an artist out of necessity," believing all the while that he was paying a compliment to African Americans.[77]

Even with his revisionary plan Andrew Ross still presents a more or less traditional *literary* history, which concentrates on a few writers and intellectuals of the 1950s and 1960s, most notably Norman Mailer and Lenny Bruce. With a keen eye and relatively broad purview, Ross accounts for popular culture usages in a way that the "bohemian" thesis never could. But what Ross misses (I think primarily because he slights the white Negroes who preceded Mailer's essay and were its putative subject matter) is that the history of white Negroism in the American twentieth century is a cultural field defined primarily by middle-class Jews engaged in significant acts of individual and group identity formation.[78]

Because he is interested in underlining the connections between the white Negro and the intellectual, Ross detaches the former from the physicality which is so crucial to the performance of white Negroism. Intent on situating the white Negro in the *post*–World War II economy, Ross argues that the quality of "hip" which betokens the white Negro is mostly a matter of following appropriate consumption patterns. To be hip, as Ross puts it, "always involves outhipping others with similar claims to make about taste."[79] Accurate as far as it goes, Ross's analysis downplays the significance of the body of the white Negro as a site of *production:* the white Negro's consumption of "Blackness" (as music, clothes, marijuana, and so on) is secondary to his direct physical and expressive embodiment of it in easily recognizable forms.

The difference I am trying to underline here should be familiar to any viewer of American television of the 1970s who remembers the advertisements for Star-Kist tuna. In a long-running series of cartoon ads, a self-conscious hipster tuna named Charlie (as in "Mr. Charlie"?) tries to convince an invisible representative of the tuna company that he has a highly developed appreciation for the hip things in life, and as a result is worthy of incorporation into the Star-Kist line. No matter what Charlie says or does, however, it will never be enough for Star-Kist. As the unseen representative of the company always tells Charlie at the end of each ad: "Sorry, Charlie. Star-Kist doesn't want tunas with good taste; Star-Kist wants tunas that taste good."[80] The case is just so for the white Negro, who must also taste good: he must satisfy all audiences that the Blackness he transmits comes from within and is the product of a self which has an organic connection to African American life. This is demonstrated mostly through acts of verbal agility (along with bodily power, spontaneity, and grace): the key figures of Jewish white Negroism had no access to the visual repertoire of stage black-face, and so relied in large part on language fluency to ratify their authenticity: the "descent" into, and convincing adaptation of, Black-ness by Jewish white Negroes is most effectively communicated through their authoritative discussions and reproductions of "Black" slang.[81] While such moves might be authenticating and liberatory for the Jewish white Negro, embedded in them is a hierarchical assumption about the direction the Jewish subject must travel in order to arrive at the vernacular.

With this in mind, it is worth mentioning the contemporary move made by Harlem stride pianist Willie the Lion Smith to incorporate Yiddish into his performances and daily conversations. While claiming some genealogical connection to Jewishness, Smith never explained in a satisfying way how he came by his ability to speak Yiddish. Smith's Yiddish speech acts thus stand as a wickedly apt reversal of the Jewish white Negro's appropriation of "low" Black talk. Yiddish is Hebrew's Other in Jewish culture—it is the language of the street, the market-place, and most of all the kitchen—and Smith makes it clear at a few moments in his memoirs that he reaped some financial gain through his access to Yiddish.[82]

In the first half of the twentieth century, Jewish men were more likely than any other "white" people to claim (and sell) a natural relationship to Blackness. Jews in the entertainment business of the first two decades of the century were actively engaged in debate over what their involvement with Black forms had to say about their closeness to African Americans. The dominant attitude among these Jews (to reduce numerous careers to one scheme) was one of ambivalence, if not outright hostility, toward the idea that Jews had a natural propensity—racial and/or religious—to produce "Black" music. Between the equivocal poses of these stage and Tin Pan Alley Jews and the bluff immersion dramas of Mezz Mezzrow and Artie Shaw stands the key figure of George Gershwin. While the more "authentic" jazz players such as Mezzrow and Shaw would certainly have disavowed taking inspiration from Gershwin (representative of a type Mezzrow referred to as a "hamfat"), the composer created and helped spread a remarkable rhetoric about his own relationship to African Americans and their music.[83] Gershwin—unlike Irving Berlin—had the confidence and the worldliness to insist that he belonged *as a Jew* in African American music.

Although he rarely romanticized the attractive dangers of Blackness, a move which now seems central to white Negroism, George Gershwin, with his luster of high-art respectability, helped organize a critical modality for explaining and justifying the presence of Jews in African American music. I am most interested in exploring how and why Gershwin publicized himself—his body, really—as the ideal site for the production of Blackness while also maintaining plausible deniability: Gershwin's "Blackness" was temporary, detachable, and merely functional. His bravura public relations coup reveals most of all a Jewish man's confidence in his white manhood, as well as his ability to demonstrate it. Such was not the case for Gershwin's predecessors in blackface or for Irving Berlin.

George Gershwin was making claims on African American life and music by the late 1910s and early 1920s. From the time of his first "mini-opera," *Blue Monday*—which Gershwin referred to in a letter to biographer Isaac Goldberg as his "nigger opera"—Gershwin situated himself, *when he wanted to*, as *within* African American music.[84] Traditional musicology depicts Gershwin as Janus-faced, staring off across the ocean to the musical modernists of Europe while also keeping his eyes fixed firmly on the vernacular forms surrounding him. But it should be clear by now that Gershwin's greatest talent was for staking out African American music (arrived at in the vehicle of his vague but vital Jewishness) as the grounds for modernist innovation—whether in *Porgy and Bess*, *An American in Paris*, or *Rhapsody in Blue*.

Gershwin no doubt approved of the racially inflected interpretations of his music advanced most vigorously by his Boswell, Harvard professor Isaac Goldberg. In a 1936 article Goldberg wondered whether it was "the Jew in Gershwin" which "helped to make him our foremost writer of American-Negroid music"; earlier Goldberg had speculated on a "common Oriental ancestry in both Negro and Jew."[85] Gershwin's most important productions rested on the widely circulated idea that as a Jew he had more or less *inherited* African American music, and that out of these materials he was legitimately developing an American art music. *Rhapsody in Blue*, as we saw, conferred significant energy on this notion that Gershwin came to African American music through his own racial identity. But it was with Gershwin's crowning achievement, *Porgy and Bess*, that white Negroism—as personal style and musical approach—was installed as the explanation for his success at making African American–inspired music.

Gershwin and DuBose Heyward had first discussed adapting Heyward's novel *Porgy* (1925) as early as 1926, but the composer did not begin work on the music until 1934. The intervening years had seen a stage version co-written by Heyward and his wife, Dorothy, as well as a bid by Al Jolson to play Porgy in blackface in a musical version; Jolson bought the rights to *Porgy* in 1929.[86] Soon after Gershwin finally did clear the time to work on the project, he made the important decision to travel to the South Carolina Sea Islands in order to mine that "inexhaustible source of folk material."[87] With this trip Gershwin borrowed directly from a public relations move established much earlier in the development of blackface minstrelsy: as Eric Lott writes, minstrel performers often "claimed they did 'fieldwork' among southern blacks, while on tour, though in fact this required at most a trip to the East River waterfront; it was to their professional advantage to make such claims."[88]

A central component of white Negroism is the immersion ritual. Full symbolic identification with the African American, usually initiated by some personal crisis or professional challenge, is cemented by the subject's entry into a closed social space defined almost exclusively by its racialness and maleness.[89] Conceptions of class position and sexuality certainly infuse the white person's move, but race and masculinity (that is, Black manhood) always remain as the principal markers of difference and affiliation for the white Negro. For most Jews carving out a personal niche within white Negroism, the city (usually Chicago's South Side or New York's Harlem) provided all the necessary apparatus. Gershwin harked back to an older model for his immersion ritual: going native.[90]

Gershwin went to South Carolina in 1934 with his cousin, the painter Henry Botkin, who was painting "Negro subjects" at the time.[91] They were preceded by Gershwin's manservant, Paul Mueller, who brought all their luggage, art supplies, and golf clubs.[92] The men settled in on Folly Beach, which was adjacent to James Island and heavily populated by Gullahs. Although Gershwin's trip south was certainly novel for a Broadway or Tin Pan Alley composer, in some important respects he was merely participating in a cultural movement which had broad appeal in the 1930s: the rediscovery of the American "folk."[93] But unlike those who explored the world of the folk in order to expose and protest injustice, Gershwin was of a more celebratory bent. Of course his cousin Benjamin Botkin was himself a leading folklorist, with a particular interest in African American materials, and Gershwin might well have understood his work on *Porgy and Bess* to be a fulfillment of Botkin's 1934 call for a conscious blending of native and cosmopolitan artistic forms.[94] In 1935, in fact, Gershwin was quoted in a *New York Times* article as saying that *Porgy and Bess* exemplified "the typical American proletariat point of view in its fundamentals, regardless of race or color."[95]

It will simply not do, however, to imagine that Gershwin was some leftist cultural worker out to compile African American folk materials in order, ultimately, to further the cause of racial justice. Even so, he presents an excellent example of the kind of "racial romanticism" which Kobena Mercer considers central to the white Negroism of Norman Mailer and others. Mercer asks a cogent series of questions about the causes and effects of expressions of "racial" affinity: "At what point do such identifications result in an imitative masquerade of white ethnicity? At what point do they result in ethical and political alliances? How can we tell the difference?" Gershwin's Sea Island trip can hardly be considered to have contributed materially to what Mercer calls "ethical and political alliances." But as more optimistic critics have reminded us, it is also necessary to note how important the works of Gershwin and other Jewish composers have been to African American musicians—if only as subject of parody.[96]

It is sometimes hard to give Gershwin this credit, especially when examining the superficial and romantic clichés he used to describe his trip. Soon after arriving in South Carolina, Gershwin wrote to his mother that the "place down here looks like a battered old South Sea Island," going on to complain of the "flies and gnats and mosquitoes."[97] But any hint of displeasure had disappeared by the time Frank Gilbreth, a reporter from the *Charleston News and Courier*, showed up for the first of two interviews; Gershwin gushed at being at such a "back-to-nature" place and even offered up a sample of a local corn whisky known as "Hell Hole Swamp."[98] At this initial meeting Gershwin was clean-shaven and neatly dressed in a "light Palm Beach coat and an orange tie."

When Gilbreth returned for the next interview, Gershwin had already gone native. According to Gilbreth, "Gershwin's hair was matted and uncombed, his beard was an inch thick," and he greeted the reporter shirtless—"bare and black above the waist," as Gilbreth put it. This reporter was so taken with the Blackness of the composer that he wondered whether Gershwin intended "to play the part of Crown, the tremendous buck in 'Porgy' who plunges a knife into the throat of a friend too lucky at craps and who makes women love him by placing huge black hands about their throats and tensing his muscles."[99] The headlong rush of this sentence, its breathless syntax, indicates that at least this one reporter was nearly overwhelmed by Gershwin's "native" act. The content of the description also reminds us, as Marianna Torgovnick has written, that within Western culture "the idiom 'going primitive' is in fact congruent in many ways to the idiom 'getting physical.'"[100] This is certainly the case for Gershwin: writing "Black" music in this Black place enabled him, at least for a while, to leave his body—his New York Jewish body with its stomach problems—back home. In its place he presented to the reporter a healthy and powerful Black body.

Gershwin reveled in what he took to be the "freedom" of Folly Beach, writing in a letter to Emily Paley that he, Botkin, and Mueller "go around with practically nothing on, [and] shave only every other day."[101] (Of course, as a Jewish man Gershwin could not go totally naked/native; while he might black up "above the waist," the telltale mark of the male Jew is, of course, located below the waist.)

The most significant moments of this trip came when Gershwin actually had contact with local Gullahs on James Island. A story recounted in a *New York Times* article on *Porgy and Bess* in early October 1935, and told more fully by DuBose Heyward in a piece published in the theater magazine *Stage*, furnished an interpretation of Gershwin's sojourn in South Carolina which has formed the heart of the Gershwin *Porgy and Bess* legend. In Heyward's version, Gershwin's trip to James Island was "more like a homecoming than an exploration."[102] The crucial mystical moment in Heyward's account comes when he and Gershwin observe a "shout," a religious ritual which combines vocalization, hand-clapping, and movement; Gershwin could not remain a spectator, and began to "shout" with the Gullahs. To the "huge delight" of the participants, Gershwin stole the show. Heyward concludes that Gershwin is the "only white man in America who could have done it."[103] The Jewish composer is certified here by Heyward—a *real* white man—as "white plus."

Like the "little colored boy" story, this anecdote carried (and continues to carry) much rhetorical weight. Heyward's article was first published almost simultaneously with the New York debut of *Porgy and Bess*, and has been republished and cited extensively. The arguments in Heyward's piece quickly lost the appearance of being arguments—just as Heyward must have wished. Instead, Heyward's insights have come to serve as givens in the reception of not only *Porgy and Bess* but indeed Gershwin's whole career. Typical of this process is the conclusion of one Gershwin biographer who suggests that Heyward's story clearly demonstrates "Gershwin's empathy with the music of the Gullahs."[104] But the careful design of Heyward's chronicle makes it clear that he was trying to authorize Gershwin as composer of "Black" music for his own "Black" libretto. Heyward, as a southern white man, did not need such validation, ostensibly because of the geographic access he had to the African Americans who populate his story.

Heyward's journalistic article–cum–publicity release may have been inspired by the fact that *Porgy and Bess* was a shaky proposition commercially. A major public relations effort pitched this "folk opera" as both high art and the authentic yield of African American folk music; but even with this push *Porgy and Bess* did not have much success until its revival in the early 1940s, after both Gershwin and Heyward had died.

Contemporary discussions about Gershwin's relationship to African Americans in South Carolina suggested that the Jewish composer *really* had become one of them. A good friend of Gershwin's recounted that after experiencing the excitement of African American churches and schools, the composer would walk around Folly Beach singing spirituals. The reporter Gilbreth wrote that during his visit Gershwin sat at the piano to play "I Got Rhythm" and before long "two black servants, back in the kitchen, were beating time." The performance ended with "30 or 40 people—mostly servants from nearby cottages" gravitating toward Gershwin's playing.[105] Kay Halle, another Gershwin friend, provided the white Negro capper: "George had become so deeply identified with the black life around Folly Beach and Charleston" that he began to find whites boring and unemotional. Gershwin, speaking about the characters in *Porgy and Bess*, but obviously making a broader point as well, told the reporter from the *News and Courier* that he found whites "dull and drab," but was impressed that with "the colored people there is always a song."[106]

Gershwin's white Negroism had a life beyond Folly Beach, and the rehearsals for *Porgy and Bess* vouched for Gershwin's nearness to African Americans and their culture.[107] Alexander Smallens, the conductor of the *Porgy and Bess* orchestra, noted that many of the actors "born and educated in the North, hadn't the slightest trace of the essential Negro lingo, and were obliged to learn the dialect of the South.[108] George Gershwin himself, fresh from his plunge into African American life, was more than happy to act as tutor for these performers. In this anecdote we find Gershwin serving as a source—rather than a beneficiary—of African American culture. Indeed, the American popular culture industry has frequently offered up the spectacle of African American people marveling at white performances of Black styles.[109]

Gershwin's trip south suggested a sort of reunion between northern and southern whites activated by a Jew who understood himself to be a shareholder in American whiteness. In this the creation of *Porgy and*

Bess appears as a late entry in the process of sectional reunification which started at the end of federal Reconstruction, but in which Jews were not always welcome participants: during the Leo Frank case, for instance, much was made of Frank's position as a latter-day carpetbagger—a northern Jew come to enjoy the fruits of New South labor.

To pull off the white Negro act Gershwin had to believe, first of all, that he was white. He must have been fairly certain that there would be general agreement that he had a solid claim to whiteness. Essential to the enactment of white Negroism is a shared knowledge of the voluntarism which lies at its core: one does not *become* "just like them" unless one begins as something else altogether. The performance of white Negroism also offers a subtle argument against the possibility that a person could actually be both Black and Jewish. In any case, Gershwin's execution of white Negroism around the time he was writing *Porgy and Bess* was obviously provisional. During his career he more consistently cultivated a high-art cosmopolitanism far removed from Blackness.

I should note that there was nothing programmatic or uniform about the "race moves" made by Gershwin and his advocates. What was being worked out here in a lurching manner was a modality for Jews to snare both whiteness and Blackness—in different amounts and for different reasons—without repudiating Jewishness. When the composer Harold Arlen was described as really having become one of them (African American, that is)—absorbing "their idiom, their tonalities, their phrasings, their rhythms"—a few important messages were being communicated.[110] First and foremost, the songwriter who described Arlen in this way knew that Arlen was white; otherwise this compliment—and it is a compliment—would not have had the stable foundation it needed. At the same time the implication is that Arlen had an access to Blackness—perhaps because of his Jewishness—which allowed him to make great music (and also to make a lot of money).

This was the central meaning of Gershwin's Jewish white Negroism. As the conductor of the orchestra for the first version of *Porgy and Bess* put it, Gershwin's Jewishness "enabled him to understand" the African American materials he was transforming.[111] Gershwin biography has stuck to this line: a recent life of Gershwin approvingly quotes a source very close to Gershwin (Emily Paley, sister of Leonore Gershwin, Ira's wife), who suggests that the composer's affinity for African American forms derived from his belief that "blacks and Jews [were] the same in relation to the rest of society." The British critic Wilfrid Mellers has articulated a similar position, suggesting that although Gershwin, unlike Porgy, was not "a physical cripple, he was a psychological cripple: an archetypical white Negro, a poor boy who made good, a Jew who knew about spiritual isolation." Of course this misses the key point that even if the white Negro is responding to some perceived lack in his home culture or to some personal disability, he also always operates from a position of power.[112]

I have focused on Gershwin's little-noted performance of white Negroism as a corrective to those critics who evaluate his significance only through allegedly disinterested readings of his finished products. Having said this, I want to turn briefly to one musical moment of *Porgy and Bess* in order to explore in more, and different, detail how Gershwin positioned himself as an interpreter of African American culture not only through the events surrounding the production of *Porgy and Bess*, but also within its own musical story and language.

Based on DuBose Heyward's novel *Porgy* and the play he co-wrote with his wife, Dorothy (1927), *Porgy and Bess* tells the story of the poor Black residents of Charleston's Catfish Row.[113] The opera's libretto was by Heyward, with lyrics by him and Ira Gershwin. The opera begins with Clara, a young mother, singing "Summertime" to her baby while a group of men, including her husband, Jake, shoot craps. In "Summertime" Gershwin is able to ventriloquize simultaneously an African American mother and an African American orphan, because within his lullaby is a quote from "Sometimes I Feel Like a Motherless Child." Earlier writers and singers of Mammy songs (Gershwin included) usually routed their musical evocations of the African American family through the figure of the nostalgically forlorn child. Gershwin, by offering the hint of a well-known spiritual within his own song, instead voices an intact relationship, reuniting mother and child in the sung moments of "Summertime." In one respect, we might merely note that in his usual savvy fashion Gershwin had tapped into a going concern; as Sam Dennison notes, the lullaby form had become increasingly popular around the time of *Porgy and Bess*.[114] Even more, Gershwin's inventive positioning makes it seem as if the African American spiritual is a product of his own lullaby. In the familiar white Negro way, Gershwin speaks a Blacker-than-thou Blackness.

According to his own description, George Gershwin did not use any previously composed pieces of African American music in his opera. One highly competent listener, J. Rosamond Johnson, praised Gershwin for adapting the idiom of the spiritual rather than importing spirituals wholesale into his opera.[115] Here is how Gershwin put the matter: "When I first began work on the opera I decided against the use of traditional folk music because I wanted the music to be all of one piece. Therefore I wrote *my own* spirituals and folk songs" (emphasis added). But where Johnson suggests moral integrity and Gershwin emphasizes aesthetic concerns, Hollis Alpert, who has written a history of *Porgy and Bess*, suggests a different motivation for Gershwin's decision not to use spirituals in his score: it had been done already, and recently at that. Marc Connelly's *Green Pastures* (1930) and Hall Johnson's *Run, Little Chillun'!* (1933), not to mention the original *Porgy* itself, all highlighted the use of spirituals onstage. (*Porgy* featured Clara singing a snippet of "All My Trials" to her child: "Hush li'l baby, don' yo' cry. / Fadder an' mudder born to die.")[116]

It is misleading to accept that Gershwin did not use spirituals in his score, for "Summertime" does incorporate a distinct musical quotation of "Sometimes I Feel Like a Motherless Child." "Summertime" is the first major song introduced in *Porgy and Bess*, sung initially by Clara to her infant son as the action of the opera opens, and later sung by Bess to the same child. The spiritual "Motherless Child" ended the play version of *Porgy*, which Gershwin had seen. The director of the play, Rouben Mamoulian (who also directed the opera), had heard "Motherless Child" during an earlier research trip of his own to Charleston.[117]

Samuel Floyd, Jr., explains the similarities which link the two songs by suggesting that Gershwin consciously "tropes"—or makes knowing reference to—the spiritual's intervallic structure, its rhythm, and its melodic structure.[118] Without delving too far into the musicology of the matter, I want to note, as Gideon Pollach has suggested, that the "overall shape, or arch" of certain phrases in both tunes makes their resemblance fairly plain.[119] "Summertime" was the first Heyward lyric Gershwin set to music; Gershwin began work on it in 1934, well before his trip to Folly Beach. In this light it is not surprising that Gershwin would draw from a familiar African American sacred text, having as yet no *appropriate* ethnographic store from which he could draw.[120]

It is worth speculating how Gershwin got from Heyward's lyric for "Summertime" to "Sometimes I Feel Like a Motherless Child." One explanation is that Gershwin saw the word "summertime" and, trying to *think* Heyward's verse into what he imagined as the proper vernacular, chose to recode it as "sometime."[121] On top of this, the song Gershwin had to write was supposed to fit into the opera in the place where "All My Trials" had been in the play; "All My Trials," stands, then, as the generative text behind Heyward's current lyric, which could in turn have pointed Gershwin toward the musical thematics of "Sometimes I Feel Like a Motherless Child." The importance of this latter spiritual is fully revealed in the final two vocal lines of the opera. As Porgy gets ready to leave for New York to search for Bess, he sings an "invented" spiritual: "I'm on my way to a Heav'nly Lan' oh, Lawd. / It's a long, long way, but You'll be there to take my han'." The spiritual Gershwin draws on in "Summertime" not only turns on the phrase "a long ways from home" but also features the lines "Sometimes I feel like I'm almos' gone; / Way up in de heab'nly lan,' / Way up in de heab'nly lan.'"[122]

What is most striking about Heyward's lyric for "Summertime" is that it gives dignified voice to the African American mother, usually present in stage and popular song only as an etherealized object of fantasy. Equally interesting is that when faced with the challenge of this lyric, Gershwin produced music which conjures up another song, this one sung from the position of a child. If Gershwin had simply returned here to the site of his first and biggest commercial success, "Swanee," and written music which evoked the usual Dixie/Mammy clichés, we could write this display off as a rather pathetic instance of musical repetition compulsion. But instead, Gershwin matches Heyward's lullaby with an example of the type of music which inspired it: Heyward's original lyric for "Summertime," we recall, replaces "All My Trials," a spiritual which states plainly the future "motherless" condition of the child which is only portentously hinted at in the new lullaby. Within this confused genealogy, then, Gershwin's "original" music for "Summertime" gives birth to "Motherless Child," which simultaneously stands as the "authentic" spiritual responsible for giving birth to "Summertime" itself.[123]

Gershwin's coupling of "Summertime" with "Motherless Child" might be read as an inventive, self-authenticating move. As his opera begins, that is, Gershwin places his own music in an allegedly natural relationship with a sacred African American song. Naturalizing materials which did not originate in the African American community by placing them in "Black" contexts is not Gershwin's innovation, but dates back at least as far as the advent of stage minstrelsy. Perhaps the most relevant contemporaneous example comes from the set piece which introduces the Jerome Kern–Oscar Hammerstein II song "Can't Help Lovin' Dat Man" in *Show Boat* (1927). Julie, a woman the audience understands to be white, sings a song which is obviously Black; Queenie, the African American domestic worker, is surprised also, and tells Julie that she has heard only "colored" people sing this song before. This interruption is rendered temporarily irrelevant as the musical number continues and we see that Julie really does know, and feel, a strong attachment to this song. Queenie is ultimately moved to join in to sing this "Black" song. As this scene ends, the audience has a few options to choose from as it considers how truly Black "Can't Help Lovin' Dat Man" actually is. The two most likely choices are either that this song which came from the African American community has been taken up by white people (and here Julie's status as a "show" person who travels in the South makes it likely she would have access to such materials). Or else the song comes from white minstrels—and recall that the featured performance on the showboat includes a blackface act—which has struck a chord with at least one African American listener, Queenie.

The retrospective punch line delivered by *Show Boat* is that Queenie was right after all. It turns out that only "colored" people do (so far) sing this song, for Julie's secret is that she is Black herself. In the early scene featuring "Can't Help Lovin' Dat Man," Julie passes for white while she sings a song which passes for Black. Edna Ferber's passing/miscegenation plot serves, then, as a hook on which Oscar Hammerstein II (as lyricist, then screenwriter) can hang the racial legitimacy of the music written by himself and Jerome Kern. George Gershwin's opera opens similarly, as it stitches a whisper of an African American sorrow song into "Summertime."[124]

"Summertime" is sung at three critical points in the opera, twice by Clara and once by Bess. Clara sings it first in scene 1, and then again during the hurricane scene, as she waits anxiously for her husband, Jake, who has been caught in the storm. The final rendition of "Summertime" is delivered by Bess after both Jake and Clara have died in the hurricane, and after Clara has entrusted the baby to the care of Bess. When Bess sings to the baby, she thinks that Crown too has died in the storm, and the implication is that now that this villain is out of the way, she and Porgy will become a family with the baby. Immediately after Bess sings "Summertime" (act 3, scene 1), Crown miraculously reappears, and Porgy strangles him.

These vignettes are pivotal, for they reveal *Porgy and Bess* to be concerned deeply with the question of what kind of African American family will make it in the modern world. Gershwin's scoring of the ominous lullaby with reference to "Motherless Child" suggests that the composer was amplifying the family drama of DuBose Heyward's libretto. Heyward has Clara's infant end up in the arms of Serena, the symbol of religious tradition in Catfish Row, after eradicating the healthy but doomed nuclear family (by killing off Clara and Jake in the hurricane) and briefly testing the possibility that unconventional African Americans (Porgy and Bess) can form a new family of choice. This chance is spoiled as Bess, rendered unfit by her association with urban ways (in the person of Sportin' Life), abandons the child.[125]

Gershwin's lullaby foreshadows much of the action of the opera. The "Summertime"/"Motherless Child" performance achieves a few important effects. To begin, the "spiritual" heart of the lullaby serves to instruct the child that he will remain in the sacred folk community which is represented by Serena—the woman destined to be his mother. Additionally, insofar as "Motherless Child" is the baby's unacknowledged theme in the opera, "Summertime" itself acts as the vehicle for the child's implied communication. The baby of Clara and Jake cannot speak for himself: he is the one significant character who can articulate only through the music Gershwin writes for him. The music he is given contains a folk spiritual; thus within "Summertime," the baby is coded as belonging only to the world of Catfish Row, religion, and Serena. In one musical moment, then, Gershwin can effect the "mother and child reunion" which it takes the opera's libretto hours to accomplish.[126]

It might almost go without saying that Sportin' Life and Bess belong in New York. Cab Calloway insists in his autobiography that Gershwin based the music for Sportin' Life on his own performances at the Cotton Club. True or not, Gershwin was certainly drawing from styles he had heard in Harlem clubs and cabarets.[127] Bess, too, although she makes an attempt to fit in with Porgy at Catfish Row, obviously belongs in the faster world of New York City with Sportin' Life. (And it might be worth noting that Gershwin had his own favorite "Bess" in New York: according to one account Bessie Smith was one of the "few people . . . George would desert the piano to hear" when he was playing at parties.)[128] Porgy is thus rendered marginal. As the opera ends and he heads off to New York, it matters little if he will make it or not. What is clear is that he can no longer be at home in either his southern birthplace or the northern metropolis. But the baby must remain in Charleston, mostly so that he can be seasoned properly. Gershwin's entire project in and around *Porgy and Bess* depends, after all, on there being a reliable store of African American religious folk he can "return" to in order to discover musical ideas and find personal rejuvenation—all as a part of his public drama of racial affiliation with African Americans. Given that he had already written a lullaby (while still in New York) in which he impersonates an African American mother and child in Charleston, it becomes easier to see how Gershwin's own trip to the South Carolina Sea Islands could be described as a homecoming.

It seems clear that Gershwin's involvement with *Porgy and Bess* stands in a unique place in the narrative of Jewish orchestrations of Blackness in the music business. At once an apotheosis of minstrel and Tin Pan Alley usages, Gershwin's *Porgy and Bess* also looks forward to the immersion rituals of the white Negro.

Coda: Sick White Negroes

George Gershwin's complicated performances of white Negroism ran parallel to even more extreme stagings of it arranged (and, just as significantly, codified in autobiography) by his Jewish jazz contemporaries. I want to turn briefly to two of these men, Artie Shaw and Mezz

Mezzrow, in order to explore how Jewish white Negroism came to take its most lasting form as a mode for rejecting some of the trappings of middle-class Jewish life via an embrace and stylization of Blackness, while also subtly fortifying the whiteness of the Jew. But my claims here for this formalization of the stance of the Jewish white Negro are not meant to imply fixedness. For Jews, the activity of white Negroism always implies the flexibility necessary for the maintenance over time of meaningful interracial forays and the working out of intraethnic generational spats. Taken independently of the tradition I have been tracing out, Mezzrow and Shaw provide an instance of what Michael Rogin has claimed is the exclusively "Americanizing" function of "imaginary blackness" for Jews; as heirs and competitors of Irving Berlin and George Gershwin, they remind us yet again that one major use of Blackness in twentieth-century America has been to delineate and reinforce Jewish identity itself.[129]

The autobiographies of Milton "Mezz" Mezzrow and (to a lesser extent) Artie Shaw are sourcebooks on Jewish white Negroism.[130] Both men were clarinet players—although a more precise evaluation might indicate that Mezzrow was best known as a white Negro marijuana dealer and unofficial jazz promoter, while Shaw was primarily a bandleader and celebrity. Shaw's musical reputation is fairly solid; he is remembered particularly for giving Billie Holiday a job with his band in 1937.[131] Mezzrow's personal and musical legacy is perhaps best summarized on the one hand by a line from Pops Foster's autobiography and on the other by a definition from Cab Calloway's 1944 edition of his *Hepster's Dictionary:* Foster wrote, "I like him but man he can't play no jazz," while Calloway defined "mezz" as "anything supreme, genuine."[132]

Most often Mezzrow, Shaw, and their cohorts (among them Bud Freeman and Max Kaminsky) are understood, as Burton Peretti has put it, as "ideal types" of second-generation Americans, using "African-American culture to incorporate themselves more fully into a new kind of American urban life."[133] One central constituent of this "new kind" of city life was Jewishness.

It is misleading to assume that a simple linear path existed by which "Jew" moved through "African American" to become "American." By the time Mezzrow recounted his journey to white Negroism, this social modality had become not only (or maybe even mostly) a move "away" from Jewishness, but an expressive form of Jewishness itself. This is not to say that the Jew somehow speaks an essential Jewishness through the liberating possibilities of white Negroism (as Irving Howe and others have said of Jews in blackface); rather, my point is that the articulation of this stance itself became an important feature of a recognizably "Jewish" idiom. There have always been plenty of non-Jewish white Negroes. Even so, in the interwar period this stance emerged as a specialized way for Jewish men to establish public identities.

George Gershwin's performance of Blackness depended on a both/and construction. His "descent" into South Carolina was constructed and interpreted as a version of tourism, whereby he could obtain (and even embody) a usable amount of raw Blackness while maintaining his claim on a cosmopolitan white identity. Mezzrow and Shaw, on the contrary, insisted on an either/or white Negroism. For both—especially Mezzrow—dissatisfaction with a "home" culture leads the subject to immerse himself in Blackness and ultimately opt for living a "Black" life rather than accept the inadequacies of living a "Jewish" life.[134] Mezzrow in particular rejected the trappings of middle-class life, selling his sister's fur coat to a brothel's madam in order to buy his musical instrument; he was not, as Andrew Ross has suggested, a poor boy (54).[135] A minor point, perhaps, but telling: needing Mezzrow to be a lower-class analogue to the hip middle-class (Jewish) intellectual, Ross misses the point that the two could have been brought up in the same family. More to the point, Ross's formulation makes it impossible for the two—the musical and intellectual hipsters—to be the same person: go tell it to Artie Shaw.[136]

Both Shaw and Mezzrow had concrete immersion experiences which solidified their felt connections to African American culture. Shaw's immersion ritual takes place on the streets and in the music clubs of Harlem. As such it helps establish a safer and more accessible paradigm for modern white Negroism than the examples of Gershwin, with his expensive southern vacation, or Mezzrow, whose conversion was energized by a stay in reform school.[137]

Shaw's journey to white Negroism began with his discovery of anti-Semitism. His first response was simply to evade the issue of his Jewish identity, a move which caused him such guilt, he claims, that it was "impossible . . . to enjoy whatever success [he] was later to achieve" (90). Shaw presents his concrete move into white Negroism as a last-ditch option when he hits bottom: after killing a pedestrian with his car, Shaw suffers a deep depression (223). During this period of despondency he enacts his conversion: "Through some accident I can't remember, I found my way to Harlem; and there I found a temporary haven, a place to light for a while . . . I felt at home here, for the first time since I had arrived in New York" (223–224). Fortunately for Shaw he is befriended by Willie the Lion Smith, the Harlem stride pianist, who considered himself a Jew. From here Shaw's description becomes predictable and rote. He is accepted among "these Negroes" in Harlem and "treated as one of them." Ultimately, he comes "to feel more like a colored man . . . than an 'ofay'" (228). Shaw pauses to explain the meaning of "ofay" ("Harlemese for 'white man'") and give an etymology of it. The lexical interruption is vital: the white Negro signifies his achievement of grace not only by the revelation of his *faith* in things Black but also with *acts* of Blackness—frequently just this sort of demonstration of idiomatic fluency. (Mezzrow attached a quite detailed glossary to his text which explains the "Black" words such as "hincty," but not the "Jewish" words such as "yomelkeh."[138]

The one remarkable aspect of Shaw's text is how quickly and completely he believes himself to have adopted "Negro values and attitudes, and . . . the Negro out-group point of view not only about music but life in general" (228). Up until this point of his conversion narrative Shaw has mentioned one actual, living and breathing African American—his guide to a brothel. But even so, Shaw is able—once convinced that he cannot "break into the white world"—to imagine himself as belonging to "these people" who emanate that "warmth and enthusiasm and friendliness" absent from his "own race" (229).

Where Shaw's white Negroism was temporary, Mezz Mezzrow never surrendered his claims on Blackness. Indeed, according to his co-writer, Bernard Wolfe—a former aide to Trotsky—Mezzrow believed his metamorphosis to have become biological rather than simply a case of "transculturation" (390).[139] Mezzrow's belief that he had come to look physically "Black" is a definitive act of one-upmanship which makes an absurd final comment on white Negroism as a voluntary stance. After marrying an African American woman and living in Harlem for so many years, Mezzrow wanted to believe that a crucial act of transubstantiation had taken place whereby desire changed into matter and nearness into sameness. More like the Broadway "hamfats" than he would like to admit, Mezzrow articulates a strategy for Black-Jewish relations whose main move is to reimagine spatial proximity as a state of being. But what is central here, as I have been arguing throughout, is rhetorical performance. The heart of "Black-Jewish relations," as we have come to understand it, is not ontology or epistemology but oratory. As he insists on some mysterious yet decisive exchange of bodily fluids, Mezzrow trumps any comers who might still imagine white Negroism to be a game for amateurs. For Mezzrow (in this aspect of his self-making anyway), true success at white Negroism comes only with the total erasure of racial difference—which is to say the elimination of just those conditions which made his striking performance possible in the first place: he might not have been much of a musician, but no one can cut Mezzrow's white Negroism.

This strand of Mezzrow's life and self-representation—his abandonment of a smothering Jewish upbringing for the promise of African American life—is familiar and oft-cited. Consciously distancing himself from Al Jolson, Eddie Cantor, and so on, Mezzrow notes that most of the big names of his day "were heebs" who "played a commercial excuse for the real thing" (49). As Mezzrow comes to understand the shortcomings of his family life, he searches for a "new language" and feels his "way to music like a baby fights its way into talk" (7). A turning point comes for him when a close African American friend (Big Six) in the reformatory is attacked for having a white lover, a "punk," and Mezzrow—without judging Big Six's homosexuality—feels allegiance to the African American man. From here Mezzrow knows his future is as a musician, "a Negro musician, hipping the world about the blues the way only Negroes can" (18).

Mezzrow became a member of a loose assemblage of authenticity-mongering white Chicago jazz musicians which included Eddie Condon, Jimmy McPartland, and Bud Freeman. But Mezzrow distances himself from his white friends as he describes his final initiation into Blackness. Condon and some of the other white musicians decided to move to New York to try to hit the big time, but Mezzrow stayed behind in order to "be true to the spirit" of African American music

(163). At a going-away party for Condon and company, Jimmy Noone's band of African American musicians is asked to play the blues for the departing white men; they decline to do so until the white men get up to leave, and then Doc Poston sings a mocking blues whose message is one of support for Mezzrow. Mezzrow, forsaken by his friends, feels as if he is "saved that night, and in the nick of time" (162). Mezzrow finally follows his friends to New York, where, in Harlem, he "became" a "Negro." Like Artie Shaw, he proves his Blackness by speaking the "special lingo" reserved for "the race" (210).[140]

But within *Really the Blues* is the utopian possibility that Mezzrow's inherited (and usually scorned) Jewishness might harmonize with his acquired Blackness. Indeed, this reconciliation of Jewishness and Blackness is enacted with a powerfully sacred inflection. Early on in his narrative Mezzrow recounts that soon after he decides to live as a "colored" man, he is delighted to learn from a friend that King Solomon, Moses, and the Queen of Sheba were also "colored" (18). The unifying impulse of this insight is neglected for much of the autobiography but recurs in two key places. In a rhapsodic disquisition on jazz as a people's music which appeals to all types ("even the pampered pedigreed poodles in the penthouses"), Mezzrow notes how "the Lower East Side took the colored man's music to its heart, especially the blues" (202). Mezzrow observed this phenomenon when the Minsky brothers broadcast phonograph records over a public address system in order "to attract customers into their cabaret: Man, those records caused a traffic jam for blocks around. All day long the lobby was packed tight with little old bearded grandpas in long black pongee frock-coats and cup-cake-shaped yomelkehs, rubbing their hands behind their backs and shaking their heads sadly at Louis' moans, like they understood everything he had to say" (201). Mezzrow's conclusion is that these Orthodox Jews comprehend Louis Armstrong's music because "the language of the oppressed is universal, and hops right across those boundaries of nationality" (201). Here, a grammar is being worked out within which Jewish attraction to African American music is interpreted as a natural outgrowth of Jewish traditions.

Mezzrow repeats and extends this conclusion in discussing an incident which takes place when he is back in prison on a marijuana bust. The Jewish holidays are approaching, and the Jewish men in the prison ask Mezzrow ("me, a colored guy") to lead their choir: "I find out once more how music of different oppressed peoples blends together. Jewish or Hebrew religious music mostly minor, in a simple form, full of wailing and lament. When I add Negro inflections to it they fit so perfect, it thrills me . . . I give it a weepy blues inflection and the guys are all happy about it. They can't understand how come a colored guy digs the spirit of their music so good" (316). This discovery of such racial likeness between Jews and African Americans—particularly in their music—was a familiar part of the landscape by the time of Mezzrow's writing. White Negroism, as well as the less extreme forms of "racial" sympathy Jews had for African American forms (as expressed by Samuel Ornitz and others), were astonishingly functional: while these moves most obviously signaled a renunciation of Jewish heritage, they also left open the possibility of reunion.[141]

In this chapter I have focused most closely on George Gershwin, but in many ways Irving Berlin is really the pivotal figure in the story of musical Jews using Blackness. Berlin's great early successes came at around the same time as the rise of the blackface Jews, who operated in the already established and relatively restricted world of stage repre-sentations, but before the advent of George Gershwin, who developed a complex apparatus for advancing claims about his organic connection to African American forms. In Berlin's career, and especially in the "little colored boy" story, "Black-Jewish relations" surfaced as an in-tensely ambivalent and sometimes hostile tale of involuntary intergroup affiliation.

But George Gershwin (with a lot of help from Al Jolson, Harold Arlen, and others) made it possible to imagine that the movement of Jews toward African American music was itself a "Jewish" activity—and not only in the secularized urban manner I have so far discussed. A widely circulated rhetoric accompanying and sanctioning the Jewish involvement with African American music suggested that this affiliation had deep roots in Jewish religious tradition. Before examining this "sacralization" of Jews in African American music, I want first to ex-plore how some African American intellectuals and cultural leaders viewed the landscape of musical interaction which Jews would come to occupy as hallowed ground.

4

"Lift Ev'ry Voice": African American Music and the Nation

Two years after Samuel Ornitz published *Haunch Paunch and Jowl*, James Weldon Johnson made an interesting comment in his introduction to the groundbreaking collection *The Book of American Negro Spirituals*. Johnson noted that in studying ragtime music, he had come to find it "interesting, if not curious, that among white Americans those who have mastered these rhythms most completely are Jewish-Americans. Indeed, Jewish musicians and composers are they who have carried them to their highest development in written form."[1] There is much to comment on in this description alone—not least of which is the sly distinction Johnson makes with those last three words; with a wink for those in the know, Johnson hints at the countless African American ragtime musicians who had yet to publish—either because of their lack of technical training or their lack of access to the appropriate outlets.

My primary interest with Johnson here is in his role as perhaps the preeminent African American intellectual of the World War I era to concern himself with the world of popular culture. Johnson participated fully in discussions of the condition of African Americans in the United States which situated popular expression—whether called "folk" or "mass" or "low"—as a main text. This cultural conversation circled obsessively around the question of nationality; its central question had

141

to do with whether African Americans were to be understood as a "folk," a "race," a "nation," or some combination of these terms.

James Weldon Johnson exemplified an integrationist stance in African American thought which has enjoyed, for easily grasped reasons, little cachet in recent years. For Johnson and many others, "nation" contained little ambiguity: it meant the United States of America. The key question was how the "race" was going to attain its rightful place in that corporate body. This frankly integrationist position helped to create and maintain a congenial environment for the Jewish involvement in African American popular music which I have been describing. Johnson believed, as David Levering Lewis and others have noted, that the social status of African Americans could be materially improved through the agency of art; a 1913 *Chicago Defender* headline for an article on James Reese Europe argued that the bandleader was "Jazzing Away Prejudice."[2] One result of this approach is that Jewish cultivation of African American "folk" materials could be seen as a sort of civil rights activity and indeed find justification from members of the African American community.

The Real American Folk Song (Is a Rag)

In the first line of the preface to his massive study of slavery, Eugene Genovese notes that the "question of nationality . . . has stalked Afro-American history from its colonial beginnings."[3] A few basic positions have defined this discourse. As already noted, James Weldon Johnson gave voice to the possibility that African Americans were to be understood as a recognizably distinct group in America, but one which was destined to move up to equal status in the extant nation. A structurally similar approach holds that African Americans are already fixed as vital members of the American nation, but that their standing has been, and will continue to be, as a peasantry of sorts. The final two modes can both be termed "nationalist": the emigrationist, "nation to be" stance which reached its height of popularity with Marcus Garvey in the 1920s, and the harder-to-define "cultural nationalism" which has argued various degrees and versions of the "nation within a nation" thesis.

This last approach has inspired a vigorous contemporary critical project which focuses our attention on the ways in which "race" and "nation" can be understood to have achieved, at times, synonymity in African American life and thought. While the Black Aesthetic call for "Nation Time" in the 1960s has not materialized (but has been significantly revived and revised in hip-hop culture), a number of cogent arguments have been made as to the pervasiveness of cultural nationalist stances.[4] For instance, in his reformulation of the Harlem Renaissance, Houston Baker, Jr., emphasizes that turn-of-the-century African American intellectuals participated in the construction of an "emergent Afro-American *national* enterprise" and refers to *The New Negro* (with some ambiguous pronoun usage of his own) as "our first *national* book."[5] Bernard Bell, Arnold Rampersad, and Eric Sundquist have all noted that for W. E. B. Du Bois the terms "folk," "race," and "nation" overlapped in significant ways.[6]

I should note that since at least the late nineteenth century, both major forms of African American nationalism have fostered comparisons of African Americans and Jews. Of course Marcus Garvey frequently compared his movement to that of the Jew's Zionism, suggesting that, like the Jew, the African American needed a "strong nationalism."[7] Even moderates such as Alain Locke took up the proto-nationalist analogy; he wrote in his introduction to *The New Negro* that Harlem is another name for the "Negro's 'Zionism.'"[8]

The complexities of African American nationality and nationalism are beyond my purview. What I am most interested in is calling attention to the critical place occupied by artistic productions—particularly music—within these various discourses of "race" and "nation." Ardent nationalists, racist whites, communists, and moderate African Americans have all agreed that African American music provides vital data on the relationship of the African American and the United States. Nineteenth-century America generated an intense debate about the relationship of art and nationality which focused most sharply on how a national "high" literature was to be developed. African Americans were routinely ignored in this discourse, except for scattered mentions of the potential contribution of their music. H. Bruce Franklin has pointed out that the idea that African Americans (and their artistic productions) might be omni-American was already being parodied by a white critic in 1845. In an article titled "Who Are Our National Poets?" J. K. Kennard wrote: "What Class is most secluded from foreign influences, receives the narrowest education, travels the shortest distance from home, has the least amount of spare cash, and mixes least with any class above itself? Our negro slaves, to be sure . . . From them proceed our ONLY TRULY NATIONAL POETS."[9] Only a few years after this Bayard Taylor was indeed contending that African Americans were crucial to America's artistic nationhood: "Ethiopian melodies well deserve to be called, as they are in fact, the national airs of America."[10] Taylor, of course, is referring to minstrel songs here, but even so, he represents the growing consciousness that the music of African Americans might have something to donate to artistic nationhood.

For about 150 years now a controversy has raged about the place of African American music—both secular and sacred—in the American nation. Interest in African American music has followed an obviously politicized ebb and flow. A broad charting of major expressions of notice might begin with the period which saw the publication of *Slave Songs of the United States* in 1867 and the first tour of the Fisk Jubilee Singers in 1871; the next peak on the graph, and the one I am most interested in, comes in the last decade of the nineteenth century and first decades of the twentieth century. As Eric Sundquist has pointed out, it was just around the time of *Plessy v. Ferguson* that a renewed interest in collecting the objects of African American folk life developed. A sense that the "folk" were passing gave urgency to this quest.[11] We should not be surprised, then, to find Du Bois, in 1903, insisting that "the Negro folk-song" is the "sole American music," for one way to validate an interest in African American folk expression was to insist on its centrality to the broader American culture.[12]

But this same era in which the significance of African Americans to the nation was confirmed—as its musical "folk" if nothing more—was also the age of the "coon song." One obvious message of these songs, with their razor-toting, watermelon-eating, unfaithful "coons," was that African Americans were subhuman, certainly not worthy of citizenship.[13] At least one "coon" song, "Every Race Has a Flag but the Coon" (1901), addressed directly the national status of the African American:

> Just take a flannel shirt and paint it red
> Then draw a chicken on it, with two poker-dice for eyes,
> An have it wav-in' razors 'round its head;

> To make it quaint, you've got to paint
> A possum with a pork chop in its teeth;
> To give it tone, a big ham-bone
> You sketch upon a banjo underneath.[14]

The conflation of race and nation in this song returns "nation" back to its roots in "race" in order to exclude the African American from the (white) realm of the United States.[15] A year later the same songwriters tried to undo the damage by offering up "The Emblem of an Independent Coon," which held that Abe Lincoln had extended the United States flag to include all: "No coons should be neglected 'cause no other race it bars; / For ev'ry man on earth, of ev'ry shade and birth, / Is welcomed and protected 'neath the noble Stripes and Stars."[16]

Even given the terms of racialized discourse circulated by "coon" songs, it still remained possible to imagine a different relationship between race and nation than that proposed by "Every Race Has a Flag but the Coon." This was done, most simply, by imagining the African American as the folk of the United States. A summary statement of this position can be found in the first Ira Gershwin song ever to be performed onstage, called "The Real American Folk Song (Is a Rag)." To grant significance to African American music, as Gershwin's lyrics do, frequently meant to interpret it as unmediated folk expression; Ira Gershwin makes no mention of it, but a common follow-up to such a claim is that this folk material was most important as a building block for higher art.[17] By 1926 Gilbert Seldes was able to articulate a question which brought together Jews and African Americans, as well as race and nation: "Can the Negro and the Jew stand in the relation of a folk to a nation? And if not, can the music they create be the national music?"[18]

Gene Bluestein has shown that Johann Gottfried von Herder's advocacy of national forms of high art based on (so-called) raw folk materials was hugely influential in America.[19] To apply this theory to American art was complicated, however, because the United States did not have the conspicuous peasant class found in Herder's Europe (which is not to say that Herder was a complete authenticity monger), and because the "folk" and the "popular" were, from early on, mixed together. The absence of "peasant" folk material was, of course, partially due to an unwillingness to acknowledge the offerings of African Americans; early folk song collecting (for example, the work of Francis James Child and Cecil Sharp) ignored African Americans because of a belief that if a song was Black, it was either "copied from white tradition or had no real connection with American developments."[20]

But Bernard Bell has noted how Herder's main thrust was adapted by African American intellectuals (especially Du Bois) in order to call attention to the potential value of African American folklore.[21] Alain Locke, for instance, in answering his own question whether the African American folk idiom should be considered racial or national, concluded that the "answer is both, because it is only a difference of degree." Claiming that African Americans formed the peasant class of the United States, Locke found it obvious that they would "furnish the musical sub-soil of our national music."[22]

Communists and socialists also took part in defining African Americans as America's folk and their music as America's folk (or only) music. As early as 1923 the Yiddish *Forward* was arguing that "if one is talking about American music today, one is really talking about Negro music."[23] And while American communists certainly reached no easy consensus about the relationship of African Americans to the American nation, some very influential writers agreed that jazz represented the purest form of American folk music.[24] But this does not mean that American communists agreed on what the "Black Belt" thesis said about African American music. Michael Gold, for instance, argued in 1933 that any "real" jazz that existed was "not jazz; that's the African nation."[25] This position set off a flurry of criticism, most of which held that two kinds of jazz existed: the authentic, proletarian music of the African American masses, and the Tin Pan Alley corruptions.[26] The fullest statement of this position came in Charles Edward Smith's "Class Content of Jazz," in which he argued that Tin Pan Alley produced "wish-fulfillment music . . . folk music 'from above'" in order to "lull to sleep class consciousness."[27] After receiving some criticisms of his initial claim, Gold too came around to accept the "two kinds of jazz" theory and even quoted approvingly a letter writer who suggested that the "overlay of filth" which Tin Pan Alley applied to pure folk materials "is what the Russians have rightly tabooed." Nonetheless, Gold still held out that George Gershwin "might be able to write native proletarian music, because he comes from the jazz soil."[28] Indeed, Gershwin did write that he regarded jazz to be "an American folk-music; not the only one, but a very powerful one."[29] The major irony which accompanied the installation of African Americans as America's folk, and their music as *its* music, was that it undercut any specific claim of ownership which African Americans had on their own "folk" materials.

The Optimism of James Weldon Johnson

James Weldon Johnson was driven most strongly by his conviction that the most vital American popular culture products in the modern world were distinctly of a blended nature. Sometimes these blends occurred horizontally (as with the cross-ethnic Jewish adaptation of African American musical forms), and sometimes vertically (his fictional ex-colored man's defining search for a high culture/low culture fusion), but one consistent characteristic of Johnson's thought is that pure ethnic and racial products belonged to a "folk" world that was quickly receding into the past. For Johnson, it was a given of the modern urban world that any vision of discrete ethnic property had to give way to the realities of porous boundaries. Not only did Johnson view popular culture as the breeding ground for experiments of ethnic mixing, but also he at least tacitly suggested that Jews and African Americans were the avatars of this process.

For Johnson, a "plurality of voices" was inevitable.[30] He spent less energy discussing the moral implications of this situation (that is, the rip-off of African American culture by outsiders) than he did trying to answer two basic questions. First, what were the implications of such a total infusion of African American forms into mainstream white culture? And, then, what should the relationship of the African American artist to African American folk culture be, given its status as a negotiable commodity?

To answer the first question, I want to concentrate on a passage from Johnson's "real" autobiography, *Along This Way* (1931), which revises and adds to the observations he made about Jewish musicians in *The Book of American Negro Spirituals*. *Along This Way* occupies a special place in the James Weldon Johnson canon as the last major work he completed before his accidental death in 1938. Johnson was frequently self-referential in his nonfiction writing (often without citing his earlier work), and it is always fascinating to observe how his commentary appears when it reaches its (provisional) final form.[31] In this autobiography, which shares numerous passages with the fictional *Autobiography of an Ex-Colored Man* (1912) and with other of his published writings, Johnson contends that it is not with the spirituals but in

> his lighter music that the Negro has given America its best-known distinctive form of art. I would make no extravagant claims for this music, but I say "form of art" without apology. This lighter music has been fused and then developed, chiefly by Jewish musicians, until it has become our national medium for expressing ourselves musically in popular form, and it bids fair to become a basic element in the future great American music. The part it plays in American life and its acceptance by the world at large cannot be ignored. It is to this music that America in general gives itself over in its leisure hours, when it is not engaged in the struggles imposed upon it by the exigencies of present-day American life. At these times, the Negro drags his captors captives.[32]

Johnson travels an extraordinary route in this passage. He begins with an opposition of race and nation, and a clear suggestion that "Negro" signifies a distinct, actively participating member of a larger composite known as "America." From there he subtly weaves "the Negro" into the fabric of "American life."

Johnson was always a precise writer, and his use of pronouns in this excerpt bears special attention. He begins with two third-person pronouns, "his" and "its"; the first "his" positions Johnson outside the discussion even though as a songwriter he was an early participant in the process he is discussing. The use of "its" as the referent echoing "America" in this sentence further places "the Negro" as outside the nation. In the next line Johnson's choice of pronouns signals his personal entrance into the argument, with the second "I" carrying a sense of deep investment in the issue.

The following sentence is perhaps the most remarkable of all: "This lighter music has been fused and then developed, chiefly by Jewish musicians, until it has become *our* national medium for expressing *ourselves* musically in popular form, and it bids fair to become a basic element in the future great American music" (emphasis added).[33] With the introduction of "Jewish musicians" Johnson adds a third element to his opposition of "Negro" and "American," an element which has not been mentioned previously. The second part of this compound sentence should give us pause. It is as if Johnson has been playing some subtle version of literary three-card monte: he first shows us the three different cards—"Negro," "American," and "Jewish"—and then shuffles them and makes each face appear as American! Johnson has craftily transformed what he initially described as "lighter music" into "our national medium for expressing ourselves."[34]

Along with the intricate changes Johnson rings on his pronouns, a general argument comes clear. With Jews serving as intermediary, African American music has become the only truly national art that exists in America.[35] The form of this argument is particularly characteristic of Johnson's thinking; one constant of Johnson's aesthetic system was that transcendent art came from a group process filtered through an appropriate medium to become singular expression. Of course, in major respects there is nothing new about the main thrust of Johnson's argument. Since at least the 1890s numerous calls had been made to base a classical American music on African American (as well as Native American) themes.[36] In this particular case—the development of ragtime song—Jews served in the role of go-between. Even Johnson's discussion of the texts of the spirituals pointed to the centrality of cross-cultural development: "Hebraic paraphrases are frequent . . . But in those paraphrases we have something that is not exactly paraphrase; there is a change of, I dare to say it, style; something Hebrew—austerity—is lessened, and something Negro—charm—is injected."[37] The outline of ragtime song's development is a fine example of Johnson's making a positive from a negative. Instead of focusing on the implied theft that is embedded in his discussion of Jews as cultural middlemen, or on the lack of recognition afforded to the African American originators of this music, Johnson emphasizes that for an African American form to come to be recognized as American music is a triumph in itself. Paul Joseph Burgett has carefully examined how "vindication" of the value of African American culture was a major theme in Alain Locke's music writings.[38] A similar case could be made for James Weldon Johnson, with one crucial difference: where Locke focused on racially pure moments (such as James Reese Europe's "coming-out party" for jazz at Carnegie Hall in 1912), Johnson tends to concentrate on the significance of African American contributions to products generally construed as "American."

"Commercial Slavery": Dissenting Opinions

James Weldon Johnson was convinced that the contested space of popular culture was a likely arena for the negotiation of ethnic expression. It was not only in his autobiography that Johnson made a case for the inescapably mixed nature of American popular culture, but he was sometimes less optimistic about the meaning of the infusion of Blackness into white culture than he was in *Along This Way*. In his preface to *The Second Book of Negro Spirituals* (1926), Johnson lamented the outright appropriation of Negro creation: "The first of the so-called Ragtime songs to be published were actually Negro Secular folk songs that were set down by white men, who affixed their own names as the composers. In fact, before the Negro succeeded fully in establishing his title as creator of his secular music the form was taken away from him and made national instead of racial."[39] The differences between this passage and Johnson's later meditations on the blending which had occurred in recent American musical history is striking. Here Johnson describes a theft, an act of cultural imperialism with a clear negative valence. Not surprisingly, the players in this version of the development of ragtime song have lost their specificity; by generically fixing "white men" as the colonizers of African American music, Johnson avoids the responsibilities and pitfalls which might accompany a direct attack on Jews. In a sense, the ellipsis implied in the unacknowledged later translation of "white men" into "Jewish musicians," with the attendant change to a generally positive outlook on the production of racially mixed cultural products, suggests that for Johnson "Jewish" signified an improvement on "white." Recall that the Jewish musicians of the later description did not merely affix their names to existing creations but "fused and then developed" them.

Some other African American intellectuals were much less sanguine than Johnson about outside interventions into African American music. Alain Locke, for instance, called for "a class of trained musicians who know and love the folk music and are able to develop it into great classical music, and a class of trained music lovers who will support by appreciation the best in the Negro's musical heritage and not allow it to be prostituted by the vaudeville stage or Tin Pan Alley, or to be cut off at its folk roots." In case the full implications of Locke's position are not clear, we need only look at the specificity with which he named the debasers of African American music: "One of the handicaps of Negro music today is that it is too popular. It is tarnished with commercialism and the dust of the marketplace. The very musicians who know the folkways of Negro music are the very ones who are in commercial slavery to the Shylocks of Tin Pan Alley."[40] Not only were Jews responsible for perverting "authentic" African American music by directly commercializing it themselves, but also their control of the music industry allowed them to obstruct the artistic labor of those African American composers who were able—by talent and inclination—to produce folk-based masterworks. Locke made explicit here one of the arguments held inside the anecdote about Irving Berlin's "little colored boy": by denying African American artists the fruits of their labor in urban spaces, Jews had come to function as oppressors.

Locke was not alone among African American writers in expressing concern over "adaptations" or "improvements" of African American music. Sterling Brown, for instance, used the appropriation of African American musical materials to lodge a sharp protest in his poem "Real Mammy Song" (from the mid-1930s). Here Brown reads the conditions of musical production in the context of an extreme moment of racial oppression. To begin, the target of Brown's protest is marked off in the mock dedication of this poem, which is made with "proudful apologies" to "Irving Berlin et al. and all the Tin Pan Alley Manipulators." The use of "Manipulators" in this last phrase connects the songwriters of Tin Pan Alley with their predecessors in minstrelsy; Brown's intention in this poem is to examine how culture industry productions of Blackness work to draw attention away from the realities of African American lives. "Real Mammy Song" tells the story of an African American man who prepares to kill himself rather than surrender to a lynch mob which hopes to punish him for shooting a sheriff and another white man. The poem juxtaposes lyrics which sound "authentically" African American ("Sun shines east, sun shines west, / Moon shines on de boy / She loved de best") with those which are obviously parodies of Tin Pan Alley songs, especially those inspired by Stephen Foster. The confusion of genres is resolved in the last four lines as Brown gives voice to the absent subject of most Mammy songs—the African American mother herself:

> They done took
> Poor Jim away . . .
> They done took
> My son away . . .[41]

A subtext of Brown's poem, introduced by his dedication, is that "real Mammy" songs are rendered inaudible by the "manipulations" of Tin Pan Alley composers. The ideological violence done by Mammy songs, from minstrelsy to Tin Pan Alley, stems from their proposition that fissures in the African American family were benignly normative—the product of the usual (non–race specific) intergenerational dramas which trouble all families. In other words, Mammy songs rewrite the unique history of African American families in America, a history which includes enforced separations and lack of legal recognition for marriages. In his poem Brown argues that the stereotypes of musical minstrelsy played an active role in concealing racial oppression and thus became a form of persecution in themselves.

But James Weldon Johnson argued that recognizing the "Black" *sounds* in American popular music would facilitate the increased visibility of African Americans as citizens, Brown made a more pessimistic claim. For Brown, the "misrecognition" of African Americans through the stereotypes of musical minstrelsy played an active role in concealing racial oppression and thus became a form of persecution in itself. The romantic ventriloquism of Mammy songs not only silenced African American artists but obscured the realities of African American life as well.

George Schuyler, in his novel *Black No More* (1931), also fixed on Mammy songs as a significant site of cultural negotiation, but Schuyler's mode is burlesque rather than tragedy. This satirical work lampoons everything in view as it tells a story of the effect of a product which can make even the darkest African American look white: after great anxiety is caused by this leveling device, racists can only find comfort in the fact that faux whites can be discovered because they are *too* light. The book is dedicated to "all Caucasians in the great republic who can trace their ancestry back ten generations and confidently assert that there are no Black leaves, twigs, limbs or branches on their family trees." Ostensibly this is a dedication to no one (since no Americans would be able to defend such an avowal), but we might also read it as an appeal to more recently arrived Americans—including eastern European Jews—to resist the temptation of claiming the privileges of "whiteness."[42]

Black No More makes a few direct references to Jews—including one jibe about "canny Hebrews" who manufacture most of the skin-whitening and hair-straightening products—and pauses to parody the Jewish Mammy song. Before a speech is delivered by the Imperial Grand Wizard of the Knights of Nordica, the radio audience is entertained by "Mr. Jack Albert, the well-known Broadway singer and comedian." "Jack Albert" refers, of course, to Al Jolson, stitching together as it does Jolson's own first name with the first name of Jack Robin, the "jazz singer." Jack Albert introduces the song by noting that he likes it "because it has feeling and sentiment. It means something. It carries you back to the good old days that are dead and gone forever. It was written by Johnny Gulp with music by the eminent Japanese-American composer, Forkrise Sake." With this last joke ("For Christ's Sake"), Albert launches into his song, entitled "Vanishing Mammy":

> Vanishing Mammy, Mammy! Mammy! Mammy! of Mi-ne,
> You've been away, dear, such an awfully long time
> You went away, Sweet Mammy! Mammy! one summer night
> I can't help thinkin', Mammy, that you went white.
> Of course I can't blame you, Mammy! Mammy! dear.[43]

To imagine the young "Black" boy unable to recognize his mother is a neat reversal of Jolson's famous interpolation in his song "My Mammy": "Mammy, look at me. Don't you know me? I'm your little baby."[44] The humor of the "Vanishing Mammy" song derives from a formal racial travesty which relies on the acknowledgment of difference. It is funny because it figures a white man singing in blackface about his Black mother whom he cannot find because she is now white. Whatever Schuyler thought about James Weldon Johnson's hope that the art of African Americans would aid their translation from race into nation, he certainly found the position of Jews (and others) in blackface (and Black music) deserving of contempt.

James Weldon Johnson, unlike Brown, Locke, or Schuyler, saw some benefit in "outside" intervention in African American music; nonetheless he still had real concerns about the manner of this involvement. What seems to have piqued Johnson most was the lack of recognition by America of the pedigree of its most (or perhaps only) distinctive art form. In the preface to *The Book of American Negro Poetry* (1922), Johnson complains that for "a dozen years or so there has been a steady tendency to divorce Ragtime from the Negro; in fact to take from him the credit of having originated it. Probably the younger people of the present generation do not know that Ragtime is of Negro origin . . . Ragtime is now national rather than racial. But that does not abolish in any way the claim of the American Negro as its originator."[45] One task, then, for the African American intellectual at this point was to secure for the mute "folk" the entitlements they deserve, at the very least as important figures in the historical record of America's music. Johnson acted in just this fashion in the yeoman service he undertook in his role as collector of African American spirituals and poetry, in the historical survey *Black Manhattan* (1930), as well as in his own collection of poetry, *God's Trombones* (1927). The unspoken moral of all this is that for good or ill, much of African American folk culture had merged with other strains in American culture. Still, it remained important to guarantee that the progenitors of the composite culture be recognized.

There were, for Johnson, compelling reasons to name the African American contribution to the American cultural scene. Johnson entertained the notion that with the intervention of Jewish musicians, the growth of an African American musical form might result in a hidden victory for African Americans, a surreptitious colonization of American popular culture. But Johnson was ultimately a pragmatist and would not have paid so much attention to music had he not held out hope that its influence would be far-ranging. Arguing against the tendency to view the Negro's musical gift as a kind of "sideshow," Johnson claimed instead that this gift is the "touchstone, it is the magic thing, it is that by which the Negro can bridge all chasms."[46]

Johnson's faith in the ameliorating influence of art on racial discord was seen by many as naive. To cite just one example, in 1934 Langston Hughes published his collection of stories *The Ways of White Folks*, which included "The Blues I'm Playing." In this story, Hughes, through pianist Oceola Jones, takes on Johnson's argument:

> And as for the cultured Negroes who were always saying art would break down color lines, art could save the race and prevent lynchings! "Bunk!" said Oceola. "My ma and pa were both artists when it came to making music, and the white folks ran them out of town for being dressed up in Alabama. And look at the Jews! Every other artist in the world's a Jew, and still folks hate them."[47]

Hughes neatly reverses Johnson's formula here with his suggestion that art has no power to make inroads against racism.

Johnson never made explicit just how an appreciation of the African American origins of American art would affect race relations. He might inscribe ragtime song as the modern expression of "the blare and jangle and the surge, too, of our national spirit,"[48] but he did not consider seriously if it was simply one more resource of the African American to be exploited within the functional racial hierarchies of American capitalism. Neither did he consider the possibility that its adoption by white America was at the debased level of minstrelsy.[49]

The Example of James Weldon Johnson

The other reason for Johnson's interest in naming the African American contribution to American culture brings us back around to what I earlier located as the second of two important questions Johnson tried to answer vis-à-vis cultural production (the first being what the merger of African American and white forms in America signified): What should the relationship of the African American artist to folk culture be?

Sometime in 1922 or 1923, during a trip to Russia, Claude McKay wrote an essay, "Negroes in Art and Music," in which he asked, "Why, among contemporary American Negroes, is there this tendency (which always ends unsuccessfully) to improve . . . works which are as finished and complete as spirituals or the melodies of Negro plantation slaves?"[50] James Weldon Johnson, for one, was fascinated by the possibilities of a vertical integration of "low" folk art resources with what he considered to be higher forms of cultural expression; his emphatic belief that great (African) American art would be built upon folk sources helped construct a field of activity in which Jews who "improved" folk materials could be understood to be actively helping African Americans.

Johnson offers us a prime example of the emerging consciousness in the early decades of the twentieth century that the folk art of premodern people had to be transformed into a newer, urban, conscious art. These new forms would be marked by their complex genealogies, merging, as they would, high and low, and in-group with out-group. Many Jews and African Americans came to see themselves as placed in the front ranks of this campaign, and thus as partaking in the construction of a kinship of art.[51]

In his career as a songwriter, Johnson (along with his brother Rosamond and Bob Cole) was actively engaged in the cultural work about which he would later theorize. Eugene Levy has argued that the time Johnson spent in Venezuela as a consular officer cemented the vision of race and nation he had been groping toward all along. There, as Johnson saw it, "the black race had given up its identity to become part of the Venezuelan people." If the loss of racial identity heralded by this process left Johnson feeling "wistful," he could maintain his race pride by continuing to champion both folk music and more modern forms of art.[52]

In 1905 Johnson wrote an article about African American music for a national magazine in which he heaped praise on classical composers (Harry Burleigh and Samuel Coleridge-Taylor), and on some popular musical figures (Bert Williams, George Walker, and Ernest Hogan), but ignored those practicing ragtime pianists and composers (Scott Joplin, James Scott) who were contemporaneously exploring the blend of high and low, African American and European, which Johnson so often invoked.[53] That Johnson could so neglect the very artists whom later observers would canonize as the central figures of instrumental ragtime brings us again to the troubling issue of just what Johnson and his contemporaries meant when they called a music "ragtime." In this case we might turn to Johnson's own declarations on music, to get an idea of the various things he used this label to describe. Through this lens it will be possible to obtain a sense of Johnson's vision for a high art/folk art synthesis.

For Johnson, "ragtime" (whatever he meant exactly by it) occupied a middle ground between the folk art of the spirituals and the high art collected in his anthology of African American poetry. The potency of ragtime as an image for Johnson was as both echo and omen. It echoed the authentic, collective, and decidedly racial aspects of the spirituals (as his "Under the Bamboo Tree" would work a variation on "Nobody Knows de Trouble I See"),[54] and pointed toward innovations such as Johnson's own *God's Trombones*, all serving the ultimate goal of reaching a broader audience. Johnson made these connections explicit when he recalled in *Along This Way* how he wanted to

> take the primitive stuff of the old-time Negro sermon and, through art-governed expression, make it into poetry. I felt that this primitive stuff could be used in a way similar to that in which a composer makes use of a folk theme in writing a major composition. I believed that the characteristic qualities: imagery, color, abandon, sonorous diction, syncopated rhythms, and native idioms, could be preserved and, at the same time, the composition as a whole be enlarged beyond the circumference of mere race, and given universality.[55]

Johnson had a personal stake in promulgating a theory of art which not only allowed for but actively encouraged liberal borrowings from anonymous folk creations since many of his own greatest successes were achieved just so.

This is not to suggest that Johnson's theoretical writings on African American art forms were transparent apologies for his own inclination to utilize folk materials; I see his speculative writings rather as part of the project that Valerie Smith has called "self-discovery and authority"—the attempt, given specific social contexts, to develop fruitful modes of self-authentication.[56] The particular aspect of the cultural world that fascinated and indeed inspired Johnson was his sense that the age of folk creation had come to a close. Since Johnson believed that the new art should be constructed on the foundation of earlier collective expression, and in view of his oft-repeated dictum that "an artist accomplishes his best when working at his best with the material he knows best," it is not surprising to find him situating the African American artist in a particularly promising and demanding position.[57]

Johnson declared the folk era closed in his preface to *The Second Book of Negro Spirituals* (1926). He wrote of a process just then taking place, submitting that "with the close of the creative period of the Blues, which appears to be at hand, it is probable that the whole folk creative effort of the Negro in the United States will have come to an end." Johnson pointed to urbanization and technological advance, and most of all to consciousness as the primary culprits:

> The production of folk-art requires a certain naïveté, a certain insouciance, a sort of intellectual and spiritual isolation on the part of the producing group that makes it indifferent to preconceived standards. All of these, the Negro in the United States is fast losing, and inevitably. The bulk of this Aframerican folk production has been music . . . but the urge and necessity upon the Negro to make his own music, hisflown songs, are being destroyed not only by the changing psychology but by such modern mechanisms as the phonograph and the radio.[58]

Although Johnson does demonstrate some regret at the passing of the "folk," he is decidedly not of the sobbing school of nostalgia. In fact, his optimistic integrationist agenda makes it possible to read his phrase "urge and necessity" as a hushed reminder of past oppression.[59] If "folk" in Johnson's lexicon implies the experience of racism and oppression, then the products of African American folk culture come to appear as the rightful inheritance of the African American artist, and the artistic development of them becomes a modern act of filiopiety, the remembrance in art of the social conditions of folk culture under which earlier generations suffered.

The demand for creative art erected on the remains of folk culture became, as we have seen, Johnson's ideal. Johnson elaborated on this point so often and so emphatically that I need cite only a few examples of his general theorizing before moving on to a look at the special problems ragtime presented for him.

In *Along This Way* Johnson recalls how during his early years in New York, when he was actively writing songs, he "began to grope toward a

realization of the importance of the American Negro's cultural background and his creative folk-art, and to speculate on the superstructure
of conscious art that might be reared upon them."[60] Johnson avoids
making blatant value statements about collective versus individual art
(apart from his acceptance of the values implicit in the high/low dichotomy), but simply takes as given that the age of group expression had
ended. What African Americans now wanted (for art's sake, and ultimately for the amelioration of race hatred) was a "master" who would
gather "from the hearts of the people" their now silenced expression
and then run "it through the alembic of his genius."[61] Eugene Levy
suggests in his biography of Johnson that this was a formulation toward
which Johnson had been journeying for years. According to Levy,
Johnson was able to synthesize and formalize his thinking on the subject
only after being directed by certain white critics to observe the recent
flowering of Irish literature which built on folk expression—particularly
the work of the Irish playwright J. M. Synge.[62]

But ragtime song and ragtime piano problematized Johnson's scheme
for reclamation of folk materials. When Johnson considered the spirituals, folk preaching, or folk tales, he was clear and direct about their
continuing use as sources for new artistic creations. Ragtime was not a
folk music (though Johnson sometimes treated it as such) and therefore
was not technically the type of raw material to be improved by "conscious art." And while ragtime did make use of folk themes, it was not
received as high enough to be encouraged as useful in "contributing to
the breakdown of racial separation in American society, thus pushing
society closer to his goal of integration."[63] Ragtime occupied an uncom-
fortable middle ground for Johnson, representative structurally of the
very process he valorized in his definitions of art, but unacceptable as a
final product. Johnson summarized this tension by contending that
ragtime and the cakewalk may be "lower forms of art, but they are
evidence of a power that will some day be applied to the higher
forms."[64] It is just this sort of confusion about ragtime that has allowed
it to become the turf on which numerous contests over group ownership and racial identification have been played out, both during its
heyday and among generations of observers to follow.

Johnson's musical career provides an interesting lens through which
to view his later pronouncements on artistic production.[65] Johnson,

with his brother and Bob Cole, was a successful author of popular "ragtime" songs. While they were certainly not producing the complex pianistic work of a Scott Joplin or James Scott, they were consciously attempting to "refine" and "elevate" the music without losing its "racial identity." Levy argues that in the hands of Cole and the Johnsons, "coon song lyrics [became] noticeably more genteel" and that Johnson's music did portend "an ultimate loss of racial identity." The loss Levy points to is in the text of the songs; he suggests that the songwriting team replaced the "obnoxious racial stereotypes of the coon song" with "the equally stereotyped, though essentially nonracial" elements of Tin Pan Alley song.[66] Levy ignores, however, the strictly musical component of popular song; more important, he does not evaluate "racial identity" in the same context as Johnson would have. For Johnson, American music was suffused with African American elements, and it was becoming increasingly difficult to separate out which contributions to the grammar of popular song had come from which participants. So even if ragtime song moved thematically away from African American subjects, it could never escape its African American subjectivity.

But Johnson was inconsistent in his pronouncements on ragtime, never quite sure where it was situated on the folk art/high art continuum. At times Johnson viewed ragtime as an inchoate representative of his deepest wishes for African American art; at other times he described it as raw material ripe for higher development. In *The Second Book of Negro Spirituals* Johnson drew explicit parallels between the spirituals and other "lower" forms which ought to be transformed into high art:

> It is safe to say that for many generations the Spirituals will be kept alive as folk songs. I think it equally safe to say they will some day be a strong element in American music. They possess the qualities and powers; the trouble, so far, has been their almost absolute neglect and rejection by our serious composers. Our lesser musicians have been wiser and more diligent; they have taken the music the Negro created in lighter moods—Ragtime, Jazz, Blues—and developed it into American popular music. Indeed all the major folk creations of the Negro have been taken up and developed, except the Spirituals.[67]

As we again note the movement from race to nation in this passage, we should also pay attention to the demotion ragtime has suffered here.

No longer is ragtime a provisional, middle-ground prototype of a "developed" art; now it is merely more Black grist for the mill.[68]

Perhaps this ambivalence was due to Johnson's own experience in adapting popular song to a "higher" form. After all, Bob Cole and the Johnsons might have imagined themselves, as one reviewer did, in the role of "Musical Moses to lead the coon song into the Promised land."[69] While occasionally the team adapted the musical theme of a spiritual, their approach was to take the general form of a "coon song" and make it less offensive racially and more sophisticated lyrically.[70] Johnson did not take part in updating, transforming, or elevating what is usually recognized as folk music. Whereas he did later utilize an analogous technique in writing the poems in *God's Trombones* (published together in 1927), his musical oeuvre was characterized by adaptations of an already commercialized version of folk material.[71]

In *The Book of American Negro Poetry*, Johnson discusses directly the evolution of ragtime, with an unacknowledged paraphrase from what he had already written in *The Autobiography of an Ex-Colored Man*. Here he writes: "Ragtime music was originated by colored piano players in the questionable resorts of St. Louis, Memphis, and other Mississippi River towns. These men did not know any more about the theory of music than they did about the theory of the universe. They were guided by their natural musical instinct and talent, but above all by the Negro's extraordinary sense of rhythm." And "this," Johnson writes, "was the beginning of Ragtime song."[72] From here Johnson traces the development of the music, mentioning as Ornitz did the importance of the Chicago World's Fair of 1893 to the popularization of ragtime.[73] Then Johnson writes something really interesting: "The earliest Ragtime songs, like Topsy, 'jes' grew.'"[74] (Recall the claim in the program for Paul Whiteman's 1924 "Experiment in Modern Music" which held that jazz "sprang into existence about ten years ago from nowhere in particular.")[75] Rather than foreground Scott Joplin, James Scott, or Artie Matthews, or even more popular "coon song" writers such as Ben Harney or Ernest Hogan, Johnson instead reinvented ragtime as a more or less spontaneous folk expression. Like Harriet Beecher Stowe's Topsy, then, this music has unknown parentage, and perhaps also like Topsy (in the hands of Miss Ophelia), it may be worth trying to cultivate.

James Weldon Johnson and his colleagues took part in this process of blending old melodies with new words and arrangements, and were proud of the improvements wrought by their blends. Johnson traced the writing of "Oh, Didn't He Ramble!" to an appropriation of "about the last one of the old 'jes' grew' songs."[76] Given the lack of access to the copyrighting process or the sheet music industry which plagued many African American artists, Johnson's attitude here seems cavalier and self-serving. But I think more than personal gain or self-aggrandizement, Johnson was interested in setting an example for African American artists to emulate. Johnson's master narrative was one of improvement and uplift; his dominant tropes included combination, merger, collaboration. But Carl Van Vechten's famous suggestion that James Weldon Johnson's ex-colored man predicted George Gershwin's *Rhapsody in Blue* points up the central paradox of Johnson's position: in the 1920s and 1930s the artistic project drafted in Johnson's fictional and theoretical work became the special province of Jews.[77]

While Johnson accepted this condition as provisionally necessary, he continued to display a deep ambivalence with regard to the relative status of Jews and African Americans. Perhaps this comes most clear in another passage from *Along This Way*. Here Johnson fantasizes that a genie ("jinnee") has appeared to him to offer him the satisfaction of various desires. Johnson imagines that after bestowing riches and equal opportunity upon him, the genie becomes more controlling:

> If, coming to the principal matter, he should say, "Name any person into whom you would like to be changed, and it shall be done," I should be absolutely at a loss. If, continuing, he should say, "Name any race of which you would like to be made a member, and it shall be done," I should likewise be at a loss. If the jinnee should say, "I have come to carry out an inexorable command to change you into a member of another race; make your choice!" I should answer, probably, "Make me a Jew."[78]

This one moment which contains pained hesitancy and grudging embrace sums up nicely Johnson's stance on the prominence of Jews in African American music.

Highbrow, Lowbrow, "He-brow"

Of course James Weldon Johnson's project of designating certain African American forms as "folk" to be built on by a higher art betrayed anxieties about "brow" level which have been endemic to discussions of African American music. Lawrence Levine reminds us that highbrow/lowbrow distinctions in art derived from phrenology; to name a particular artistic production lowbrow was also to imply that its maker was an example of an inferior species.[79] For Johnson, it made sense to present ragtime as unmediated folk expression: before any enemies of the race and its music could score points by deriding ragtime's pretensions to high art, Johnson (and many of his contemporaries) made sure to locate it as kindling rather than the fire itself.[80]

George Gershwin was especially well served by this emphasis on the *potential* value of African American music; he wrote that he expected "a number of distinctive styles to develop in America, all legitimately born of folk-song," which to Gershwin included "Jazz, ragtime, Negro spirituals and blues."[81] But Gershwin lacked either the self-awareness or the forthrightness to comment directly on what it meant for him, as a Jew, to make interventions in African American music. Gershwin's brother Ira, by contrast, offered an interpretation of Jewish uses of African American "low" music in the form of a parodic song, "Mischa, Jascha, Toscha, Sascha" (written in 1922 and published in 1932). This song told of "four internationally renowned violinists then living in New York" (Elman, Heifetz, Seidel, and Jacobsen) and imagined that these concert performers, in their private moments, liked to "shake a leg to jazz." The final published form of the second refrain carried this moral: "High-brow He-brow may play low-brow / In his privacy." But an earlier version of this refrain told a different story:

> We're not high-brows, we're not low-brows,
> Anyone can see.
> You don't have to use a chart
> To see we're He-brows from the start.[82]

While the final rendering cautiously envisions the high culture Jew as comfortable playing ragtime or jazz only in seclusion, the first version tells the truer story: even invoking the phrenologist's "chart," Ira Gershwin humorously celebrates the ability of the Jew to occupy a dynamic middle ground.[83]

We should remember that such claims of Jewish artistic "chosenness" have not been uncontested. The most obvious response has come from jazz musicians who quote from and cover Tin Pan Alley song. Albert Murray suggests that "the endless list of outstanding blues-idiom compositions derived from the songs of Jerome Kern, Irving Berlin, George Gershwin, Cole Porter, Harold Arlen . . . among others . . . clearly indicates [that] blues musicians proceed as if the Broadway musical were in fact a major source of relatively crude but fascinating folk materials!"[84] Krin Gabbard adds to this insight, noting that jazz musicians "can now signify" on pop music from "above" just as they once signified on classical music from "below."[85] Wynton Marsalis has closed the circle with a fine piece of rhetorical signifying; according to the trumpeter, jazz "has always been a fine art in that it addresses a song, like a Gershwin song, as if it's a piece of folk material. You take the melody and perform the art of jazz on it, and turn it into a piece of jazz."[86] Marsalis must have enjoyed articulating this punch line, a payback to all those people over the years who insisted that ragtime and jazz were mainly valuable for donating raw material to Jewish artists.

5

$\frac{4}{7}$

"Melancholy Blues": Making Jews Sacred in African American Music

James Weldon Johnson's historicizing and prescriptive interventions into African American music in the 1910s and 1920s stand as prime examples of realpolitik. Given that Jewish success at "Black" music could not be ignored, Johnson conceded the significance of Jews at this moment, but still insisted that "Black music" itself (and not "Jews") be understood as the subject of his discussion. In Johnson, then, we find a culture worker remarkably conscious that while "Black-Jewish relations" is above all a rhetorical tendency, it is still one which can be manipulated for practical ends. In his expressive acts—be they poems, songs, or historical works—the pragmatic Johnson acted as an advance man for Black art, and he utilized the available languages of Black-Jewish relations in order to try to cultivate a more receptive audience for Black art made by African Americans.

Johnson's method was diachronic, rational, and analytical; he wrote Jews into the history of African American music and carefully explained their contribution, all the while setting the stage for a Jewish exodus from the field as African Americans exercised fuller control. So, even as Johnson's work reinforced Jewish claims for special proficiency in this sphere, it also interpreted this mastery as a surmountable, if necessary, moment in the evolution of African American music.

Sharing some ground with Johnson's approach, but ultimately competing with it, was a narrative of Jewish adaptation of African American forms which plotted Jews themselves as the subject—indeed as the heroes—of this story. While it should be apparent by now that Jews and African Americans shared an enormous amount of musical terrain, it is still necessary to explain *how* a consolidation of the two groups was achieved through the sacralization of Jewish involvement in African American music.

Lawrence Levine has described a general process in the last few decades of the nineteenth century (and into the twentieth) by which some arts were consecrated as "high" and thus lifted above mass entertainment. In the decades after that process made itself felt in American life, there was a corresponding move by well-placed cultural figures to reclassify—that is, dignify—forms previously understood as low or popular.[1] Such forms—mixed in "racial" origin and appealing to a mass audience—were, according to Levine's convincing analysis, unlikely additions to the high culture canon. But George Gershwin and company did not enact the unglamorous compromise suggested by "middlebrow." Rather, the sacralization of Jewish participation in popular music made a unique claim, not unlike that made in Ira Gershwin's punning on highbrow/lowbrow: situating "He-brow" as a triumphant synthesis of high and low, the Jews in popular music could avoid the elitism of the former while rising "above" the suspect "mass ethos" of the latter. For high culture credibility, the music of these Jews pointed "eastward toward Europe";[2] at the same time their music was obviously rooted in American soil. And, in their conspicuous public lives, these Jews embodied a vaguely sacred racialness at once attractively exotic as well as unthreatening.

What I call "sacralization"—essentially the conflation of cantorial singing and jazz playing—forms the secret heart of the conversations about musical similarity linking African Americans and Jews. While much of the surrounding rhetoric claimed that Jews were especially good at "improving" African American materials, sacralization made it possible to understand African American music as a product of the Jew's Jewishness.

The sacralization of Jews in African American music worked to interpret the activities of a group of mainly second-generation Jews as a double victory. Even while conspicuously (and successfully) engaged in the most secular of activities, these Jews could continue to appear as true to the religious tradition of their ancestors. As a consolation prize of sorts, this rhetoric also implied that the same "Black" music which had come under constant attack since at least the turn of the century could be sanctified, and therefore, in a sense, protected by Jews.

One obvious reason why the Jewish adaptation of African American materials had such great impact is that "Black" sounds were imagined to be reproducible only by racial insiders.[3] Since African and African American music cannot easily be made to fit into Western systems of notation, it had long been assumed that no logical system underlies the manufacture of African American song.[4]

It was the first attempts to collect and analyze African American spirituals in the nineteenth century which established that this music could not be accurately written down, and certainly could not be copied by outsiders.[5] At the end of the century a witness to a performance of the Fisk Jubilee Singers noted with resignation that in "writing the notes one has to compromise"; a folklorist writing in 1903 called the lullaby of an African American woman "quite impossible to copy, weird in interval and strange in rhythm"; and as late as 1926 a critic for *The New Republic* argued that the singing style of an African American performer would "furrow the brow of anyone who might attempt to set the tune down on paper."[6]

The literature on African American music is filled with words such as "quaint," "weird," and "strange," and "spontaneity" has always been a crucial term for explaining (and often disparaging) the production of African and African American music.[7] But "spontaneity" has had extreme functionality for both whites and African Americans: it allows white observers, even the most sympathetic, to at once appreciate and depreciate African American music as a primitive folk expression, while also enabling African Americans to mark off the boundaries which, ostensibly, will protect their cultural stuff from theft.[8]

The other major reason why the sacralization of Jewish success in African American music was so welcome is that it acted as a response to the widely held belief that the religious traditions of both Jews and African Americans were being diluted in urban America. Around the turn of the century it became clear to many that even as interest in collecting and cataloguing African American spirituals grew, the power of the religious impulses which contributed to their creation was rapidly diminishing. One writer described the shift from spirituals to ragtime as proof of "the release of the Negro from his own addiction to holiness." Part of the achievement of Jews was to refashion such obviously secular African American sounds into forms which at least hinted at religious feeling.[9] With this, amazingly, Jews were boldly offering up the sort of blatant mixture of sacred and secular which has been so commonly censured—yet never effectively suppressed—in African American culture as to become almost a folkloric motif. The popular singer Nina Simone was, in a sense, summarizing decades of such concern in the late 1960s when she told an interviewer, Phyl Garland, that "Mama and them were so religious that they wouldn't allow you to play boogie-woogie in the house, but would allow you to use the same boogie-woogie beat to play a gospel tune."[10] Jews, of course, operated under no such ban with regard to African American music.

One of the side benefits of the Jewish sacralization of "Black" music is that it allowed Jews to transcend, if only temporarily, their own struggles with religious and cultural decline. As the lapdogs of Ornitz's Allrightniks Row make clear, Jews—like African Americans—were consciously and painfully negotiating how to pass on their cultural and religious heritage to the next generation. One of Irving Berlin's earliest successes, "Sadie Salome, Go Home" (1908), addressed just this issue of how to resist "the threat of seduction away from the old paths into the godless and immoral behavior of American urban life."[11] That Jews were able to depict their involvement in African American music as an outgrowth of their own religious traditions, then, served the dual function of purifying both the Jews and the music in question, and thereby easing the pressures caused by the thorny issue of secularization.[12]

Cantoring

In the early 1920s, at the peak of a blues craze, two African American musicians, Porter Grainger and Bob Ricketts, published a booklet titled "How to Play and Sing the Blues Like the Phonograph and Stage Artists." In it they offered this advice to budding performers: "To render a 'Blues' song effectively, it is necessary to possess a fair knowledge of the spirit and circumstances under which this type of publication was created. If one can temporarily play the role of the oppressed or the depressed, injecting into his or her rendition a spirit of hopeful prayer, the effect will be more natural and successful."[13] Of all the non–African Americans who made "Black" music in the first half of this century, Jews seemed to be most "natural and successful" at infusing "a spirit of hopeful prayer" into their productions. As with later attempts to interpret the presence of Jews in the civil rights movement as the natural yield of Jewish prophetic tradition, the process of sacralization in popular music operated from the assumption that Jewishness had immense characterological significance even for the most secular Jews.

Sacralization depended heavily on biography. Many of the Jews participating in the production of popular music were sons of cantors. The fact of biography, however, was only a starting point. The melancholy of the cantor's art displayed a striking resemblance, for many, to the pathos of African American music, which suggested that because centuries of suffering had instituted lamentation as a dominant expressive form in Jewish culture, individual Jews were particularly able to give musical voice to affliction. African American music—as James Weldon Johnson said of African American dialect poetry—was commonly understood to express primarily pathos and humor, and Jews, as a result of their own religious history, appeared well equipped to handle the pathos.[14]

Correlating sacred Jewish with secular and/or folk African American sounds formed a reply to those enemies of popular music who found too much sin in syncopation. This process also played a major role in installing the rhetoric of shared group oppression, and worked to establish quite broad ground for comparison, and finally conflation, of African Americans and Jews. The emphasis on cantors also served to reinforce the rigid gender segregation which has been crucial to the concept of Black-Jewish relations by insisting on a particular conduit of Jewish sympathy for African Americans which was not open to women.

Biographical reality was the major determinant for the development and endurance of this linkage of Jews with Black music. Al Jolson, along with the composers Harold Arlen and Irving Berlin, were all the sons of "cantors," although the fathers reached quite different levels of success in their profession.[15] Some American Jewish folklore holds that Eddie Cantor's father served in this role also, a claim which is difficult

to substantiate. Moreover, Cantor's father died when Eddie was still a
toddler, which undercuts any suggestion that the performer was
influenced by his father's art. What is more interesting for our purposes
is that when this Jewish blackface comedian was searching for a stage
name, he gave up Isidore Itzkowitz (or Iskowitz) in favor of Eddie
"Cantor."

There is only meager evidence that any of the young Jews learned
important musical lessons from the cantors. Berlin achieved his musical
education on the streets and in the rathskellers, while Arlen's most
influential teachers were other Jewish composers and straight-ahead
jazz bands. The Jewish composers and performers did, however, publicize their roots in the synagogue. Irving Berlin insisted that going to
religious services with his father powerfully shaped his musical education, and Harold Arlen attempted to make connections between his
blues-inflected compositions and his father's performance style. Al Jolson also frequently mentioned his father's musical stylings during his
stage shows and radio broadcasts.[16] By 1925 George Gershwin was able
to generalize from the particular examples provided by these musical
Jews to conclude that good music "must have feeling," a quality "pos-
sessed to a great degree by the Jewish people." According to Gershwin,
"the Hebrew chants possess a peculiarly plaintive wail which give [sic]
them a universal appeal. Men like Al Jolson and Eddie Cantor . . . owe
their great success to the intense Jewish feeling they possess for melody."[17] Whatever these men learned from their fathers, more
significant was the critical mass which they and other Jews constituted
which gave rise to a confident linkage of their music with the religious
music of their fathers and with the popular music of African Americans—their brothers, as this line of thinking proposed.

The cantor analogy also worked well for historical and musicological
reasons. To begin, as Mark Slobin has noted, there was a "cantorial
craze" of sorts in America during the 1880s and 1890s; liturgical recordings continued to sell well on the Lower East Side as late as the 1920s,
and cantors were sometimes included as part of vaudeville packages.
Even as the role of the cantor diminished in importance for Jewish
religious communities in the United States, he remained the most
available symbol of the "soul" of his people.[18] Slobin remarks that the
"cantorate lies close to the core of the culture, particularly *expressive*

culture," a notion which circulated widely as cantors served as icons of
Jewishness in America through concert appearances and popular culture imagery. The cantor's performative role fitted him especially well
to serve as an analogy to the jazz musician. Like the improvising African
American musician, the cantor combined "fixity and freedom" in his
performance of the liturgy and was valued for his ability to aestheticize
holy texts. Cantorial patterns, according to Eliyahu Schleifer, "are
flexible enough to allow for regional and personal stylistic differences.
In this respect they resemble jazz patterns."[19]

Moreover, as J. Hoberman writes, even in Europe "the cantorate was
a major site for the struggle between the sacred and the secular."
Hoberman goes on to explain how the cantor presented an image of
Jew as middleman—but not in the usual usurious sense; he argues that
the cantor was a major carrier of modernity to Jews who acted as a
"spiritual middleman, negotiating the realm between religion and show
business as well as God and the congregation." When secular American
Jews drew on the cantor as the definitive image of Old World piety,
they were, to paraphrase the apt title used by Eric Hobsbawm and
Terence Ranger, "inventing tradition."[20] The "Old World" music that
these American Jewish men were purportedly returning to did not
really exist: Slobin notes that cantors tended to be among the most
cosmopolitan of European Jews—often with slightly shady reputa-
tions—performing eclectic repertoires which combined materials from
a variety of sources, Jewish and non-Jewish, secular and sacred. In order
for the Jews of Tin Pan Alley to be sacralized, then, it was also necessary
to consecrate the decidedly impure liturgical wellspring from which
they allegedly drew their inspiration.[21] Melting pot rhetoric, then, had
to give way—at least for these moments—to language which highlighted ethnic and religious discreteness.

Because many well-known Jewish performers and composers were
sons of cantors, they could be imagined as harmlessly atavistic, rever-
sions to just the sort of cultural/religious type from which these musicians were actually distancing themselves. To put it more concretely,
Irving Berlin's lineage might permit listeners in 1912 to hear his song
"When I Lost You" as a by-product of a vague and atemporal yet
artistically rich Jewish melancholy; a side benefit was that they could
ignore the fact that it specifically commemorated the sudden death of

his first (Christian) wife.[22] Calling attention to fantasized versions of
their embattled first-generation fathers, these Jewish musical figures
created more suitable genealogies for themselves than their actual fathers could furnish. At the same time the musicians were able to draw
attention away from the racially mixed, competitive urban milieu which
they inhabited as professionals. As a result, these composers and stage
personalities could perform the delicate balancing act of expressing
Blackness while also embodying Jewishness.

Al Jolson's own life, and the fact-and-fancy dialectic he staged with
Samson Raphaelson, donated a wealth of energy toward the sanctifying
of Jews in popular music. Writing what was essentially a publicity piece
for *The Jazz Singer* in *American Hebrew* magazine in 1927, Raphaelson
recalled that when he was an undergraduate in 1916, he brought a date
to see Jolson perform and thought, "My God, this isn't a jazz singer.
This [is] a cantor!"[23] This insight, as Raphaelson's self-penned legend
has it, led him to write the short story on which the play and movie of
The Jazz Singer would be based. In that story, "The Day of Atonement," Raphaelson describes Jack Robin as "no ordinary singer of
ragtime": "Those dark eyes of his might have been the ecstatic eyes of
a poet in the days when the chosen people lived sedately in the land of
Canaan. They might have been prophetic eyes, stern and stirring in the
years of Zedekiah, son of Josiah . . . They might have been deep wells
of lamentation even one generation ago had his lyric voice been born
to cry to the sorrows of Israel in a Russian synagogue."[24] By the time
of Jolson's death, this analogy had come to seem completely natural—in
fact, it no longer seemed to be an analogy. At Jolson's funeral Rabbi
Max Nussbaum maintained that whatever Jolson was "came to him
from his father": "It is from Rabbi Yoelson that he received the form
and content of his singing. When you listened to any of his songs, you
noticed the half and quarter tones, the sigh and the sob, the sudden
inflections of the voice and the unexpected twist—all these are elements
that come out from the Cantorial singing of our people."[25]

The agency of such acts of reception and translation was rarely
addressed. This account (like most) preferred to imagine that the "sigh
and the sob" of the Jew in music represented a spiritual inheritance. But
around the time of the release of the movie version of *The Jazz Singer*,
the direct influence Jolson's father had on him was more widely dis-

cussed. Here is how one Jewish magazine described the process in a 1927 article: "Years ago an unhappy little boy used to sit at Sunday School in his father's class and sing mournful Jewish hymns. He had a melodious, pathetic voice with a wail in it which his father was training for the synagogue." Because of this instruction, Jolson's jazz songs always have "a haunting, plaintive note . . . reminiscent of the Jewish chants that his father taught him to sing."[26]

Usually the explanations were abstracted from any concrete situation. Alexander Woollcott describes Irving Berlin's singing voice as "a clear, true soprano voice—a plaintive voice tuned to the grieving" of the synagogue which had been mystically bestowed upon Berlin by the "generations of wailing cantors" standing behind him. Among other things, Woolcott's remarks reveal how sacralization worked its complex magic, granting status to Jewish composers and performers through their connections to other culturally powerful men—cantors—while also insisting that musical careers for men mark them as effeminate.[27] Woollcott also encouraged a descent-based reading of Berlin's art which was picked up and developed by Harold Arlen as he described his father's style: "I can remember improvisations of my father's that are just like Louis Armstrong's . . . He knew nothing about jazz, but there was something in his style that's in the style of jazz musicians . . . I know damned well now that his glorious improvisations must have had some effect on me and my own style."[28] The more obvious conclusion—that Arlen's own style was influenced by the African American musicians he loved as a youth—is sidestepped here in favor of the mystical-genetic argument. Additionally, Arlen elides the important differences between improvisatory vocal and instrumental technique on the one hand, and composition strategies on the other, as he folds all musical creation into one analogy. In other words, even if one accepts the terms of the comparison which connect Louis Armstrong and the cantor, there is still no clear explanation of how all that gets into Harold Arlen's songwriting.

In the 1920s and early 1930s the "cantor" motif moved into the territory of cliché and satire, even as it retained its effectiveness in naturalizing Jewish interventions in African American music. By the time that Raphaelson adapted his short story into its dramatic version (1925), he was already gently parodying his own conceit. When Jack

Robin refuses to give an eager journalist background information for a
puff piece, the newsman decides to "fake" a story with "the usual East
Side background," which includes a "pious old father."[29] Edmund Wilson's 1929 novel *I Thought of Daisy* presents a more sober example.
Wilson's protagonist hears a good song—of course in a minor
key—which he remembers is by Harry Hirsch, a conflation of Berlin
and Gershwin. He imagines Hirsch to be "a small young Jew with very
large, intense, black eyes, like motor headlights," who was "no doubt
the son of a Rabbi or of the Cantor in a Synagogue." But from where
did Hirsch get his remarkable sounds?

> From the sounds of the streets? the taxis creaking to a stop? . . . some
> distant and obscure city-sound in which a plaintive high note, bitten
> sharp, follows a lower note, strongly clanged and solidly based? Or had
> he got it from Schoenberg or Stravinsky?—or simply from his own
> nostalgia, among the dark cells and the raspings of New York, for
> those orchestras and open squares which his parents had left be-
> hind?—or for the cadence, half-chanted and despairing of the tongue
> which the father had known, but which the child had forgotten and
> was never to know again?[30]

In this passage, which serves no narrative function in the novel, the
music of the Jew is first situated as belonging to the "real world" of the
city and then the European avant-garde, only to be explained, finally,
by the more obscure workings of inheritance.

A few years later Ben Hecht daringly interpreted the sacralizing of
Jews in music as a cynical business ploy. In his novel *A Jew in Love*
(1931), which is usually cited only as the pinnacle (or is that the nadir?)
of Jewish self-hatred, Hecht introduces Gabe Solomon, "a semitic
pagan" who conducts a "jazz band in a gaudy cabaret":

> Solomon was of the tribe of Jews who dominate the night life of
> Broadway, who stamp their legendary sophistication as a trademark on
> American entertainment . . . They sing of mothers, babies, faraway
> homelands, of breaking hearts and last joys, but to this eternal scenario
> of middle class art they add a set of histrionics filched from the
> dwindling synagogues. Their songs quiver with self-pity, are full of the
> unscrupulous wailings of ancient Jew griefs tricked out in Negro,

Russian and oriental rhythms, and pounded home with the rabbinical slobber of an atonement prayer.[31]

In this surprisingly nuanced, if exaggerated, reading Hecht properly defines the Jewish performance of pseudo-sacred nostalgia as being in the idiom of denial. The religious overtones of this expressive mode deflected notice from the profit-making interest of the secular Jew in the music business and from the loss of piety of contemporary Jews. An even less sympathetic British critic writing a few years after Hecht complained that "Al Jolson's nauseating blubbering masquerades as savage lamenting" and that Tin Pan Alley "has become a commercialized Wailing Wall."[32]

But even these negative evaluations make it clear that the rhetorical figuration which had originally been the specific yield of biographical circumstances had become a supple and effective cultural metaphor only loosely connected to genealogical fact. Expressed frequently enough, these metaphors themselves come to seem as if they are the biological facts. Because some very prominent Jews in the entertainment world were sons of cantors, and because their life stories were so widely circulated (and here Jack Robin is probably as important as Al Jolson himself), it became possible to see all Jewish men as at least vaguely connected to a positively valued sacred past.

One way to chart the influence of the popular-songwriter-as-cantor motif is to note that a number of otherwise responsible modern-day accounts of Jews in music include George Gershwin in the list of cantors' sons. Both Irving Howe and the jazz critic Gary Giddins make this claim, a revealing mistake which accurately evokes the climate surrounding Gershwin even as it plays loosely with the historical record.[33] Gershwin's father was no cantor; rather, he was a classic luftmensch, a man who held jobs too numerous to mention. But still many of Gershwin's contemporaries heard his music as an outgrowth of Jewish liturgical styles. Isaac Goldberg, for instance, listened to some musical phrases Gershwin had written for his aborted opera of *The Dybbuk* and thought that the "room became a synagogue and this was the indistinct prayer of those to whom prayer has become a routine such as any other." (Gershwin, according to all accounts, did not spend much time praying or in synagogue; unlike his brother Ira, he did not undergo the bar mitzvah ritual.)[34] A friend of Gershwin's named Nanette Kutner invoked similar religious imagery as she described a man who sat next to her at Gershwin's funeral: "Whoever he was, butcher, barber, tailor, neighbor, he sobbed with a cry that had retched its way past throats of many cantors, echoing itself in the melodic wails of the boy he loved."[35] This description sketches a neat if mystical circle in which the cries of the cantor inspire the cries of Gershwin which inspire the cries of the mourner—and then back around again. A final example of how broad the sacralizing tendency could become is found in a eulogy written by Rouben Mamoulian, the stage and film director who worked with Gershwin on *Porgy and Bess*. Mamoulian recalled that although Gershwin sometimes seemed to be like a child, he was "also like a patriarch. I would look at him and all but see a long white beard and a staff in his hand."[36] Such stereotyping epitomizes a refusal to acknowledge the real spaces Jews occupied in the modern city, a move which helps remove the taint of opportunism and commercialism from Jews in the music business. In this redrawn field, "cantor," "rabbi," and "Khassid" (however it was spelled) came to stand metonymically for all Jews. This rhetoric also desexualizes the men in question: it is impossible to imagine one of these bearded patriarchs visiting prostitutes (Gershwin) or marrying Christian women (Berlin).

Given that the 1910s and 1920s gave rise to some broad rhetorical attacks on secular urban Jews—as factory managers, white slavers, Reds, World Series fixers, bootleggers, and so on—it was quite savvy for Jews and their friends to construct a public narrative which decontaminated American Jews by making them over in the (invented) image of their Old World ancestors. If, as this rhetorical construct had it, all Jewish men were cantors, then it was religious destiny that led Jews to find a congenial place in the music business. Earlier I outlined a collaborative public project which emphasized the racial flexibility of Jews in order to create a space for Jewish contributions to American popular culture. The rhetoric of sacralization shared the same aim, but did its work by insisting that Jews were fixed into a static (if fruitful) social position rooted in their *religious* identity. Together these two strands of a single cultural project helped to naturalize Jewish power in the entertainment industries; sacralizing was a particularly effective tool for Jews to use because it helped them erase the commercial taint which looms as the terrifying repressed of Black-Jewish relations.

"Khassid and Negro Join Hands": Black-Jewish Musicology

The sacred metaphors which offered a general explanation for why Jews figured so prominently in making "Black" popular music also helped account for the similarities between African American and Jewish music. Samuel Ornitz—and Mezz Mezzrow, among others—maintained that Jewish liturgical music shared important characteristics with African American popular and folk forms.[37] Of course analogies drawn between the expressive cultures of African Americans and Jews began not with the advent of Jolson and Berlin, but with the resonance that the Jewish Old Testament had for the African American slave.[38] But the assumed synonymity between these two *religious* cultures gave way by around the turn of the century to the revised notion that the significant consonance was really between the sacred culture of the Jews and the secular folk culture of African Americans. It comes as no surprise to find Abraham Cahan in 1898 approvingly citing the words of a "Hebrew spectator" at a cakewalk at Madison Square Garden who observes that the African American man who wins the contest reminds him of a "certain type of orthodox Rabbi."[39]

It has become something of a commonplace to point out the similarities which link Jewish liturgical music and African American popular music. The tacit assumption guiding most modern scholars, following closely the narrative established in the early years of this century, is that these remarkable musical correspondences demonstrate how closely the histories of the two groups resemble each other. These musicological insights—which themselves need to be examined critically—then give rise to an even broader characterological reading of the correspondences of African Americans and Jews.

Gary Giddins presents a typical checklist of the "similarities between cantorial singing and the blues tradition," making special mention of "the ubiquitous minor third, vocal wailing, spare harmonies, [and] improvisation." Deena Rosenberg, a Gershwin scholar, relates that many historians continue to argue that blue notes "came into the American musical vernacular from two sources: the African-American blues and Jewish liturgical music." Rosenberg also makes a point of noting the similarity between scat singing and cantorial improvisation.[40] These more recent accounts reproduce those analogies developed in the 1910s and 1920s which used music as a main support for the thesis that Jews and African Americans were linked by their past experiences of suffering. Isaac Goldberg favored this cultural metaphor, suggesting that in Gershwin's "My One and Only," "the Khassid and the Negro join hands melodically."[41] What is interesting here is that the distance separating the music of the "Khassid" from mainstream Jewish liturgical music is never addressed; in fact, that gap is completely ignored as all Jews are imagined to be ghettoized and religious Old World figures.

The energy for these comparisons derived in large part, although not exclusively, from the life and career of Al Jolson. In the early 1920s the *Forward* ran an article on Jolson which played up the cantorial angle:

How is it that the most famous black face singer in the world, Al Jolson, should be the son of a cantor? How is it that the second most popular black face artist should be an East Side boy, Eddie Cantor and that Irving Berlin, author of so many Negro songs, should be an East Side scion of a line of *Chazonim* [cantors] . . . Is there any incongruity in this Jewish boy [Jolson] with his face painted like a Southern Negro singing in the Negro dialect? No, there is not. Indeed I detected again and again the minor key of Jewish music, the wail of the *Chazan*, the cry of anguish of a people who had suffered. The son of a line of rabbis well knows how to sing the songs of the most cruelly wronged people in the world's history.[42]

The Jazz Singer actively encouraged such confidence in musical similitude, and even included demonstrations of the analogy. In the play version, Jack Robin attempts to convince his pious old father that "our songs"—the popular and the religious—are "very much alike." As the stage directions put it: "He sings 'Ain Kelohenu,' a Hebrew prayer tune. He sings four bars of it, swiftly, with feeling. And then, suddenly, to exactly the same tune and with exactly the same plaintiveness but with a new rhythm and shaking his shoulders, he sings a popular song."[43] In the original screenplay for the movie, this scene (ultimately left out of the film version) is slightly revised; now Moey, a favored student of

Cantor Rabinowitz—a substitute son, actually—is the one who demonstrates the similarity of "ragtime" and liturgical music. Playing "Yes, Sir, That's My Baby," on the piano, Moey segues fluidly into "Eli, Eli"—a Yiddish song of deep religious feeling—when Cantor Rabinowitz enters the room.[44] The moral of this moment has already been prepared by an earlier juxtaposition of title cards. Just after Mary Dale has told Jack Robin that he will make it big as a jazz singer because his voice has a "tear" in it, we see Cantor Rabinowitz telling Moey that he must sing "with a sigh—like you are crying out to your God."[45]

Such thematics of return announce themselves again and again in these narratives of Black-Jewish musical sympathy. The second-generation Jews who were themselves most responsible for articulating these analogies were making the canny argument that their work in "Black" music should be interpreted not as a dilution or renunciation of Jewishness but rather as its quintessence.[46] The either (jazz)/or (religion) choice posited by the ambiguous endings of the short story and dramatic versions of *The Jazz Singer* is resolved, then, in the both/and scenario of the movie. Jakie now has an answer for his father, who in Raphaelson's original short story cannot understand why Jakie is a "ragtime singer with the bums" even though he comes from ten generations of cantors. The reverence Jakie ultimately demonstrates in the movie is matched in a souvenir program which the Warner brothers released along with it. Here the moviemakers note that "the faithful portrayal of Jewish homelife [in the movie] is largely due to the unobtrusive assistance of Mr. Benjamin Warner, father of the producers and ardent admirer of *The Jazz Singer*."[47] Sacralizing their involvement in popular music, Jews could *be* their own fathers insofar as they were singing not a "new" song in this strange land but the same old one. At the same time they could not help but emphasize their social authority in the American scene, a power alien to their weaker first-generation fathers.

All of the sacred metaphors gained force because there was also some evidence that the musical understanding ran both ways. Not only were Jews "naturally" attracted to African American music, but African Americans in turn seemed drawn to the songs of the Jews. Both stride pianist Willie the Lion Smith and Duke Ellington performed Yiddish songs for appreciative audiences. Whereas Smith claimed to have a

"Jewish soul," and to have experienced an actual conversion after hearing a Jewish cantor sing, Paul Robeson offered a more conventional rationalization for why African Americans might have special sympathy for Jewish music. As Hasia Diner recounts, Robeson explained to the Yiddish *Morgan Journal-Tageblatt* why he wanted to sing in a Jewish opera but "did not like to sing in French, German, or Italian": "I do not understand the psychology of these people, their history has no parallels with the history of my forebearers who were slaves. The Jewish sigh and tear are close to me . . . [I] feel that these people are closer to the traditions of my race."[48] In another interview Robeson argued for a more concrete link. When told by a music writer in 1927 that a spiritual he sang resembled Jewish synagogue music, Robeson pointed out that New Orleans had a large Jewish population, and African Americans might have picked up the melody there.[49]

Leslie Fiedler and others have also described how in Newark and on the Lower East Side there were African Americans who sang in Yiddish and Hebrew. The Yiddish song "Eli, Eli" was a particular favorite: by 1920 the practice of African Americans singing "Eli, Eli" was parodied in a *Forward* cartoon which showed a Jewish cantor singing from *Aida* while an African American man sang the Yiddish song. In her autobiography the African American singer Ethel Waters recalls how she added the song to her repertoire during an Orpheum vaudeville tour in the early 1920s. A song plugger persuaded Waters to sing "Eli, Eli" by telling her that "another Negro performer, George Dewey Washington, who was then with Paul Ash's Band, was getting wonderful results with it." Waters kept the song in her set: "I always loved to sing it. It tells the tragic history of the Jews as much as one song can, and that history of their age-old grief and despair is so similar to that of my own people that I felt I was telling the story of my own race too." As a postscript, Waters admits the commercial logic for continuing to perform "Eli, Eli": "Jewish people in every town seemed to love the idea of me singing their song. They crowded the theaters to hear it."[50] Jules Bledsoe (of *Show Boat* fame) also included the song in his repertoire during a 1929 tour on the RKO vaudeville circuit.[51]

Written for a Yiddish play which had its New York debut in 1896, this song was popularized by Boris Thomashefsky, Cantor Yosele Rosenblatt, the vaudevillian Belle Baker, and Al Jolson himself.[52] "Eli,

Eli" begins with the words "My God, My God, why hast thou forsaken me?"—the same words which begin the Twenty-second Psalm, and which Matthew and Mark recount as the last spoken by Jesus Christ on the cross—and ends with the Hebrew Shema ("Hear, Oh Israel, the Lord is our God, the Lord is One!"). The song, it was assumed, appealed to African Americans because of its lyrical content, an expression of faith even in the most trying circumstances, as well as for its minor-keyed pathos. It also seems significant that the song's lyrics move from a phrase best known from a New Testament usage to an ending which makes unequivocal reference to the Old Testament religion of the Jews: the performance of these words by an African American singer, then, mirrors the historical process by which African American slaves, instructed mostly in New Testament Christianity, found their deeper associations with the Israelites of the Old Testament. Significantly, the song quickly shed its theatrical association and was produced and received as if it were an ancient prayer.[53] For a final turn of this screw, I should note that when the goodwill tour of *Porgy and Bess* landed in Israel in 1955, the cast made a point of singing "Eli, Eli" at a reception in Tel Aviv.[54]

Melancholy Babies

The process of musical sacralization during the 1910s and 1920s pivoted on the idea that parallel experiences of suffering produce identical musical sounds. Fundamental questions are begged by this proposition: why, for instance, did Native American music not share these defining characteristics with African American and Jewish forms? While Mac-Donald Moore has introduced an Orientalist thesis which argues that the linking of African Americans and Jews grew from a perception that the groups were racially connected by a common origin in the East, it seems clear that the impulse driving this discourse was the belief that common experiences of suffering over time concretely shape the sound of music. Cynthia Ozick has written that a central tenet of "Black-Jewish relations" is that "wounds recognize wounds"—that is, comparable suffering leads to conscious mutual sympathy.[55] To evoke the assumptions underlying this musical discourse, we might paraphrase Ozick to suggest that wounds also *mimic* wounds. The keywords which unite

African Americans and Jews in this musical narrative—among them
"plaintive," "exile," "lamentation," and "pathos"—all suggest that the
historical pain of each group had been directly translated into conso-
nant characterological formations which then stimulated analogous collective musical growth.[56]

This syllogism rests on the assumption that the tonal and melodic
effects that we hear as emotion—here "pathos" or "plaintiveness"—are
constituted by the unmediated feelings and experiences of the musical
author. The persecution of African Americans and Jews, it is thus
widely believed, is expressed in blue notes and minor keys. This musical
premise acknowledges that hurts have been inflicted on both groups,
while also limiting the musical prospects of each group to lamentation
and defensive humor. Furthermore, the musical metaphors which connect African Americans and Jews imply that individual members of each
group are carriers of certain inherited character traits which require
that they express themselves in circumscribed ways. A summary of this
"common sense" might read as follows: the historically determined
"melancholy" of the young Jewish composer or singer allows
him—forces him, really—to gravitate toward pathos-ridden liturgical
music. This ultimately leads him to write and perform adaptations of
the African American popular music which so resembles cantorial song.

A necessary postulate for the effective sacralization of Jews in African
American music was that melancholy inhabited both Black sounds and
Jewish men. By the time of ragtime and jazz it had been long established
that African American music was almost always sad, except when it was
comical. Before much reporting on African American music had been
published, a visitor to West Africa took special notice of the "sweet and
plaintive" music he heard there.[57] Thomas Wentworth Higginson's
contention that virtually all the songs he heard in his army regiment
during the Civil War were religious reveals to us how small a portion
of African American music could be made to stand for the whole; given
this limitation, it makes sense that Higginson focused on the "minor-
keyed pathos" of African American song.[58]

The insistence on melancholy as the definitive characteristic of slave
music was also encouraged by African Americans. This was first done
in part to overturn the notion that singing and dancing were "proof"
that slaves were "the most contented and happy laborers in the world":

thus Frederick Douglass's famous contention that it was only when he was no longer "within the circle" of slavery that he could understand that "songs of the slave represent the sorrows of his heart."[59] Later, the highlighting of melancholy was at least in part a response to the depredations of minstrelsy and the coon song craze. W. E. B. Du Bois, of course, identifies slave music as "distinctly sorrowful" and approvingly quotes Higginson's description of "I Know Moonrise" as being the most "plaintively" uttered instance of a "longing for peace" in history.[60]

Melancholy was easily transferred as a descriptive from folk spirituals to professional blues and jazz. Albert Murray has shown how blues music has come to seem "synonymous with lamentation and commiseration," even though most "people who sing, play, dance to, or just listen to blues music" do so mostly "to get rid of the blues." And, too, as Murray insists, most blues entails a *performance* of melancholy rather than a direct expression of it.[61] Nonetheless, early accounts of ragtime and jazz, whether written by its creators, partisans, or critics, frequently claimed that these forms directly articulated the pain of African Americans. A typical portrait of jazz written in the 1920s argued that "the plaintive kind of pathos which obtrudes itself from time to time in these dance tunes is undoubtedly inherited from the wistful longing of an enslaved and exiled people."[62] Paul Whiteman also acknowledged that jazz was full of "nostalgia, lament and longing" but argued that even these "create a form of happiness because they express something that lies deep in the soul."[63]

In the first few decades of this century, the sense that African American music was defined by its pathos coincided and merged with a fixation on the melancholy of the Jewish musician. In writing about what he perceived to be a streak of sadness in George Gershwin, Isaac Goldberg whimsically coined the phrase *"melancholia judaica"* to define "that *Weltschmerz* which the Jew seems to acquire with circumcision."[64] Here Goldberg makes concrete the diffuse cultural sense that all Jews are men, and that these men are specially equipped (through their lack of a foreskin, if nothing else) to give voice to pain. Whether regarding such melancholy as inherited or acquired, a gift or a handicap, a wide range of observers took it as an article of faith that the Jewish artist—in his life and his work—expressed pathos above all.

The image of the melancholic Jewish artist did not originate with

Berlin and Jolson of course. At least one nineteenth-century commentator believed that readers could tell that Goethe was a Jew because of the "melancholy expression" in his work.[65] The critic and composer Lazare Saminsky wrote in 1934 that melancholy is defining of the Jewish composer in the West: according to Saminsky, with a "soul split and aggrieved," the Jewish composer in the West cannot help but be "a deeply troubled, a dolorous figure."[66] But whereas Saminsky imagines an expulsion from some musicological Eden of the East as the major injury inflicted upon the Jewish composer, the discourse surrounding Gershwin and company fastened on melancholy as the racial/religious destiny of all Jewish men.

The specific application of melancholy to the Jewish male musician was the crux of the sacralizing tendency. By the late 1920s and early 1930s it was taken for granted by novelists such as Ben Hecht and Edmund Wilson that the "wail" in popular song was particularly Jewish; this "fact" was evaluated quite differently by the two, with Wilson ennobling it as an exalted heritage and Hecht parodying it as a cynical manipulation of the populace by Jews. More than any other quality, melancholy was what removed the Jew from the secular present and ensconced him safely in a mythic sacred past. It was good public relations, if nothing else, for George Gershwin to have his biographer—and Gershwin did feed Isaac Goldberg much of his important information—portray the composer as "prone to regard himself as a rather sad young man, adrift in a universe foredoomed to unhappiness."[67] This depiction, as opposed to one which, say, called attention to Gershwin's tortured sexuality, business acumen, or egomania, took part in establishing the *preferred* reading of Gershwin's artistic productions. Audiences and critics were thus instructed to understand Gershwin and his work as motivated by the purest instincts.

Examples of the "melancholizing" of the Jewish musician are legion. Alexander Woollcott envisioned Irving Berlin as being overtaken by this melancholy in private moments: "He would probably admit that the moment he is left alone and the sounds of the city die down, he begins to turn Russian, growing a long beard and feeling sorry for himself."[68] Woollcott also contended that the "generations of wailing cantors" behind Irving Berlin were responsible for the "enjoyable melancholy" in his work.[69] Of course this description runs contrary to everything we know about Berlin's personality, but Woollcott was trading in cultural metaphor, not actual biography. Harold Arlen, too, was remembered by a friend and colleague as a "very, very melancholy person" whose music—including his comic songs—was infused with pathos.[70]

Again, the terms for this metaphor were articulated most clearly by Samson Raphaelson. In "The Day of Atonement," the short story which would evolve into *The Jazz Singer*, Raphaelson connects Jolson and Berlin as he writes that if Jakie "had a sentimental grief, what better relief than sitting in the dark of his bedroom . . . and howling dolefully the strains of 'Down by the Old Mill Stream' . . . If the joys of being alive smote home, what could more sweetly ease the ache of happiness than the plaintive blare of 'Alexander's Ragtime Band'?"[71] This formulates a perfect Jewish analogue for Albert Murray's idea that African Americans often play the blues to get rid of the blues: Jews wail to relieve their melancholy.[72] Raphaelson also stitches together the production and reception of melancholy—as Mezz Mezzrow did—arguing that "instinctively the East Side responded" to Jakie's modern interpretations of "the tradition of plaintive, religious" music of his forefathers.[73] A few commentators understood these melancholy sounds to be restorative. Paul Whiteman elbowed his way into this mostly Jewish discourse by declaring that he had "dozens of experiments to make with jazz," and especially wanted to test his hypothesis that it had "therapeutic value": "I believe a way will be found to use [jazz] in curing diseases of mind and body, especially melancholia." Much earlier, in 1903, a writer in *Ladies' Home Journal* had suggested that "in cases of despondency and melancholia the minor chords are the most effective and act as a tonic."[74]

The catalyzing agent in this formula for melancholy was nostalgia. Nostalgia, as Fred Davis writes, frequently serves as a significant mode for "constructing, maintaining, and reconstructing our identities."[75] In the case of these hugely successful musical Jews, the nostalgia was of two related varieties. First, the actual bodies of these Jewish men were effaced and made to function as signs of a remote world. Al Jolson was billed in a 1939 show as singing the "past the way you want to remember it," and he could deliver on this promise because as a Jew, his home country *was* the past.[76] Ethnicity has often functioned as a carrier of tradition in American culture, and these Jewish musicians were able to shoulder their own apparently sacred past, as well as a sanitized version of America's racial history.

Where the Jewish white Negro learned to cloak himself in ultramodern aural and physical productions of Blackness, the musical evocations of nostalgia produced by Al Jolson and Irving Berlin helped to distract attention from the actual bodily presence of the Jewish man. In addition to making them appear *themselves* as throwbacks, the music made by these Jews was heard by many to evoke a hazy and idealized past. According to Davis, the use of minor key is a favorite tool for invoking nostalgia: the publicity surrounding Jews in music maintained that access to minor keys was the birthright of Jewish men.[77]

The access these Jews had to African American music allowed them to contribute an especially serviceable version of what Renato Rosaldo calls "imperialist nostalgia" to the American scene. Rosaldo argues that while we praise innovation, still we "yearn for more stable worlds, whether these reside in our own past, in other cultures, or in the conflation of the two."[78] The achievement of the Jews under study here was to join a scenic, largely irrelevant Old World history with a gratifying version of the African American experience. Michael Rogin has shown that Jews in blackface marginalized African Americans by depicting them as remnants of a peaceful rural past; the same is true of Jews who composed "Black" music.[79] By treating all African American music as "folk," and through lyrics which upheld Plantation School fantasies of the South, many of the most successful Jews in music depended on the power of nostalgia. Joined to these projections of Blackness was a parallel self-stylization of Jews as charming old (world) men.[80] Jews were so capable of contriving a musical poetics of loss and lack, then, because they seemed to be telling their own true life stories.

The "melancholy" I have been describing must be understood not as a clinical diagnosis but as an expressive mode particularly available to powerful men.[81] Juliana Schiesari points out that the performance of melancholy has been "historically legitimated" for male artists, whose genius has been assumed to be verified by their melancholy. As Schiesari argues, displays of disempowerment come to stand as a form of cultural prestige—a mark of "inspired artistry and genius."[82]

The presentation of melancholy and nostalgia by these Jewish musicians encloses a complicated terrain of gender and sexual politics. For Gershwin, Jolson, or Berlin, such performances could serve to head off any damage that might result if their own masculinity and sexuality did not measure up to contemporary standards.[83] Berlin's "little colored boy," the rumors about Jolson's bisexuality (which one friend denied, saying he "liked colored girls, though"), the "pansy-like Negroes" of Cantor and Jolson, and Gershwin's desperate exhibitions of his masculinity with prostitutes all could be read as instantiations of what was widely believed to be the strange sexuality of the Jewish man. Whether seen as submissively effeminate or pathologically oversexed, the body of the Jewish man was often understood as a deformation of manhood.[84] One way to preempt such problems was to adopt "'feminine' positions" such as "'sensitivity' or 'nostalgia' or 'loss.'" It is thus possible to understand Berlin's female narrator songs (or even his melancholy "When I Lost You") and Jolson's extravagant performances of orphanhood as forms of masculine power (cloaked in images of weakness) in the symbolic order.[85] Another way to head off attacks on Jewish masculinity was to perform "race"—whether as a white Negro or an Old World Jew—in public. In doing so, Jewish men were able to highlight racial fitness rather than gender and sexual dysfunction.[86]

These performances—the "melancholy" music itself as well as the surrounding rhetorical acts—had profound results. The production of melancholy authorized the claim that Jews had made on African American music despite (or maybe because of) an accompanying denial that they were active players in the modern city and the burgeoning culture industry. Jews could mobilize this connotative chain to increase the perceived distance between themselves and African Americans; if Jews came to "Black" music through their Jewishness, then nobody had to worry that the two groups were actually fraternizing, or were very much alike. Meanwhile, Jewish men could also shore up their own masculine position, most strikingly by triumphing over their nearest competitors in the cultural arena, but also by rendering a melancholy which would link them with a tradition of great male artists.[87] White Americans could enjoy these Jewish mediations of Blackness without being reminded of the realities of the mass migration and immigration which were responsible for bringing African Americans and Jews together. In an age when the Leo Frank case convinced many white people that closeness of African Americans and Jews held great dangers, the work done by the Jews of Broadway and Tin Pan Alley was especially comforting. The promise of Jewish performances of Blackness—in Jolson's blackface rendition of "Let Me Sing and I'm Happy," for instance—is that Jewish demands would stop here: taking over the entertainment industry did not mean that Jews would make claims on other forms of cultural power.

It would take until at least the 1940s for African Americans to come to be recognized generally as the best interpreters of "Black" music (and even then the greatest rewards did not usually redound to them). Some African Americans—James Weldon Johnson, for instance—saw considerable benefit in the Jewish involvement in "Black" music, but there is no doubt that the cultural metaphors which grew up around and acted to sustain this relationship undercut the impact of the unprecedented innovations and syntheses generated by African American musicians at the same time.

Black Hens, White Eggs

The sacralization of musical Jews which I have been tracing constitutes a prime example of what Herbert Butterfield called the "Whig interpretation of history": "the tendency . . . to emphasize certain principles of progress in the past and to produce a story which is the ratification if not the glorification of the present."[88] Even as sacralization depended on the notion that African Americans and Jews were at least spiritually close, the "glorious" present which received sanction in this discourse was not the contemporary development of a strong alliance between African Americans and Jews; that particular "Whig interpretation" would not crystallize until the late 1950s and early 1960s as a chronicle of cooperation (mainly in civil rights activity and labor relations) began to take shape. Rather, these loosely organized but effective rhetorical practices which naturalized the success of Jews in "Black" music served *most of all* to mold a success story of Jewish assimilation and filiopiety. The achievement of Jews in popular music did bring them into an intimate contact with African Americans which strongly—if surreptitiously—influenced Black-Jewish relations. This sacralization did not highlight intergroup contact—for good or bad—but instead effaced

African Americans while advancing the "model minority" interpretation of Jewish American history. The irony of all this should not be lost.
The success of Jews in the entertainment industries relied heavily on
adaptations of "Black" forms and subject matter, and contributed to the
rising status of Jews as they became white ethnics. As the social standing
of Jews improved, it became more and more common for them to be
held up as an instructive example to African Americans.

The musical relatedness of African Americans and Jews could be so
productively mobilized because it was established in such intensely
metaphoric terms. Physical nearness is the significant term which most
often dropped out of discussions of Black-Jewish sympathy. It is worth
remembering that Jews were not the only ethnics whose music bore
similarities to the music of African Americans. Nicholas Tawa has
surveyed a variety of musical innovations on the American scene which
were introduced by African Americans and other ethnics, including
"'blue' notes, rubato, complex syncopation, polyrhythms, and improvisation":

> All one has to do is listen to a cantor "bend" notes as he sings in one
> of the synagogal modes; a Hungarian violinist and cimbalonist freely
> introduce flexible alterations of note values in a melodic phrase; a
> Greek vocalist persistently displace metrical accents over the steady
> beat of an accompanist; a Syrian instrumental ensemble glory in the
> whirring counterpoint of subtly inflected rhythms; or a Sicilian, Por-
> tuguese, or Armenian musician extemporize on traditional melodic
> patterns to realize that black Americans have no monopoly in these
> areas.[89]

Of course African Americans have been by far the most important
contributors of these "non-standard" musical effects to American music. Even so, Tawa's catalogue helps make clear how it might be possible to complicate the metaphors of musical sameness which link Jews
and African Americans.

But such cultural metaphors have continued to be hugely popular,
although (or because?) they frequently lead to a conflation of African
American and Jew which suppresses the voices of African Americans.
David Ewen recounts the story of how George Gershwin took it upon
himself to drill the cast of *Porgy and Bess* when he discovered that many

of the actors had no trace of the necessary "Negro" dialect: "With his protruding full lips and plaintive voice he seemed more Negro than many members of the cast."[90] This sort of implicit blackface performance, where Jews completely displace African Americans, was the common yield of the tendency to overemphasize the similarities of African American and Jewish music. Sacralizing the Jewish path to "Black" music made it possible to exclude African Americans from genealogies of blues and jazz by arguing that Jewish cantorial music preceded and in fact engendered them: George Brunis, a white Dixieland player, suggested that "the blues comes from the Jewish hymn, like Eli, Eli . . . Then they took the African bongos, the tom-tom, and they made rhythm to it."[91] A similar contention competes with a more realistic interpretation in Harold Arlen's anecdote about the resemblances between his father's cantorial music and jazz which I previously quoted in part:

> I brought home a record of Louis Armstrong, I don't remember now which it was. My father spoke in Yiddish. And you have to remember, he was brought into this country originally to Louisville, Kentucky, so he must have picked up some of the blacks' inflection down there. Anyway, I played him this record, and there was a musical riff in there—we used to call it a "hot lick"—that Louis did. And my father looked at me, and he was stunned. And he asked in Yiddish "Where did he get it?"[92]

Here is a prime example of how nearness (Arlen's father's living among African Americans) could be supplanted by a claim for mystical similarity. Surely Arlen intended this humorous anecdote to underscore how all cultural productions rely on materials being passed back and forth through a variety of porous boundaries. Nonetheless, giving his cantor father the last word acts both as the kind of easy filiopiety native to this discourse and as a contribution which posits the Jew's liturgy as previous to (and perhaps responsible for) African American secular performance. Samson Raphaelson made the same argument when he claimed in "The Day of Atonement" that "Jakie was simply translating the age-old music of the cantors . . . into primitive and passionate Americanese." So did the Jewish swing player Max Kaminsky much later, in 1963, when he shared his opinions of bebop in his autobiography:

> Charlie Parker's music never bothered me the way some of the other music did, with its bad tone and taste and intonation. For as far as the "modern" chords are concerned, I'd been listening to them in the classical music ever since the late twenties—in fact, I'd been hearing that kind of atonal melody in the Torah singing ever since I was a child, and when I first started to improvise on the trumpet as a kid, I used to go off into these atonal intervals that I heard in the temple chants simply because they were so familiar to me and so easy to do.[93]

Again, rather than let jazz remain in the category of art along with "the classical music," Kaminsky reinvented it as a product (at least spiritually) of liturgical music—which he had already been playing for years! In Kaminsky's description, as is usual in such discussions, Jews end up looking completely *at home* with avant-garde innovation and jazz performance.

The attraction of explaining the impact of an amazing assortment of music by its connection to sacred Jewish music has demonstrated great stamina. Some lines near the end of Part 1 of Allen Ginsberg's *Howl* (1956), for instance, might be read with the rhetoric of sacralization in mind, as Ginsberg writes of the "madman bum and angel," who "rose reincarnate in the ghostly clothes of jazz in the goldhorn shadow / of the band and blew the suffering of America's naked mind for love / into an eli eli lamma lamma sabacthani saxophone cry." And in a 1958 novel, *The Enemy Camp* by Jerome Weidman, we find a character who describes the power of a female Jewish cabaret singer by noting that if "that dame was a man, she wouldn't be working in dumps like this for coffee and cake. If that dame was a man she could walk into any synagogue in the world and take over as a cantor. She's got that thing . . . Like on Yom Kippur, when they hit the *Kol Nidre.*"[94]

In 1994 a feature writer for the *New York Times* used the same old imagery in an article on Don Byron, an African American clarinetist who plays klezmer, a Yiddish music which "evokes celebration, cheekiness, frivolity." Although this writer makes it clear that klezmer is "not what one would call sacred music," still he cannot resist this description of Byron performing: "As he pumps his torso back and forth to the music, his dreadlocks sway, and Byron looks to all the world like a rabbi davening."[95]

Perhaps the most complete conflation of sacred Jewishness and secular "Blackness" can be found in an even less predictable place: Jean Toomer's story "Fern." In this character sketch, found in his modernist masterpiece *Cane* (1923), Toomer compactly illustrates this major theme of Black-Jewish relatedness as he transforms metaphor into pure identification.

"Fern" was published originally in the autumn of 1922.[96] Toomer tells here of a woman whose identity is invented, shaped, described, and refigured by men—most notably the narrator. Fern is first explicitly rendered in the language of cross-ethnic metaphor: "Her nose was aquiline, Semitic. If you have heard a Jewish cantor sing, if he has touched you and made your own sorrow seem trivial when compared with his, you will know my feeling when I follow the curves of her profile, like mobile rivers, to their common delta."[97] There is an obvious clue in this introductory description that Fern's connection to Jewishness is genealogical as well as metaphorical: she has a Jewish nose, the most easily recognizable of Jewish features (for a woman, at least).[98] The narrator makes clear, however, that Fern is socially identified only as Black ("it is black folks whom I have been talking about thus far"[15]), regardless of the mixed heritage he discerns in her. While Toomer himself was deeply interested in the promise of an "American" race which would transcend existing racial categories, Fern's narrator can imagine her only in social spaces marked as Black—whether Georgia or Harlem. But even if Fern is "Black," the key metaphor used to describe her compares this African American woman's eyes with the sound of Jewish liturgical music.

Toomer employs this metaphor again when the narrator recounts his first meeting with Fern: "At first sight of her I felt as if I heard a Jewish cantor sing. As if his singing rose above the unheard chorus of a folk-song" (15). Now the cantor's song is placed above "the unheard chorus of a folk-song." Up until now, the design of this metaphor has been on a horizontal plane: Fern's eyes/Black folk = Jewish cantor. With this new twist, however, a vertical dimension is added. This new image partakes in that by now familiar rhetoric which called for new art forms to be erected on the bases of folk materials.[99]

In Toomer's sketch the metaphor becomes even more complex as Fern begins to lose whatever agency she had in the original construction. Soon after recounting this first sighting of Fern, the narrator describes his dream of somehow helping her. He quickly dispenses with the idea that a change in scenery would change Fern's life for the better: "I have knocked about from town to town too much not to know the futility of mere change of place. Besides, picture if you can, this cream-colored solitary girl sitting at a tenement window looking down on the indifferent throngs of Harlem. *Better that she listen to folk-songs at dusk in Georgia*, you would say, and so would I" (15; emphasis added). With this intricate revision Fern is demoted. From being at least the inspiration for—if not the actual producer of—the cantorial song as first presented by the narrator, Fern is transformed into a consumer. Even more, she is the audience now for "folk-songs," a category of music "below" art and belonging to the past. It is also clear that, like Porgy, Fern would be entirely lost if she ever left the country for the city.

Fern's identity is completely effaced in the final appearance of this figurative pattern. The narrator has taken her for a walk down the Dixie Pike. After they pass through a canebrake, the narrator instinctively takes Fern in his arms, "without at first noticing it." Next comes the climax of the story:

> Then my mind came back to her. Her eyes, unusually weird and open, held me. Held God. He flowed in as I've seen the countryside flow in. Seen men. I must have done something—what, I don't know, in the confusion of my emotion. She sprang up. Rushed some distance from me. Fell to her knees, and began swaying, swaying. Her body was tortured with something it could not let out. Like boiling sap it flooded arms and fingers till she shook them as if they burned her. It found her throat, and spattered inarticulately in plaintive, convulsive sounds, mingled with calls to Christ Jesus. And then she sang, brokenly. A Jewish cantor singing with a broken voice. A child's voice, uncertain, or an old man's. Dusk hid her; I could hear only her song. It seemed to me as though she were pounding her head in anguish upon the ground. I rushed to her. She fainted in my arms. (17)

Fern is made to disappear in a number of ways in this key scene. At first the narrator holds her without seeing her; at the end she is made invisible by dusk. What is thematically most significant, however, is that when Fern finally begins to make sounds, to articulate her grief, it is not even her voice which the narrator hears: "And then she sang, brokenly. A Jewish cantor singing with a broken voice." Even now, as Fern attempts to voice her protest against the objectification which has silenced her and rendered her invisible, the narrator ignores the particularity of her condition as he forces her into the figurative scheme he favors.

Fern was first part of an analogy which compared the eyes of a woman socially designated as "Black" to the song of a Jewish cantor. Now she is reduced to serving as a vehicle to carry the message of the Jewish singer. Here Toomer replicates the rhetoric of sacralization in which the music of African Americans becomes most significant for the congenial way it articulates the Jewish sacred song. Finally, that the Jewish cantor's voice routed through Fern sounds like a child's voice *and* an old man's perfectly captures the ability of Jewish musicians—via the rhetoric of sacralization—to appear as both dutiful sons and generative patriarchs.

But the real moral of the story is disclosed only in the last three words, when the narrator tells us Fern's full name. Fern is revealed, in a strangely deadpan punch line, to be *literally* of mixed African American and Jewish origin: "She is still living, I have reason to know. Her name, against the chance that you might happen down that way, is Fernie May Rosen" (17). The name "Rosen" carries, of course, the strong suggestion that Fern is partly of Jewish descent. With this admission of Fern's mixed heritage comes a recognition that the defining metaphor in "Fern" has been an evasion—if not a purposeful obfuscation—of a very different relationship.[100] The narrator derives a rhetoric of sameness from his perception that Fern's eyes and a Jewish cantor's song cause similar emotions in him. As with most metaphors, the comparison seems to have the force of necessity even though it is not difficult to uncover it as provisional: the metaphor functions to box in African American culture (while still insisting on its productive value) by depicting it as both the yield of the Jewish cantor's song and something the cantor's song builds upon.[101]

In this case Toomer himself demonstrates that the metaphoric correlation of Blackness and Jewishness is a front for a more troubling discourse—one which places African Americans and Jews in close contact with each other in a real world of sexualized power relations. These metaphors were meant to explain the presence of Jews in African American music in a suitable way. Ultimately they reveal a widespread discomfort with accepting that in addition to historical and spiritual group similarities, African Americans and Jews are also related by all kinds of nearness—including geographic and sexual.

Let's Call the Whole Thing Off?

Although an uncomplicated tale of theft might be satisfyingly tidy, it cannot untangle the dynamics of the interactions between African Americans and Jews (and "Blackness" and "Jewishness") in the world of popular music in the age of ragtime and jazz. First, the sacralizing of Jews in popular music was bound up with the dignifying of African American music. Willie the Lion Smith, James Weldon Johnson, and other interested African American critics make it clear that the emergence of Jews in forms associated with African Americans advanced not only individual careers but the status of the music as well. Of course the hazards of this social interaction were immense—perhaps none greater than the very real possibility that African American music could come to appear as a subset of Jewish American music: just as Fern is made to disappear in Toomer's sketch, so too did tropes of Jewish fulfillment in African American music make it possible that the actual achievement of African Americans would get lost in the shuffle. This did not come to pass. Although Jews have continued to matter as creative artists *in* "Black" music through our own time, they rarely insist that their Jewishness plays a major role in their success. Jews have never disappeared from the African American musical landscape. Indeed Jews have continued to be prominent as producers (Jerry Wexler), songwriters (Jerry Leiber and Mike Stoller), record company executives (Herman Lubinsky, Syd Nathan), and even performers (the Beastie Boys) in fields associated with African Americans up until our own time. But if *Porgy and Bess*, in 1935, stood as the apotheosis of Jews in "Black" music, it also signified as an augury. While George Gershwin could be applauded as the "Abraham Lincoln" of African American music, bebop musicians would demand, beginning in the next few years, that the "reconstruction" of African American music had to be directed by African Americans. There is little doubt that establishing the value of African American music drew from contributions made by Jews in the first few decades of the century.

We should not ignore how much the musical associations of African Americans and Jews reveals about the relative cultural and social status of the two groups. Jews used African Americans and "Blackness" in music as part of what David Roediger has called the "sad drama of . . . embracing whiteness" by those "facing the threat of being victimized as nonwhite."[102] African Americans could use Jews and "Jewishness" in only an extremely limited fashion, and of course the "public and psychological wage" of whiteness, not to mention the material profits therein, continued to elude their grasp.[103] While both Jews and African Americans contributed to the rhetoric of musical affinity, the fruits of this labor belonged primarily to the former. Maybe most significantly, this musical relationship of African Americans and Jews helped validate the idea that in any contact between the two groups, Jews would be on top.

The sacralization of Jews in popular music—like any public reinscription of Jewishness—was not without risk. Most obviously, it had the potential to endanger the assimilationist project by foregrounding Jewish identity at a time when any conspicuous signs of the Jew's difference could have immediate negative consequences.[104] The constructed images of Jews in music were safe, though, especially when taken comparatively. These musical Jews were neither bomb-throwing Reds nor fat-cat capitalists (at least not obviously so). Only a small minority of commentators saw the musical Jews as fitting the available stereotype of parasites living off the labor of others. Rather, a careful presentation insisted that they be understood as hardworking producers, rendered safely passive by their alleged melancholy.[105] As a major contributor to the growing economic and political security of Jews in America, such confident cultural achievements would help reorganize Jewishness as a species of whiteness—even as Jewishness itself retained distinct symbolic value. In this light "Black-Jewish relations" must be understood as a functional rhetoric which has helped situate American Jews in their current position as white ethnics.

Epilogue: The Lasting Power of Black-Jewish Relations

Scholarship is rarely prophetic and then usually only by accident. Even so, I want to open this epilogue with a very modest bit of speculation. Searching for a governing metaphor to convey aptly the complex history of Black-Jewish relations, the current generation of commentators will turn to "marriage" and "divorce." I am not grabbing this prediction out of thin air: two recent essays on the subject end their ruminations on the subject of Black-Jewish relations with evocations of a marriage gone bad.

Glenn Loury activates this image in his essay "The End of an Illusion" with the suggestion that it might be best to recognize that there is little hope for a close relationship of Jews and African Americans to "ever be restored." Rather, he advises, it might be better "to recognize this, rather than to incur the anguish and disappointment that inevitably accompanies attempts to sustain a marriage from which the love has long since departed." Paul Berman covers similar ground in his *New Yorker* article which appeared at the same time, as he attempts to provide an epitaph for Black-Jewish relations: "But there is a little joke at the end of this story. Judaism allows divorce, and the mainstream black church, in its Protestant denominations, likewise permits it. But the relation between Jews and blacks does not allow divorce . . . Separate beds, separate rooms; the same house. Love, hatred; a wobbling back and forth from one to the other."[1] What is perhaps most interesting about Berman's final image is that it comes at the end of a fairly hopeful essay which imagines that it was a socialist-sponsored "Third Worldism" which formed the real heart of the troubles between African Americans and Jews. With the dissolution of the Soviet Union, Berman believes, African Americans and Jews might be able to reunite on the safer grounds of liberal democracy.[2]

Also relevant here is Alfred Uhry's Pulitzer Prize–winning play of 1986, *Driving Miss Daisy*, later (1990) turned into a hugely popular Hollywood movie. Uhry's nostalgic drama, set in Atlanta from 1948 to 1973, tells the story of Miss Daisy, an elderly Jewish woman forced by her son Boolie to accept the services of an African American chauffeur, Hoke, after her own driving skills deteriorate. After some scenes of domestic squabbling, Hoke and Miss Daisy begin what can only be called a chaste courtship. The turning point comes when Hoke drives Miss Daisy to the cemetery so she can tend her husband's plot. While there, Miss Daisy asks Hoke to place flowers on the grave of a friend's husband, and discovers that Hoke cannot read the headstones. This surprises Miss Daisy because she has seen Hoke reading the newspaper: Hoke reveals that he can "dope out what's happening from the pictures." Miss Daisy gives Hoke an impromptu spelling lesson, convincing him that he has the potential to read. From this moment on the two function very much like spouses. In the next scene it is Christmas Day and the two are intimately sharing their opinions (bad) of Miss Daisy's daughter-in-law, Florine. Miss Daisy's present to Hoke is a fifth-grade speller dating from when she was a schoolteacher; Hoke holds back the tears.[3] While Miss Daisy teaches Hoke the mechanics of reading, Hoke instructs Miss Daisy to understand how deeply they are linked by their outsider status. When Miss Daisy's Atlanta synagogue is bombed, she is shocked mostly that the attackers chose her Reform Temple rather than a Conservative or Orthodox one; Hoke reminds her that a "Jew is a Jew to them folks. Jes' like light or dark we all the same nigger."[4]

By the end of the play Miss Daisy—now senile, but revealing what we know to be her deepest feelings—is able to tell Hoke that he is her "best friend." The play ends with Hoke and Boolie visiting Miss Daisy in a nursing home on Thanksgiving Day, thus reuniting the dispersed, fictive nuclear family. As the lights fade on the play, Hoke is gently trying to feed Miss Daisy a piece of her Thanksgiving pie. This is an update, it seems, of the original American Thanksgiving story: playing Pilgrims and Indians making nice, Hoke and Miss Daisy are meant to install "Black-Jewish relations" as a national mythology. *Driving Miss Daisy* avoids any of the touchy questions surrounding the relationship of Jewish employer and African American servant in favor of presenting a fantasy of true nonsexual love. Overall, Uhry's play stands both as a retrograde case of the tendency to make facile comparisons between Jews and African Americans, and as an au courant reconfiguration of the relationship in the terms of a shaky marriage—one which might still harbor great emotions but is no longer a fulfillment of traditional romantic love.[5]

But how did we get from the almost exclusively male dramas of affection and refusal I have described in the preceding pages to these explicitly heterosexual accounts of the current day? We have observed a variety of localized instances of Black-Jewish relations which have depended on the formation (or at least the illusion) of intimate connections between Jewish and African American men. One result of this exclusively male orientation is that intense contests have developed over exactly what constitutes an American man. While previous accounts of Black-Jewish relations have paid most attention to the "American" part of this equation (such as Jews showing African Americans the road to full citizenship, or Jews achieving Americanness through the medium of Blackness), I hope to have made clear that the realization of desirable forms of manhood has been similarly crucial within this cultural field.

In retrospect, it seems ironic that the male bonding crucial to Black-Jewish relations—meant, in part, to defuse anxieties about the sexual threats posed by both Jewish and African American men—could end up looking dangerous itself. The hazards attending these all-male exchanges have been considerable, as the little colored boy rumor which followed Irving Berlin showed. Fiction writers too have explored how masculine closeness can become explosive: the obvious examples are found in Bernard Malamud's novel *The Tenants* (1971) and Saul Bellow's *Mr. Sammler's Planet* (1969), but Chester Himes was on this trail much earlier in his *Lonely Crusade* (1947). *Lonely Crusade* might productively be read as a sexualization of labor relations, particularly those which brought Jews and African Americans together.

The one virtually sinless character in the book—Abe Rosenberg, a Jewish Communist Party member—has no function in the novel outside of educating and nurturing the protagonist, Lee Gordon, an African American organizer. Gordon and Rosenberg have long, mostly stereotypical talks about African Americans and Jews. More interesting than these banal discussions of Black-Jewish relations is the simmering sexual intensity which marks the relationship of the Jewish man and the African American man as the novel unfolds.

My sense is that the heterosexualization of Black-Jewish relations in recent years serves to deflect attention from the homoerotic motive running throughout its history, and thus avoid the possibility that uneasiness about the intimacy of African American and Jewish men might turn into a full-fledged "homosexual panic" on the part of members of either group—or, more threatening yet, on the part of powerful white outsiders.[6] In this respect, then, the "marriage, then divorce" figure cultivated in recent years merely continues the work of musical sacralization I discussed earlier, by normalizing the presence of Jews in areas marked off previously as "Black." But this rhetorical work cannot close off threats to its consciously asexual bent. Cornel West, for instance, has explained the rift that developed between Jewish attorney Robert Shapiro and African American attorney Johnnie Cochran at the end of O. J. Simpson's murder trial as a matter of sexual rivalry: "I think part of the problem is that Shapiro—and this is true of certain white brothers—has a profound fear of black-male charisma . . . So you get a very real visceral kind of jealousy that has to do with sexual competition as well as professional competition."[7] The "certain white brother" Cornel West is talking about here is Jewish, and West's pronouncement is more about Black-Jewish relations than it is about O. J. Simpson. In this moment, then, we find once again a formal alliance (in this case an alliance of defense lawyers) dissolving into a discussion of sexual power. Over its approximately eighty-year history, "Black-Jewish relations" has switched registers frequently in just this way—from ritualistic negotiation between members of advocacy groups to a hostile competition of sexual outsiders.

Whatever figurative language is used to describe (and indeed enact) Black-Jewish relations, one might reasonably ask how it has managed to have such remarkable staying power—even in its attenuated modern-day form. To answer this question we have to move outside the temporal scope of this volume and ask how the Nazi genocide of Jews has been assimilated into the narrative of Black-Jewish relations. For many people, the evidence of the Nazi atrocities proved that Jews and African Americans were fellow sufferers, inevitably bound together by the racism of whites.

In our own time, Jewish leaders have insisted that African Americans acknowledge in a public way that Jews have suffered tremendously and recently. Perhaps no one has been more egregious along these lines than the self-appointed "progressive" Jewish spokesperson Michael Lerner. In his published dialogue with Cornel West, Lerner again and again tries to get his African American colleague to admit that "Blacks" have not sufficiently paid their respects to Jewish suffering. While continually abjuring victimology, Lerner seems to operate on the principle that if "Black-Jewish relations" is, as I insist, mostly a competition of rhetorics, than he can "win" it by establishing Jewish suffering (and African American recognition of Jewish suffering) as one of its major components. Here, in my view, is a sort of endgame for Black-Jewish relations: even as West compassionately responds to Lerner's demands—admitting that African Americans have, in fact, not fully come to recognize the horrors of the Holocaust—Lerner uses this "dialogue" to show why he is a better Jew than the ones at *Commentary*. Again, we discover that the *interracial* dialogue which is supposed to be at the center of Black-Jewish relations acts largely as a screen for the intraethnic and intergenerational arguments Lerner is interested in making about American Jews.[8]

Lerner does not see fit to emphasize that popular considerations of Hitler and Nazi Germany have frequently included the idea that European anti-Semitism contained a message for the United States about its own minority populations. Maya Angelou recalled that when World War II ended, she felt that there was no "need to discuss racial prejudice. Hadn't we all, black and white, just snatched the remaining Jews from the hell of concentration camps? Race prejudice was dead."[9] In Harper Lee's novel *To Kill a Mockingbird* (1960)—which reaches us today as "young adult" fiction—Scout Finch attempts, with much less confidence than Angelou, to come to terms with what the murder of

Jews in Germany has to do with the racial politics of her own town. Aptly enough Lee presents Scout's struggle in the context of an elementary school lesson. After Cecil Jacobs brings up the issue of Hitler's persecution of the Jews during current events day at school (calling him "Old Adolf Hitler"), Miss Gates assures him that Jews "contribute to every society they live in," and have been "persecuted since the beginning of history." With this Miss Gates concludes, and shifts gears: "Time for arithmetic, children."[10] For Scout Finch it is indeed time for arithmetic, but not the sort Miss Gates is teaching. Scout is left trying to figure out how to make Miss Gates's compassion for Jews and her racism toward African Americans add up. Reaching no conclusion on her own, Scout asks her brother Jem how a person can "hate Hitler so bad" but still "turn around and be ugly about folks right at home."[11]

I hope to have suggested with these few examples that in important respects the American reception of the immense suffering of European Jews during World War II resuscitated the most popular narrative of Black-Jewish relations at a moment when its future was in doubt. I do not mean to abstract the telling of the story of group similarity from the material interactions between Jews and African Americans in this era: the immediate postwar era saw sustained and successful African American–Jewish coalition activity, particularly on the judicial front of the civil rights movement. What should be emphasized is that by the middle of the century the older analogies (between Russian pogroms and American lynchings or race riots; a shared history of slavery) could not go far in explaining the very different status of the two groups in the United States. The magnitude of the Nazi genocide helped to enliven "Black-Jewish relations" as a national mythos which promised that, in the United States at least, racial and religious Others could safely do as they pleased—even make alliance with one another.

Without "Old Adolf Hitler" it would certainly have been more difficult to maintain the tale of mutual uplift at the heart of Black-Jewish relations. As early as the Leo Frank case of 1913–1915 it was becoming clear that a huge chasm separated African Americans and Jews. If Frank's plight led to some cautious alliance work between the two groups, it was much more significant for revealing how far apart Jews and African Americans could appear to be—in popular imagery, in their access to powerful media outlets, and in the vague but telling area of class affect.

Similarly, while popular culture afforded the opportunity for convincing exhibitions of African American–Jewish sympathy in the first few decades of the century, this path was also closing off in the World War II era. The bravura uses of Blackness which, for a time, suggested that Jewish composers and performers—precisely in their Jewishness—were the best interpreters of African American materials did not remain accessible to Jews for long after *Porgy and Bess*. As Jews moved further away from the social conditions which allegedly made them sensitive to the sounds and styles of African Americans, other white groups stepped into the breach to capitalize on the opportunities. Gary Giddins has written perceptively on this issue, noting that "while ghetto Jews were best able to adapt the pose and expressiveness of blacks in the 1920s, when burnt cork was still an acceptable gesture, no Jewish performer came close to the [southern white] fundamentalist rockabillies or the working-class Brits in assimilating the black rhythm and blues of the 1950s."[12] Nineteen fifty-four was the year when *Brown v. Board of Education* proved that Jewish and African American lawyers could work together with enormous success, but it was also the year of Elvis Presley's arrival on the scene, one sign that in the postwar world Jews would be eclipsed by other white people who had different routes to Black sounds.

It is even more important to recognize that more than the simple substitution Giddins implies (working-class British or poor southern whites *instead* of Jews), the post–World War II era would see a revaluation of Blackness as a nontransferable quality: Andrew Ross has remarked astutely that while "white Negro" has a familiar ring, "white black" has no currency at all.[13] Whether Blackness was represented as essential attribute or social construction, a major thrust of American racial/cultural politics in the 1950s and 1960s was to position it as unavailable to most white people. This development is beyond not only the temporal scope of my study but the geographic scheme as well: one would need to open up an international perspective to begin to show how "color" consciousness took hold during this time.

It will be interesting to see how long memories of the Holocaust will continue to energize positive contacts between Jews and African Americans. Steven Spielberg's film *Schindler's List* (1993)—inside its own narrative logic and as a cultural actor—contributed significantly to the comparative tendency. On the one hand, major concerns were raised in February 1994 when some African American high school students on a field trip to see the movie on Martin Luther King Day laughed during a particularly brutal scene. Scores of editorials were written and educational initiatives were introduced to educate African American students around the country as to why this movie should be of *particular* interest to them.[14]

On the other hand, viewed through the lens of Black-Jewish relations, *Schindler's List* itself seems to be making some covert claims about parallels between European Jews and African Americans. None was more striking to me than the monumental "good-bye" scene inside Schindler's factory: the structure and tone of this scene evoke a "kindly" slave owner's announcement of the Emancipation Proclamation. Following the familiar "great white father" scenario which imagines the slave owner/Nazi boss as ultimately filled with paternal love, *Schindler's List* is quite shocking in its imaginative conclusion: yes, it seems to say, they killed us and enslaved us, but down deep they did not really hate us. Erasing the stigmata of victimhood, *Schindler's List* ends up in an Israel cleansed of politics—a nationalist move which gives the lie to its earlier universalizing claims. In our time, then, "Black-Jewish relations" frequently offers an excuse for separatists to ply their trade.

A different sort of utopianism characterizes Gloria Naylor's 1992 novel *Bailey's Cafe*. This fascinating book is set in a fantasy space, a cosmic hash joint of sorts, where all manner of desperate people come in a last-ditch effort to find a way to keep on living. Most of the characters are women who have been the victims of sexual abuse. The novel's final vignette concerns Mariam, a pregnant Black Jew from Ethiopia who insists no man has ever touched her.

Bailey's Cafe ends with the death of the Black Jew Mariam soon after the birth of her child. The honorary father of the child is Gabe, a Russian Jew who survived through World War II in Europe. The child's honorary godfather is Bailey, the African American man who runs the diner. These two men are presented as verbal sparring partners, and their close relationship, as Bailey describes it, is remarkably free of any cant about the natural affiliation of Jews and African Americans. According to Bailey, Gabe is "not my brother . . . This man is simply someone who doesn't have to run around trying to guess what I really think about him because I tell him so. And if you're finding that heartwarming and refreshing, it shows you how far the world still is from anything that even looks like peace among men." In fact, Bailey explicitly denies the facile Russian Jew–African American analogy:

> He's a Russian Jew. I'm an American Negro. Neither of us is considered a national treasure in our countries, and that's where the similarity ends. We don't get into comparing notes on who did what to whom the most. Who's got the highest pile of bodies. The way I see it, there is no comparison. When most folks come out with that phrase, what they're really saying is that their pain is worse than your pain. But Gabe knows exactly what I mean: they're two different ball games.[15]

With this, Naylor offers a helpful way out of the comparative trap which has so frequently hindered efforts to conceptualize the relationship of African Americans and Jews.

But as the novel comes to a close, Bailey abandons the unblinking pragmatism of the passage just quoted in favor of a very different rendering of his relationship with Gabe—this one implying that a foundational Americanness resides within Black-Jewish relations. This utopian strain emerges as Bailey describes the difficulties he and Gabe face as they try to settle on a name for the baby:

> As his honorary godfather, I couldn't think of him having a better start than to give him my own father's name. But it turned out his honorary papa [Gabe] was planning on doing the exact same thing. And with personalities like ours, there was no way we could have come to a compromise. Somebody's name would have to be first, now wouldn't it? Before Miss Maple had to separate us from fisticuffs, Providence stepped in; it seemed both of our fathers were named George.[16]

Not only do Gabe and Bailey have fathers with the same name, but that name is George: the Father of Our Country. The Russian Jew and the African American have come together in the liminal space of Bailey's Cafe to name a child who has neither father nor mother, only to discover that their own true and rightful patrimony—one nation under God—is the United States of America.[17] This baby "George" is a late-model evocation of the idea that "Black-Jewish relations" is a major test case for American cultural democracy. Like the musical compositions of "George" Gershwin (named Jacob at birth), this baby is accepted as the healthy fruit of Black-Jewish relations—proof, in fact, that it is still a going proposition.[18]

Bailey's Cafe reminds us one final time that "Black-Jewish relations" endures as a powerful rhetorical formation even as "facts" pile up to prove that these two groups have little reason to believe that they should be in a special relationship. In this light, whatever skepticism I have articulated throughout this study as to the "true" nature of Black-Jewish relations should be taken mostly as an attempt to reorient a chronicle which threatens to deviate too far from lived experience to continue to have meaning in a progressive context. But "Black-Jewish relations" *does* continue to have meaning, and it is hardly satisfying to note simply that old habits die hard. "Black-Jewish relations" still has broad appeal because it is a compelling narrative, a late-model, utopian articulation of the United States as the Promised Land by the two American groups whose histories pivot on this concept.

Notes

Index

Notes

Introduction

1. Werner Sollors, *Amiri Baraka/LeRoi Jones: The Quest for a "Populist Modernism"* (New York: Columbia UP, 1978), 178.

2. Vivian Gornick, "An Ofay's Indirect Address to LeRoi Jones," *Village Voice*, 4 March 1965: 5–6, 16–17.

3. A quick run through the pages of *Commentary* for the first half of 1969 provides a good example of how this issue took center stage.

4. Henry Louis Gates, Jr., "Black Demagogues and Pseudo-Scholars," *New York Times*, 20 July 1992: A13; Benjamin Ginsberg, *The Fatal Embrace: Jews and the State* (Chicago: U of Chicago P, 1993).

5. Adolph L. Reed, Jr., *The Jesse Jackson Phenomenon: The Crisis of Purpose in Afro-American Politics* (New Haven: Yale UP, 1986), 88–89.

6. Stephen Sherrill, "Don Byron," *New York Times Magazine*, 16 January 1994: 18–21.

7. Raymond Williams, *Marxism and Literature* (1977; New York: Oxford UP, 1990), 115–116.

8. Contemporary scholarship has more or less exonerated Frank and found Conley to be the likely perpetrator of the murder.

9. David Levering Lewis, "Parallels and Divergences: Assimilationist Strategies of Afro-American and Jewish Elites from 1910 to the Early 1930s," *Journal of American History* 71.3 (1984): 543–564.

10. See my 1994 Harvard University dissertation, "Ancestors and Relatives:

The Uncanny Relationship of African Americans and Jews," for a fuller investigation of the Leo Frank case.

11. Hasia Diner, *In the Almost Promised Land: American Jews and Blacks, 1915–1935* (Westport, Conn.: Greenwood, 1977); Robert Weisbord and Arthur Stein, *Bittersweet Encounter: The Afro-American and the American Jew* (Westport, Conn.: Negro Universities P, 1970); Philip Foner, "Black-Jewish Relations in the Opening Years of the Twentieth Century," *Phylon* 36.4 (1975): 359–367; Eugene Levy, "'Is the Jew a White Man?': Press Reaction to the Leo Frank Case, 1913–1915," *Phylon* 35.2 (1974): 212–222; Lewis, "Parallels and Divergences"; Nat Hentoff, ed., *Black Anti-Semitism and Jewish Racism* (1969; New York: Shocken, 1970); Shlomo Katz, ed., *Negro and Jew: An Encounter in America* (New York: Macmillan, 1966); Isabel Boyko Price, "Black Response to Anti-Semitism: Negroes and Jews in New York, 1880 to World War II" (Ph.D. diss., University of New Mexico, 1973); Steven Bloom, "Interactions between Blacks and Jews in New York City, 1900–1930, as Reflected in the Black Press" (Ph.D. diss., New York University, 1973).

12. Paul Berman, ed., *Blacks and Jews: Alliances and Arguments* (New York: Delacorte, 1994); Jack Salzman, ed., with Adina Back and Gretchen Sullivan Sorin, *Bridges and Boundaries: African Americans and American Jews* (New York: George Braziller with the Jewish Museum, 1992); Laurence Mordekhai Thomas, *Vessels of Evil: American Slavery and the Holocaust* (Philadelphia: Temple UP, 1993); Murray Friedman, *What Went Wrong? The Creation and Collapse of the Black-Jewish Alliance* (New York: Free Press, 1993). While Thomas strangely focuses on access to coherent group narrative as the dividing line between African Americans (who do not have it) and Jews (who do), and Friedman predictably focuses on the Black Power movement as the fault line, both assume that "Black-Jewish relations" itself is a field whose database is not in question.

13. Ginsberg, *The Fatal Embrace*; Tony Martin, *The Jewish Onslaught: Despatches from the Wellesley Battlefront* (Dover, Mass.: Majority, 1993).

14. Albert Raboteau, *Slave Religion: The "Invisible Institution" in the Antebellum South* (1978; New York: Oxford UP, 1980), 311; Price, "Black Response to Anti-Semitism," 42–53.

15. This quotation, from the May 1904 issue of *Voice of the Negro*, can be found in Price, "Black Response to Anti-Semitism," 547.

16. Lawrence Levine, *Black Culture and Black Consciousness: Afro-American Folk Thought from Slavery to Freedom* (New York: Oxford UP, 1977), 175.

17. Charles Chesnutt, "Her Virginia Mammy," in *The Wife of His Youth* (1899; Ann Arbor: U of Michigan P, 1968), 36.

18. Zora Neale Hurston, "What White Publishers Won't Print," in *I Love Myself When I Am Laughing . . . And Then Again When I Am Looking Mean and Impressive* (New York: Feminist Press, 1979), 170.

19. This Du Bois quotation can be found in Marcia Graham Synott, "Anti-Semitism and American Universities: Did Quotas Follow the Jews?" in David Gerber, ed., *Anti-Semitism in American History* (Chicago: U of Illinois P, 1987), 250.

20. Karl Shapiro, "University," in *Collected Poems, 1940–1978* (New York: Random House, 1978), 10.

21. Foner, "Black-Jewish Relations," 360.

22. David Hellwig, "The Afro-American and the Immigrant, 1880–1930: A Study of Black Social Thought" (Ph.D. diss., Syracuse University, 1973), 145.

23. Ibid., 149; John Higham, *Send These to Me: Jews and Other Immigrants in Urban America* (New York: Atheneum, 1975), 149, 153.

24. Booker T. Washington, *The Future of the American Negro* (1899), in vol. 5 of Louis Harlan and Raymond W. Smock, with Barbara Kraft, *The Booker T. Washington Papers, 1899–1900* (Urbana: U of Illinois P, 1976), 369–370. See similarly in Frederick Douglass, *Life and Times of Frederick Douglass* (1881; Secaucus, N.J.: Citadel, 1983), 515.

25. Sherry Ortner, "Ethnography among the Newark: The Class of '58 of Weequahic High School," *Michigan Quarterly Review* 32.3 (1993): 427.

26. Tom Wolfe, *Radical Chic and Mau-Mauing the Flak Catchers* (1970; New York: Bantam, 1971), 46–47; Lewis, "Parallels and Divergences."

27. One of the best places to look for insights into the implications of the Bronx Slave Market is a forgotten novel by Carl Offord, *The White Face* (1943; New York: AMS, 1975).

28. See, for instance, David Roediger's pioneering work *The Wages of Whiteness: Race and the Making of the American Working Class* (New York: Verso, 1991); Robert Orsi's "Religious Boundaries of an Inbetween People: Street *Feste* and the Problem of the Dark-Skinned Other in Italian Harlem, 1920–1990," *American Quarterly* 44.3 (1992): 313–347; and above all, for my concerns, Michael Rogin, *Blackface, White Noise: Jewish Immigrants in the Hollywood Melting Pot* (Berkeley: U of California P, 1996).

29. In a series of essays (published in *Blackface, White Noise*), Michael Rogin has boldly attempted to define the representational labors assumed by race and ethnicity in early American sound film. Similarly noteworthy here is Eric Lott, *Love and Theft: Blackface Minstrelsy and the American Working Class* (New York: Oxford UP, 1993). Like Rogin, Lott explores

in detail the constitutive role played by Blackness in the creation and management of whiteness and Americanness. Rogin and Lott also supply models of how we might begin to study the ramifications of viewing the African American body as a primary site of colonization in American culture.

30. Lothrop Stoddard, "The Pedigree of Judah," *Forum* 75.3 (1926): 332.

31. Diner, *In the Almost Promised Land.*

32. Gerald Early, "American Education and the Postmodern Impulse," *American Quarterly* 45.2 (1993): 226.

33. See Orsi, "Religious Boundaries of an Inbetween People"; Roediger, *Wages of Whiteness;* Michael Omi and Howard Winant, *Racial Formation in the United States: From the 1960s to the 1980s* (New York: Routledge and Kegan Paul, 1986); Hellwig, "Afro-American and the Immigrant." Hellwig (164) notes that in 1882 one African American newspaper suggested that Jews were following the path of the Irish in America, taking almost instinctively to "democracy and negro-phobia." Also see Nathan Glazer and Daniel Patrick Moynihan, *Beyond the Melting Pot: The Negroes, Puerto Ricans, Jews, Italians, and Irish of New York City* (1963; Cambridge, Mass.: MIT P, 1965), 77, where the authors admit that everything they have to say about "Negro-Jewish relations is also true (to some extent) of Italian-Negro and Irish-Negro relations." Finally, see Robert Orsi's description (335) of current tensions between Italian Americans and African Americans, which might do just as well as a summary of Black-Jewish relations: "Even the expressions of rage that have been evoked recently by a series of tragic events in northeastern cities disclose undercurrents of attraction, disappointment, and mutual implication."

34. Michael Lerner and Cornel West, *Jews and Blacks: A Dialogue on Race, Religion, and Culture in America* (New York: Plume, 1995).

35. Gornick, "An Ofay's Indirect Address," 5–6, 16–17.

1. "Yiddle on Your Fiddle"

1. Cynthia Ozick, "Literary Blacks and Jews" (1972), in Paul Berman, ed., *Blacks and Jews: Alliances and Arguments* (New York: Delacorte, 1994), 46.

2. David Levering Lewis, "Parallels and Divergences: Assimilationist Strategies of Afro-American and Jewish Elites from 1910 to the Early 1930s," *Journal of American History* 71.3 (1984): 543–564.

3. A classic text here is the memoir by Isidore Witmark, co-written by Isaac Goldberg, who was also George Gershwin's first biographer. See Isidore

Witmark and Isaac Goldberg, *From Ragtime to Swingtime: The Story of the House of Witmark* (New York: Lee Furman, 1939).

4. The debates on the precise origins and codifying of "jazz" are old, ongoing, and not my interest per se. For recent information, see Burton Peretti, *The Creation of Jazz: Music, Race, and Culture in Urban America* (Chicago: U of Illinois P, 1992), 22; Kathy Ogren, *The Jazz Revolution: Twenties America and the Meaning of Jazz* (New York: Oxford UP, 1989), 142–143.

5. See Michael Rogin, "Blackface, White Noise: The Jewish Jazz Singer Finds His Voice," *Critical Inquiry* 18.3 (1992): 417–453.

6. MacDonald Smith Moore, *Yankee Blues: Musical Culture and American Identity* (Bloomington: Indiana UP, 1985), 74.

7. *Rhapsody in Blue*, directed by Irving Rapper, 1945.

8. After completing an initial draft of this section, I came upon Gerald Early's similar reaction to such claims for "making a lady out of jazz." Early notes that such locutions obviously include the insult that jazz was "no mere dame but an outright whore." I am pleased to acknowledge his fine essay "Pulp and Circumstance: The Story of Jazz in High Places," in *The Culture of Bruising: Essays on Prizefighting, Literature, and Modern American Culture* (Hopewell, N.J.: Ecco, 1994), 169.

9. Moore, *Yankee Blues* 108; Samson Raphaelson, *The Jazz Singer* (New York: Brentano's, 1925), 9; *Etude*, January 1924: 518.

10. See, for instance, *Musical Quarterly*, July 1918: 324–325.

11. *New Republic*, 30 September 1925: 155. Gerald Early correctly notes that intellectual Jews of the period usually heard jazz "as despair," and as a result were able to imagine it as "tragedy" rather than trash. See "Pulp and Circumstance," 177, 179. It might be worth noting that those Jews who supported jazz tended to be of east European descent while critics were likely to be German Jews.

12. Daniel Gregory Mason, *The Dilemma of American Music and Other Essays* (New York: Macmillan, 1928), 159.

13. Henry Osgood, *So This Is Jazz* (Boston: Little, Brown, 1926), 131.

14. Quoted in David Ewen, *George Gershwin: His Journey to Greatness* (1956; New York: Ungar, 1980), 112.

15. Jacques Barzun, *Music in American Life* (Garden City, N.Y.: Doubleday, 1956), 15–16.

16. Neil Leonard, *Jazz and the White Americans: The Acceptance of a New Art Form* (Chicago: U of Chicago P, 1962), 36.

17. In *Etude*, September 1924: 595.

18. On St. Louis and Sedalia, see Terry Waldo, *This Is Ragtime* (New York:

Hawthorne, 1976), 35–36, 51–52; see also Susan Curtis, *Dancing to a Black Man's Tune: A Life of Scott Joplin* (Columbia: U of Missouri P, 1994), 68–97; and Edward Berlin, *King of Ragtime: Scott Joplin and His Era* (New York: Oxford UP, 1994), 24–44. For a balanced look at Storyville, see Peretti, *Creation of Jazz*, 35–36. Hazel Carby notes that African American urban communities have often been pathologized because of the geographic propinquity of their neighborhoods to red-light districts, in "Policing the Black Woman's Body in an Urban Context," *Critical Inquiry* 18.4 (1992): 751–752.

19. Kathy Peiss, *Cheap Amusements: Working Women and Leisure in Turn-of-the-Century New York* (Philadelphia: Temple UP, 1986), 102.

20. Lewis Erenberg, *Steppin' Out: New York Nightlife and the Transformation of American Culture, 1890–1930* (1981; Chicago: U of Chicago P, 1984), 83–84.

21. Ibid.; Edward Marks, as told to Abbott Liebling, *They All Sang: From Tony Pastor to Rudy Vallee* (New York: Viking, 1934), 164.

22. *Messenger*, August 1922: 461.

23. *Messenger*, February 1925: 97, 100. A more recent analysis finds the opposite to have been true. See Ogren, *Jazz Revolution*, 61.

24. Sterling Brown, "Cabaret," in Michael Harper, ed., *Collected Poems of Sterling A. Brown* (Chicago: TriQuarterly, 1989), 111–113.

25. Terry Waldo has argued that the introduction of horns to the South can be traced to a band of itinerant Mexican musicians who appeared at the Sugar and Cattle Exposition in New Orleans in 1885. Waldo, *This Is Ragtime*, 15. On Joplin's German piano teacher see Addison Reed, "Scott Joplin, Pioneer," in John Edward Hasse, ed., *Ragtime: Its History, Composers, and Music* (New York: Schirmer, 1985), 120. A discussion of the impact of the Creole laws can be found in Ogren, *Jazz Revolution*, 32; for information on the importance of the Chicago World's Columbian Exhibition, see Edward Berlin, *Reflections and Research on Ragtime* (Brooklyn: Institute for Studies in American Music, Brooklyn College of the City University of New York, 1987), 2; Waldo, *This Is Ragtime*, 19; and Curtis, *Dancing to a Black Man's Tune*, 45–62.

26. Israel Zangwill, *The Melting Pot* (1909; New York: Macmillan, 1932), 207, 214.

27. In an oft-quoted burst of silliness from 1928, the Soviet writer Maxim Gorky wrote that listening to this music, "one involuntarily begins to imagine that it is the performance of an orchestra of lunatics, driven mad by sex, and conducted by a human stallion wielding an enormous

phallus." Maxim Gorky, "Fat Men's Music," in *Articles and Pamphlets* (1928; Moscow: Foreign Language Publishing House, 1951), 160–161.

28. Quoted in Neil Leonard, "The Reactions to Ragtime," in Hasse, *Ragtime*, 107–108.

29. Isaac Goldberg, *George Gershwin: A Study in American Music* (1931; New York: Frederick Ungar, 1958), 135.

30. Waldo, *This Is Ragtime*, 5.

31. Raphaelson, *The Jazz Singer*, 9. See also Waldo, *This Is Ragtime*, 7; Ian Whitcomb, *Irving Berlin and Ragtime America* (New York: Limelight Editions, 1988), 70; Isaac Goldberg, *Tin Pan Alley: A Chronicle of the American Popular Music Racket* (New York: John Day, 1930), 144.

32. Whitcomb, *Irving Berlin*, 44; Moore, *Yankee Blues*, 170; Berndt Ostendorf, "The Musical World of Doctorow's *Ragtime*," *American Quarterly* 43.4 (1991): 593.

33. See Chapter 2 of my 1994 Harvard University dissertation, "Ancestors and Relatives: The Uncanny Relationship of African Americans and Jews."

34. These two articles are from the *Dearborn Independent*, 6 August 1921 (8–9) and 13 August 1921 (8). For the sake of convenience, I cite them from the reprints in *Jewish Influences in American Life*, vol. 3 of *The International Jew: The World's Foremost Problem* (Dearborn, Mich.: Dearborn Publishing, 1921), 64–74. These two references are from "Jewish Jazz Becomes Our National Music," 65, and "How the Jewish Song Trust Makes You Sing," 78, 80.

35. Michael Kater, *Different Drummers: Jazz in the Culture of Nazi Germany* (New York: Oxford UP, 1992), 33.

36. Gerald Bordman, *American Musical Theatre: A Chronicle* (New York: Oxford UP, 1978), 298. The show was Sigmund Romberg's *Love Birds*. See Edward Berlin, "Ragtime Songs," in Hasse, *Ragtime*, 77. Here Berlin makes a subtle demurral from this conventional wisdom, calling "Memphis Blues" the "first important published blues." Ragtime composer Artie Matthews, for one, published a song called "Baby Seals Blues" earlier in 1912 than Handy's work. See Waldo, *This Is Ragtime*, 120–121, for full information, as well as a reproduction of Handy's sheet music. See also Gunther Schuller, "Rags, the Classics, and Jazz," also in Hasse (85). Samuel Charters and Leonard Kunstadt, *Jazz: A History of the New York Scene* (1962; New York: Da Capo, 1981), 97, describes how ragtime songs were re-released during the early 1920s blues craze with the word "blues" slapped on the end of the title—for instance, "Cataract Rag

Blues" and "Nightingale Rag Blues." See also the sheet music reprint in Albert Murray's *Stomping the Blues* (1976; New York: Vintage, 1982), 80, of W. C. Handy's "St. Louis Blues," which advertises it as the "Most Widely Known Ragtime Composition," which also included "THE FIRST JAZZ BREAK Ushering in MODERN JAZZ." And finally, see Osgood, *So This Is Jazz*, 30.

37. John Edward Hasse, "Ragtime: From the Top," in Hasse, *Ragtime*, 2–4.

38. Ibid., p. 7. On 3 August 1896 Ernest Hogan published "All Coons Look Alike to Me," an optional chorus of which was labeled "Negro 'Rag' Accompaniment." Two days later Ben Harney's "You Been a Good Old Wagon but You've Done Broke Down" was released with the claim that Harney had introduced "Rag Time."

39. Berlin, "Ragtime Songs," 73.

40. Europe's argument, which first appeared in 1909 in the *New York Age*, is quoted in Jervis Anderson, *This Was Harlem: A Cultural Portrait, 1900–1950* (New York: Farrar Straus Giroux, 1982), 70.

41. Eileen Southern, *The Music of Black Americans: A History* (1971; New York: Norton, 1983), 327.

42. Hasse, "Ragtime: From the Top," 14–15.

43. Ogren, *Jazz Revolution*, 143.

44. *Etude*, January 1924: 518; Mark Sullivan, *Our Times: The United States, 1900–1925*, vol. 4 (New York: Scribner's, 1932), 223.

45. Langston Hughes, *Not Without Laughter* (1930; New York: Collier, 1969), 94.

46. Gunther Schuller notes this in *Early Jazz: Its Roots and Musical Development* (New York: Oxford UP, 1968), 139.

47. LeRoi Jones, *Blues People: Negro Music in White America* (New York: Morrow Quill Paperbacks, 1963), 90, 148.

48. Quoted in Osgood, *So This Is Jazz*, 144.

49. Ibid., 27.

50. Waldo, *This Is Ragtime*, 57.

51. Quoted in Moore, *Yankee Blues*, 143.

52. *Etude*, January 1924: 6.

53. *New Republic*, 3 February 1926: 293.

54. Alain Locke, *The Negro and His Music; Negro Art Past and Present* (1936; New York: Arno Press and the New York Times, 1969), 87.

55. Perhaps overstating the case a bit, but still making a necessary point, Gerald Early has argued that "Jewish-created Tin Pan Alley song" became the basis of all serious American music. Early, "Pulp and Circumstance," 200.

56. Many have noted the irony of "Blackness" so successfully taking over the "mainstream" at the same time that the treatment of African Americans was hitting a post-Reconstruction low. See, for instance, Ostendorf, "Musical World of Doctorow's *Ragtime*," 590; and Wilfred Mellers, *Music in a New Found Land: Themes and Developments in the History of American Music* (1965; Boston: Faber and Faber, 1987), 263.

57. See, for instance, Ostendorf's "Musical World of Doctorow's *Ragtime*."

58. On Populist anti-Semitism, see Richard Hofstadter, *The Age of Reform: From Bryan to F.D.R* (New York: Vintage, 1955), 77–81; and John Higham, "Anti-Semitism in the Gilded Age: A Reinterpretation," a version of which can be found in *Send These to Me: Jews and Other Immigrants in Urban America* (New York: Atheneum, 1975). For evaluations of these and more (and with a decidedly alarmist tone), see Michael Dobkowski, *The Tarnished Dream: The Basis of American Anti-Semitism* (Westport, Conn.: Greenwood, 1979), 170–208.

59. Lewis, "Parallels and Divergences."

60. Rogin, "Blackface, White Noise," 441.

61. On the new media, see Charles Hamm, *Yesterdays: Popular Song in America* (New York: Norton, 1979), 337.

62. For the early years of mass entertainment, see among others Larry May, *Screening Out the Past: The Birth of Mass Culture and the Motion Picture Industry* (1980; Chicago: U of Chicago P, 1983); Russell Sanjek and David Sanjek, *American Popular Music Business in the Twentieth Century* (1988; New York: Oxford UP, 1981); Witmark and Goldberg, *From Ragtime to Swingtime*; Erenberg, *Steppin' Out*; Schuller, *Early Jazz*; Bill Malone, *Country Music U.S.A* (1968; Austin: U of Texas P, 1985); and Henry Jenkins, *What Made Pistachio Nuts? Early Sound Comedy and the Vaudeville Aesthetic* (New York: Columbia UP, 1992).

63. Rogin, "Blackface, White Noise," 439; see also Hasia Diner, *In the Almost Promised Land: American Jews and Blacks, 1915–1935* (Westport, Conn.: Greenwood, 1977), 3–27.

64. On African American consumption of "race" music in the 1920s, see Lawrence Levine, *Black Culture and Black Consciousness: Afro-American Folk Thought from Slavery to Freedom* (New York: Oxford UP, 1977), 224–236.

65. For example, see Irving Howe's claim that the Jewish takeover of blackface turned it into something "emotionally richer and more humane." Irving Howe, with the assistance of Kenneth Libo, *World of Our Fathers* (New York: Touchstone/Simon and Schuster, 1976), 563. Ian Whitcomb explains the Jewish dominance of Tin Pan Alley in part by noting

that the "corporate communities of established business—like banking, law, medicine, steel and oil—were closed to them." Whitcomb, *Irving Berlin*, 43.

66. Harold Cruse, *The Crisis of the Negro Intellectual: A Historical Analysis of the Failure of Black Leadership* (1967; New York: Quill, 1984).

67. Hasse, "Ragtime: From the Top," 22.

68. It was not the fair proper but the opportunities to play around it which were so crucial to the dissemination of ragtime. Scott Joplin was there, as were W. C. Handy and James Weldon Johnson. See Waldo, *This Is Ragtime*, 19–20, 50–51; Curtis, *Dancing to a Black Man's Tune*, 45–62.

69. Laurence Bergreen, *As Thousands Cheer: The Life of Irving Berlin* (New York: Viking, 1990), 36. Bergreen dates the Jewish takeover from 1881. See also Philip Furia, *The Poets of Tin Pan Alley: A History of America's Great Lyricists* (New York: Oxford UP, 1990), 20; and Witmark and Goldberg, *From Ragtime to Swingtime*.

70. One estimate suggests that during the last decade of the nineteenth century, it cost $1,300 to "launch" a song appropriately. Sanjek and Sanjek *American Popular Music Business*, x.

71. Witmark and Goldberg, *From Ragtime to Swingtime*, 111; Sanjek and Sanjek, *American Popular Music Business*, x.

72. Hasse, "Ragtime: From the Top," 10; David Jasen, *Tin Pan Alley—The Composers, the Songs, the Performers and Their Times: The Golden Age of American Popular Music from 1886 to 1956* (New York: Donald I. Fine, 1988), 9. The Witmark brothers' father served in the Confederate Army and had been a slave owner. See Witmark and Goldberg, *From Ragtime to Swingtime*, 30–31.

73. In addition to Witmark and Goldberg, *From Ragtime to Swingtime*, see also Berndt Ostendorf, "'The Diluted Second Generation': German-Americans in Music, 1870–1920," in Hartmut Keil, ed., *German Workers' Culture in the United States, 1850 to 1920* (Washington, D.C.: Smithsonian, 1988), 278–282.

74. Witmark and Goldberg, *From Ragtime to Swingtime*, 196.

75. On Hogan, see Waldo, *This Is Ragtime*, 100; Anderson, *This Was Harlem*, 32–33.

76. On Cook, see Thomas Riis, *Just before Jazz: Black Musical Theater in New York, 1890–1915* (Washington, D.C.: Smithsonian, 1989), 40–43.

77. Witmark and Goldberg, *From Ragtime to Swingtime*, 197.

78. Witmark and Goldberg, *From Ragtime to Swingtime*, 375–376; see also Sanjek and Sanjek, *American Popular Music Business*, 17–18. Thomas Morgan and William Barlow say that by 1920 there were only ten

African Americans on the rolls of ASCAP. See Thomas Morgan and William Barlow, *From Cakewalks to Concert Halls: An Illustrated History of African American Popular Music from 1895 to 1930* (Washington, D.C.: Elliot and Clark, 1992), 91. In addition to the low number of African Americans in ASCAP, the rankings of composers within the organization which determined royalty percentages appear not to have been very favorable to African Americans. Barry Singer, *Black and Blue: The Life and Lyrics of Andy Razaf* (New York: Schirmer, 1992), 261.

79. This is recounted by saxophonist Gene Sedric in Nat Shapiro and Nat Hentoff, *Hear Me Talkin' to Ya: The Story of Jazz as Told by the Men Who Made It* (New York: Dover, 1955), 265. Barry Singer also claims that Waller sold the complete *Hot Chocolates* score to Mills Publishing in 1929 for $500. Singer, *Black and Blue*, 261.

80. Singer, *Black and Blue*, 151.

81. Ibid., 132.

82. Quoted in Early, "Pulp and Circumstance," 195.

83. Sanjek and Sanjek, *American Popular Music Business*, xi.

84. Howe, *World of Our Fathers*, 557.

85. Singer, *Black and Blue*, 79. These thin years for African Americans in the music industries also saw the death of Booker T. Washington and the institution of federal segregation by Woodrow Wilson.

86. Singer, *Black and Blue*, 187–188; Ronald Morris, *Wait until Dark: Jazz and the Underworld, 1880–1940* (Bowling Green, Ohio: Bowling Green UP, 1980), 4. With little documentation, Morris suggests that gangsters heavily underwrote the cultural productions we have come to know as the Harlem Renaissance.

87. Singer, *Black and Blue*, 216–222.

88. Bergreen, *As Thousands Cheer*, 148.

89. Mark Slobin, *Tenement Songs: The Popular Music of the Jewish Immigrants* (Chicago: U of Illinois P, 1982), 51; see also his essay "Some Intersections of Jews, Music, and Theater," in Sara Blacher Cohen, ed., *From Hester Street to Hollywood: The Jewish-American Stage and Screen* (Bloomington: Indiana UP, 1983), 29–44. Other Jews who performed in blackface include George Jessel and George Burns, and even the Yiddish stage actress Molly Picon; Fanny Brice, according to the best account of her life, blacked up only once, for a routine she did with Eddie Cantor in 1917. See Barbara Grossman, *Funny Woman: The Life and Times of Fanny Brice* (Bloomington: Indiana UP, 1991), 105–106. Lester Friedman, *Hollywood's Image of the Jew* (New York: Frederick Ungar, 1982), 50; J. Hoberman, *Bridge of Light: Yiddish Film between*

Two Worlds (New York: Museum of Modern Art and Schocken, 1991), 14.

90. Howe, *World of Our Fathers*, 562. The *Variety* article is quoted in Jenkins, *What Made Pistachio Nuts?* 71.

91. Herbert Goldman, *Jolson: The Legend Comes to Life* (New York: Oxford UP, 1988), 40; Harry Geduld, *The Birth of the Talkies: From Edison to Jolson* (Bloomington: Indiana UP, 1975), 166–167. There is remarkably little serious work available on Jolson's life (as opposed to his stage persona and *Jazz Singer* role). My remarks on Jolson throughout rely heavily on Goldman's solidly researched if analytically suspect work. One of the few people in recent years to have anything interesting to say about Jolson is Gary Giddins, the regular jazz critic for the *Village Voice*. See especially his "Native Wits," *Village Voice*, 11 May 1993: 86. Here he writes with wonderful ambivalence that, try as you might, it is "no use trying to separate Jolson, the enduringly hypnotic performer, who wears down your defenses with a nearly violent energy, daring you to remain indifferent, from the traditions of burnt cork." Also see Michael Rogin, *Blackface, White Noise: Jewish Immigrants in the Hollywood Melting Pot* (Berkeley: U of California P, 1996).

92. Howe, *World of Our Fathers*, 563.

93. Goldberg, *George Gershwin*, 41.

94. Raphaelson recounted this in an article for *American Hebrew* (14 October 1927) which is quoted in Robert Carringer's introduction to his edited version of the screenplay for *The Jazz Singer* (Madison: U of Wisconsin P, 1979), 11. The playwright first saw Jolson when he was an undergraduate at the University of Illinois in 1916.

95. Joan Peyser, *The Memory of All That: The Life of George Gershwin* (New York: Simon and Schuster, 1993), 39; Goldman, *Jolson*, 45–59.

96. Goldman, *Jolson*, 101, 61.

97. Ibid., 62–63.

98. Ibid., 114–115.

99. Peyser, *Memory of All That*, 54–55.

100. Goldman, *Jolson*, 109.

101. For the text of "Old Folks," see William Austin, *"Susanna," "Jeanie," and "The Old Folks at Home": The Songs of Stephen C. Foster from His Time to Ours* (1975; Chicago: U of Illinois P, 1987), 246.

102. I have relied heavily here on Austin's fascinating study of Foster and his influence in American culture. See Austin, *"Susanna," "Jeanie," and "The Old Folks at Home,"* x, 123–162, 251–252.

103. Ibid., 123–162.

104. Eric Lott, *Love and Theft: Blackface Minstrelsy and the American Working Class* (New York: Oxford UP, 1993), 191.

105. On Berlin's admiration for Foster, see Bergreen, *As Thousands Cheer*, 40–41.

106. Earl Bargainnier, "Tin Pan Alley and Dixie: The South in Popular Song," *Mississippi Quarterly* 30.4 (Fall 1977): 530. Al Jolson, for instance, recorded a song titled "Down Where the Swanee River Flows" in 1916, and "Rock-a-Bye Your Baby with a Dixie Melody" in 1918, which contains lyrical reference to Foster's "Old Black Joe" and "Old Folks at Home." Goldman, *Jolson*, 378–379.

107. Robert Dawidoff, "The Kind of Person You Have to Sound Like in Order to Sing 'Alexander's Ragtime Band,'" manuscript in author's possession, 1, 17.

108. Irving Berlin, *The Songs of Irving Berlin*, vol. 2 (Miami Lakes, Fla.: Masters Music, n.d.), 3–6.

109. Austin, *"Susanna," "Jeanie," and "The Old Folks at Home,"* 331.

110. Ibid.

111. Charles Schwartz, *Gershwin: His Life and Music* (New York: Da Capo, 1973), 46.

112. Roger Hewitt, "Black through White: Hoagy Carmichael and the Cultural Reproduction of Racism," *Popular Music* 3 (1983): 33, 49. As Hewitt also notes, white reproductions of black sounds were the product both of "the contact between black and white musicians *and* of the racist practices which regulated that contact" (36). See, similarly, Robert Dawidoff, "Some of Those Days," *Western Humanities Review* 41.3 (1987): 282.

113. Ronald Sanders, "The American Popular Song," in Douglas Villiers, ed., *Next Year in Jerusalem: Portraits of the Jew in the Twentieth Century* (New York: Viking, 1976), 197. Isaac Goldberg (*George Gershwin*, 46) also notes that minstrelsy was the cradle of Tin Pan Alley. Gary Giddins puts the issue succinctly: "Minstrelsy is said to have died at the hands of vaudeville, but it was a death in form, not spirit." Gary Giddins, *Riding on a Blue Note: Jazz and American Pop* (New York: Oxford UP, 1981), 32.

114. See, for instance, Paul Oliver, Max Harrison, and William Bolcom, eds., *The New Grove Gospel, Blues, and Jazz with Spirituals and Ragtime* (New York: Norton, 1986), 23; on the translation of blackface to "blackvoice," see Dawidoff, "Some of Those Days"; Early, "Pulp and Circumstance."

115. Kenneth Kanter, *The Jews on Tin Pan Alley: The Jewish Contribution to American Popular Music, 1830–1940* (New York: Ktav/Cincinnati: American Jewish Archives, 1982), 138. For good analyses of the importance of

ragtime as metaphor, see especially Ostendorf, "Musical World of Doctorow's *Ragtime*," and Waldo, *This Is Ragtime*.

116. Laurence Bergreen furnishes this information in his biography of Berlin, pointing to Harry von Tilzer's "Alexander (Don't You Love Your Baby No More)?" as the most popular example. Bergreen, *As Thousands Cheer*, 19.

117. Alexander Woollcott, *The Story of Irving Berlin* (New York: G. P. Putnam's Sons, 1925), 40; Bergreen, *As Thousands Cheer*, 8.

118. Bergreen, *As Thousands Cheer*, 19–21.

119. On sightseers, see Woollcott, *Story of Irving Berlin*, 49; Bergreen, *As Thousands Cheer*, 20–21.

120. Kanter, *Jews on Tin Pan Alley*, 138.

121. Whitcomb, *Irving Berlin*, 161; Bergreen, *As Thousands Cheer*, 70–75.

122. Woollcott, *Story of Irving Berlin*, 215–216; Bergreen, *As Thousands Cheer*, 222–223.

123. *New Republic*, 5 August 1925: 293–294. Seldes is wrong, of course, but that is exactly the point.

124. Bergreen, *As Thousands Cheer*, 159.

125. Ibid., 321–322.

126. Goldberg, *George Gershwin*, 138–139.

127. Schwartz, *Gershwin*, 61.

128. See the movie *Rhapsody in Blue* for a fanciful re-creation. According to some reports, the stress of this production also led to the onset of the "composer's stomach"—constipation accompanied by cramps—which was to plague Gershwin from then on. Schwartz, *Gershwin*, 236.

129. For information on the Gauthier concert and the Van Vechten quotation, see Edward Jablonski, *Gershwin: A Biography* (Boston: Northeastern UP, 1987), 57.

130. Moore, *Yankee Blues*, 92–108; Cruse, *Crisis of the Negro Intellectual*, 515.

131. This phrase is from Henry Taylor Parker's review in the *Boston Evening Transcript*, quoted in Schwartz, *Gershwin*, 71.

132. The playbill is reprinted in Schwartz, *Gershwin*, 75.

133. Ibid., 72.

134. Goldberg, *George Gershwin*, 108.

135. See Deena Rosenberg, *Fascinating Rhythm: The Collaboration of George and Ira Gershwin* (New York: Dutton, 1991), 60; Schwartz, *Gershwin*, 89; Jablonski, *Gershwin*, 61–76.

136. David Ewen in Merle Armitage, ed., *George Gershwin* (New York: Longmans, Green, 1938), 207. A dissenter such as Harold Cruse might add that Gershwin "emancipated" jazz like a pickpocket emancipates a wallet.

Gerald Early notes the significance of the 12 February date, mentioning that Richard Wright sets *Lawd Today* on the same holiday. Early, "Pulp and Circumstance," 172.

137. This particular line should be taken with a very large grain of salt, because numerous Gershwin biographers cite it as having been uttered not after *Rhapsody in Blue* but at the debut of *Porgy and Bess*. Johnson himself recounted saying it after *Rhapsody in Blue* (see Armitage, *George Gershwin*, 65), but most biographers attach the quotation to the legend of *Porgy and Bess*. See Jablonski, *Gershwin*, 288; Ewen, *George Gershwin*, 232.

138. Although this time J. Rosamond Johnson thought that only 80 percent of the music was "Negroid," with the rest constituted by American Indian, cowboy, and mountain music. See Armitage, *George Gershwin*, 66.

139. For Rouben Mamoulian, see ibid., 49. For reviews of *Porgy and Bess*, see Jablonski, *Gershwin*, 288–291, and the clipping file on the opera at Harvard University's Theatre Collection.

140. Johnson quoted in Schwartz, *Gershwin*, 245; Cruse, *Crisis of the Negro Intellectual*, 103.

141. Gerald Bordman, *Jerome Kern: His Life and Music* (New York: Oxford UP, 1980), 196, 249.

142. Ibid., 7–10, 18–20. David Jasen notes that a "Trilby Rag" was written during the ragtime craze. Jasen, *Tin Pan Alley*, 92. Trilby resurfaces in Amiri Baraka/LeRoi Jones's reference to "Trilby intrigue" in his "Black Dada Nihilismus" (1964). Werner Sollors suggests that this citation is meant to call attention to the hypnotic power of American popular culture over middle-class African Americans, as well as to the deformations of the African American artist caused by bohemian norms. See Werner Sollors, *Amiri Baraka/LeRoi Jones: The Quest for a "Populist Modernism"* (New York: Columbia UP, 1986), 91, 277n8.

143. Quoted in Miles Kreuger, *Show Boat: The Story of a Classic American Musical* (New York: Oxford UP, 1977), 55.

144. Bordman, *Jerome Kern*, 400. For a good account of Robeson's involvement with *Show Boat* and "Ol' Man River," see Richard Dyer, *Heavenly Bodies: Film Stars and Society* (London: BFI/Macmillan, 1986), 105–107, 126–128. Kern's biographer Michael Freedland plays up the authenticity of "Ol' Man River." He writes that the African American chorus of *Show Boat* paid Kern an unexpected compliment: "One after another, the singers and dancers told him that they could not understand how a white man could possibly produce music like that of 'Ol' Man River.'" Several

were sure, Freedland recounts, that they had heard the song as children. Michael Freedland, *Jerome Kern* (London: Robson, 1978), 90. Louis Armstrong offers a tribute of his own in *Swing That Music* (1936; New York: Da Capo, 1993), as he describes the effect the Mississippi River has on him: "That big river has always made me a little sad and I think that is so with all the people who have lived down near the delta. Mr. Jerome Kern sure knew what he was doing" when he composed that song (19).

145. Ewen, *George Gershwin*, 230.

146. Edward Jablonski, *Harold Arlen: Happy with the Blues* (1961; New York: Da Capo, 1985), 68. See also Sanders, "American Popular Song," 197.

147. Jablonski, *Harold Arlen*, 78.

148. Ibid., 20–45. Jablonski suggests that Arlen was especially influenced by listening to Bessie Smith and Ethel Waters, with their "free, improvisational style" (34).

149. Max Wilk, *They're Playing Our Song: From Jerome Kern to Stephen Sondheim—The Stories behind the Words and Music of Two Generations* (New York: Atheneum, 1973), 152.

150. Morris, *Wait until Dark*, 108.

151. Arlen also wrote the music for the movie *Blues in the Night*, which, according to Edward Jablonski, disappointed Arlen because he had hoped the movie would be a "documentary-like study of jazz music." See Jablonski, *Harold Arlen*, 123, 125, 137–138, 142–143.

152. Wilk, *They're Playing Our Song*, 153.

153. Erenberg, *Steppin' Out*, 74. See also Sanders, "American Popular Song," 194, on the importance of the streets to Irving Berlin. Both Erenberg and Sanders overstate the amount of sway that the father managed to maintain in these immigrant families and emphasize the drama of the break away from the family and into American mass culture.

154. Ray Pratt, *Rhythm and Resistance: Explorations in the Political Uses of Popular Music* (New York: Praeger, 1990), 22.

155. *Musical America*, 29 March 1913: 27.

156. Howe, *World of our Fathers*, 558–559.

157. Woollcott, *Irving Berlin*, 6–7; see also Sanders, "American Popular Song," 197.

158. In Schwartz, *Gershwin*, 12. See also Edward Jablonski and Lawrence Stewart, *The Gershwin Years* (1958; Garden City, N.Y.: Doubleday, 1973), 33.

159. Schwartz, *Gershwin*, 12.

160. Diner, *In the Almost Promised Land*, 65.

161. On the importance of minstrel usages to Jewish performers, see Jenkins,

What Made Pistachio Nuts? 173–182; Geduld, *The Birth of the Talkies*, 147, 167; and Goldman, *Jolson.*

162. Goldman, *Jolson*, 58.

163. For Van Vechten, see Jablonski and Stewart, *Gershwin Years*, 22–24. See also Bud Freedman, as told to Robert Wolf, *Crazeology* (Chicago: U of Illinois P, 1989), 45.

164. Morgan and Barlow, *From Cakewalks to Concert Halls*, 69; Peyser, *Memory of All That*, 36.

165. Hamm, *Yesterdays*, 350.

166. Waldo, *This Is Ragtime*, 108.

167. Paul Rosenfeld quoted in Ewen, *George Gershwin*, 234; Hollis Alpert, *The Life and Times of Porgy and Bess: The Story of an American Classic* (New York: Knopf, 1990), 96.

168. Cruse, *Crisis of the Negro Intellectual*, 108.

169. Waldo, *This Is Ragtime*, 112–13; DuBose Heyward in Armitage, *George Gershwin*, 39.

170. Waldo, *This Is Ragtime*, 112–113; Walter Rimler, *A Gershwin Companion: A Critical Inventory and Discography, 1916–1984* (Ann Arbor: Popular Culture, Ink, 1991), 239–241; Peyser, *Memory of All That*, 105; Kanter, *Jews on Tin Pan Alley*, 125. Judith Grant Still, the daughter of the composer, corroborated her mother's claim, adding that her father spoke often of how Gershwin used to come up to Harlem to get ideas (Peyser, 43). Duke Ellington also suggested that Gershwin based a passage of his *Rhapsody in Blue* on the song "Where Has My Easy Rider Gone?" Quoted in Mark Tucker, ed., *The Duke Ellington Reader* (New York: Oxford UP, 1993), 115.

171. See Edward Berlin's account, originally published in 1991 as "Scott Joplin's *Treemonisha* Years," *American Music* 9.3 (1991): 260–276, esp. 267–268. This fine detective work is also incorporated into Berlin's 1994 biography of Joplin (*King of Ragtime*, 210–212).

172. Richard Hadlock, *Jazz Masters of the Twenties* (New York: Collier, 1965), 156.

173. Charters and Kunstadt, *Jazz*, 101; Schuller, *Early Jazz*, 340.

174. Schwartz, *Gershwin*, 32. Vodery, not surprisingly, is erased from the movie version of Gershwin's life: here it is Chico Marx who gets Gershwin the job. On *Blue Monday*, see Rosenberg, *Fascinating Rhythm*, 47. The patronage could go the other way as well: Gershwin helped Fats Waller land a job with CBS. See Maurice Waller and Anthony Calabrese, *Fats Waller* (New York: Schirmer, 1977), 164. On *Show Boat*, see Miles Kreuger's account of the same name (30). In 1993 a protest was

launched in Toronto against a revival of *Show Boat;* according to leaders of the action, the show made light of a painful period of African American history and represented one of many works created by Jews which malign African Americans. Clyde Farnsworth, "Blacks Accuse Jews," *New York Times,* 1 May 1993, 1:11.

175. Jablonski, *Harold Arlen,* 43.
176. Morgan and Barlow, *From Cakewalks to Concert Halls,* 40.
177. Sophie Tucker, with Dorothy Giles, *Some of These Days: The Autobiography of Sophie Tucker* (Garden City, N.Y.: Doubleday, Doran, 1943), 79, 82–84, 114–115. The African American singer Ethel Waters reports that Tucker not only came to see her act several times but also asked her for a singing lesson during the 1920s; see Waters, with Charles Samuels, *His Eye Is on the Sparrow: An Autobiography* (Garden City, N.Y.: Doubleday, 1951), 135; Giddins, *Riding on a Blue Note,* 5. Tucker has had little scholarly attention paid to her; two notable exceptions are Dawidoff, "Some of Those Days," and Erenberg, *Steppin' Out,* 176–205.
178. Grossman, *Funny Woman,* 39–40.
179. On the discovery of the "hillbilly" by the music industry, see Malone, *Country Music U.S.A.,* 31–75.

2. "I Used to Be Color Blind"

1. Nathan Belth, *A Promise to Keep: A Narrative of the American Encounter with Anti-Semitism* (1979; New York: Schocken, 1981), 23–26. One of the few times Jews did receive attention was during the Civil War, when they were temporarily kicked out of Tennessee.
2. Ann Douglas, *Terrible Honesty: Mongrel Manhattan in the 1920s* (New York: Farrar Straus and Giroux, 1995), 305.
3. Israel Zangwill, *The Melting Pot* (1909; New York: Macmillan, 1932); Werner Sollors, *Beyond Ethnicity: Consent and Descent in American Culture* (New York: Oxford UP, 1986), 92–101; Philip Gleason, "The Melting Pot: Symbol of Fusion or Confusion?" *American Quarterly* 16.1 (1964): 20–46.
4. One of the few extended ruminations on the issues raised by Jews in music is MacDonald Smith Moore, *Yankee Blues: Musical Culture and American Identity* (Bloomington: Indiana UP, 1985).
5. See, for instance, Sander Gilman, *Jewish Self-Hatred: Anti-Semitism and the Hidden Language of the Jews* (Baltimore: Johns Hopkins UP, 1986), 6–7, and *The Jew's Body* (New York: Routledge, 1991), 101.
6. The locus classicus for this position is Count Joseph Arthur de Go-

bineau's *Inequality of Human Races*, which had been published in a one-volume American edition in 1856 and, significantly, reprinted in a 1915 edition. William Stanton, *The Leopard's Spots: Scientific Attitudes toward Race in America, 1815–1819* (1960; Chicago: Midway/U of Chicago P, 1982), 174–175; See also Belth, *A Promise to Keep*, 29–31.

7. Henry Pratt Fairchild, *The Melting-Pot Mistake* (Boston: Little, Brown, 1926), 125.

8. Gilman, *Jewish Self-Hatred*, 274.

9. Quoted in Marcus Klein, *Foreigners: The Making of American Literature, 1900–1940* (Chicago: U of Chicago P, 1981), 255. In 1925 the *American Hebrew* reprinted an essay Lafcadio Hearn had written twenty years earlier on Shylock: "The truth is that the Jewish type proper disappeared with the demolition of the old *ghettos*; Jews are now Frenchmen, Germans, Americans or Englishmen, like their fellow-citizens,—nothing more." *American Hebrew*, 27 November 1925: 58.

10. Walter Benn Michaels, "Race into Culture: A Critical Genealogy of Cultural Identity," *Critical Inquiry* 18.4 (1992): 655–685.

11. Walter Benn Michaels, *Our America: Nativism, Modernism, and Pluralism* (Durham: Duke UP, 1995), 139.

12. I borrow "omni-Americans" from Albert Murray's book of that name, *The Omni-Americans: Black Experience and American Culture* (1970; New York: Vintage, 1983).

13. *Mammy* (1930), based on a story by Irving Berlin, and directed by Michael Curtiz, is now available on video.

14. I think Arnold Shaw is one of very few people to have (at least implicitly) made the argument that this Jewish cultural production was a direct rival to Harlem Renaissance productions. See Arnold Shaw, *The Jazz Age: Popular Music in the 1920's* (New York: Oxford UP, 1987).

15. Lewis Erenberg, *Steppin' Out: New York Nightlife and the Transformation of American Culture, 1890–1930* (1981; Chicago: U of Chicago P, 1984), 192.

16. Of course, as J. Hoberman notes, this debate on Jews was even more explicitly undertaken in the Soviet Union, where some tried to communicate the sense that "middleman" was indeed a productive role. J. Hoberman, *Bridge of Light: Yiddish Film between Two Worlds* (New York: Museum of Modern Art and Schocken, 1991), 171.

17. Willie the Lion Smith, with George Hoefer, *Music on My Mind: The Memoirs of an American Pianist* (1964; New York: Da Capo, 1978), 5, 246.

18. See Gilman, *Jewish Self-Hatred*, 209–210; see also "Jewish Jazz Becomes Our National Music," and "How the Jewish Song Trust Makes You

Sing," from the *Dearborn Independent*, reprinted in *Jewish Influences in American Life*, vol. 3 of *The International Jew: The World's Foremost Problem* (Dearborn, Mich.: Dearborn Publishing, 1921), 75–87; see also Eric Sundquist, *To Wake the Nations: Race in the Making of American Literature* (Cambridge, Mass.: Harvard UP, 1993), 254.

19. Isaac Deutscher, *The Non-Jewish Jew and Other Essays* (New York: Oxford UP, 1968), 27. This formulation has not been the sole property of Marxists, nor has its only subject been Jews. Its basic tenets run through Gloria Anzaldúa's *Borderlands/La Frontera: The New Mestiza* (San Francisco: Aunt Lute, 1987).

20. Thorstein Veblen, "The Intellectual Pre-eminence of Jews in Modern Europe," in Max Lerner, ed., *The Portable Veblen* (1919; New York: Viking, 1950), 474–475, 478.

21. Robert Park, "Human Migration and the Marginal Man," in Everett Cherrington Hughes et al., eds., *Race and Culture* (1928; Glencoe, Ill.: Free Press, 1950), 354. Park hangs his notion of Jew as "marginal man" on the hook of Georg Simmel's sociological formation of the "stranger." See Georg Simmel, "The Stranger," in Donald Levine, ed., *On Individuality and Social Forms* (Chicago: U of Chicago P, 1971), 143–149.

22. As Gerald Early makes clear, the stakes in this cultural work were enormous: the central question being negotiated through music was how the American self was going to be defined racially. See Gerald Early, "Pulp and Circumstance: The Story of Jazz in High Places," in *The Culture of Bruising: Essays on Prizefighting, Literature, and Modern American Culture* (Hopewell, N.J.: Ecco, 1994), 163–205, esp. 185.

23. Sollors, *Beyond Ethnicity*, 66–101, esp. 87–88; Gleason, "Melting Pot."

24. Sollors, *Beyond Ethnicity*, 64; and see his essay "A Critique of Pure Pluralism," in Sacvan Bercovitch, ed., *Reconstructing American Literary History* (Cambridge, Mass.: Harvard UP, 1986), 258–263.

25. Jules Chametzky, "Beyond Melting Pots, Cultural Pluralism, Ethnicity—or, *Déjà Vu* All Over Again," *MELUS* 16.4 (Winter 1989–90): 10; see also Gleason, "Melting Pot," 20–46.

26. Horace Kallen, "Democracy *versus* the Melting-Pot," *The Nation*, 18 and 25 February 1915: 190–194, 217–220.

27. James Weldon Johnson, *The Book of American Negro Poetry* (1922; New York: Harvest/HBJ, 1969), 11.

28. George Gershwin, "Composer in the Machine Age," in Merle Armitage, ed., *George Gershwin* (New York; Longmans, Green, 1938), 225.

29. See Berndt Ostendorf, "Anthropology, Modernism, and Jazz," in Robert O'Meally, ed., *New Essays on Invisible Man* (New York: Cambridge UP,

1988), 165. Perhaps the apotheosis of this strand of the story came with the worldwide tour of *Porgy and Bess* in the 1950s, sponsored by the State Department: one supporter of this undertaking argued that *Porgy and Bess* was "the best darned cultural ambassador we have ever sent abroad." On *Porgy and Bess* as ambassador, see the clipping from the *New York Times*, 26 April 1953, in the Harvard University Theatre Collection file on the opera. On the world tours of *Porgy and Bess*, the fullest account is in Hollis Alpert, *The Life and Times of Porgy and Bess: The Story of an American Classic* (New York: Knopf, 1990). For more personalized ac-counts, see Maya Angelou, *Singin' and Swingin' and Gettin' Merry Like Christmas* (1976; New York: Bantam, 1981); and Truman Capote, *The Muses Are Heard* (New York: Random House, 1956). Capote's book offers a more equivocal vision of the *Porgy and Bess* tour than does Angelou's, but includes at least one rave reaction from a Soviet spectator: "Powerful! Like Jack London. Like Gogol" (174).

30. Edward Said, *Musical Elaborations* (New York: Columbia UP, 1991), 53.
31. George Pullen Jackson, *White and Negro Spirituals: Their Life Span and Kinship* (Locust Valley, N.Y.: J. J. Augustin, 1943), esp. 141–227; Lawrence Levine, *Black Culture and Black Consciousness: Afro-American Folk Thought from Slavery to Freedom* (New York: Oxford UP, 1977), 19–30.
32. Werner Sollors, "Intermarriage and Mulattoes in the 1920s," *Rivista di Studi Anglo-Americani* 5 (1989): 209–287.
33. On the Paul Whiteman rumor, see Henry Osgood, *So This Is Jazz* (Boston: Little, Brown, 1926), 125. The sociologist Irving Louis Horowitz repeats this mistake in a memoir of his own youth in Harlem, *Daydreams and Nightmares: Reflections of a Harlem Childhood* (Jackson: UP of Mississippi, 1990), 3.
34. Isaac Goldberg, *George Gershwin: A Study in American Music* (1931; New York: Frederick Ungar, 1958), 139; David Ewen, *George Gershwin: His Journey to Greatness* (1956; New York: Ungar, 1980), 85.
35. Michael Rogin makes a similar point about Paul Whiteman's emancipa-tion of jazz in *Blackface, White Noise: Jewish Immigrants in the Hollywood Melting Pot* (Berkeley: U of California P, 1996), 138.
36. *The Nation*, 5 March 1924: 263.
37. Merle Armitage, *George Gershwin: Man and Legend* (New York: Duell, Sloan and Pearce, 1958), 44.
38. In Edward Jablonski, ed., *Gershwin Remembered* (Portland, Ore.: Amadeus, 1992), 107.
39. See Mezz Mezzrow and Bernard Wolfe, *Really the Blues* (1946; New

York: Citadel Underground, 1990), 49. On Fanny Brice, see Norman Katkov, *The Fabulous Fanny: The Story of Fanny Brice* (New York: Alfred A. Knopf, 1953), 205. Here Katkov recounts that Brice told Billy Rose (theater impresario and onetime husband of Brice) that "I never did a Jewish song that would offend the race, because it depended on the race for the laughs. In anything Jewish I ever did, I wasn't standing apart, making fun of the race, I *was* the race, and what happened to me on the stage is what could happen to them."

40. Armitage, *George Gershwin*, 49, 45.

41. Constant Lambert, *Music Ho! A Study of Music in Decline* (1934; London: Faber and Faber, 1947), 158.

42. Quoted in Joan Peyser, *The Memory of All That: The Life of George Gershwin* (New York: Simon and Schuster, 1993), 248–249; Alpert, *Porgy and Bess*, 118; Charles Schwartz, *Gershwin: His Life and Music* (New York: Da Capo, 1973), 245. Matthews's review, which calls Gershwin's work less accomplished than *Green Pastures*, is in the *Baltimore Afro-American*, 19 October 1935: 8. Hall Johnson's opinion is cited in the *New York Times*, 3 April 1983, clipping found in Harvard University Theatre Collection file on *Porgy and Bess*. It should be noted that Gershwin was not the only Jew to try his hand at such an undertaking; in 1925 Richard Rodgers and Lorenz Hart wrote a "jazz opera" for inclusion in *The Garrick Gaieties*. Cited in Gerald Bordman, *American Musical Theater: A Chronicle* (New York: Oxford UP, 1978), 401.

43. For the Duke Ellington and Morrow quotations, see Mark Tucker, ed., *The Duke Ellington Reader* (New York: Oxford UP, 1993), 115. See also Peyser, *Memory of All That*, 251; Alpert, *Porgy and Bess*, 121; and Schwartz, *Gershwin*, 245.

44. See *Baltimore Afro-American*, 14 December 1935: 9. This article is titled "Burnt Cork Is All Washed Up on Broadway, Writer Reveals." Rudi Blesh, *Shining Trumpets: A History of Jazz* (1946; New York: Knopf, 1955), 204–205.

45. S. A. Ansky, was a pseudonym for Solomon Rappaport (1863–1920). Schwartz, *Gershwin* 27. Irving Howe, with the assistance of Kenneth Libo, *World of Our Fathers* (New York: Touchstone/Simon and Schuster, 1976), 492. See also Edward Jablonski, *Gershwin: A Biography* (Boston: Northeastern UP, 1987), 194–195; Ewen, *George Gershwin*, xxii.

46. Introduction to S. Ansky, *The Dybbuk and Other Writings*, ed. David Roskies, trans. Golda Werman (New York: Schocken, 1992), xxvi.

47. Jablonski, *Gershwin*, 196.

48. Oscar Levant, *A Smattering of Ignorance* (New York: Doubleday, Doran,

1940), 182. See similarly Ewen, *George Gershwin*, xxii. This biographer argues that even if Gershwin had had clear access to the Ansky play, he "would soon have come to the realization that as a creative artist he was incapable of responding to subject matter so remote from his own sphere of experience." "Fortunately," Ewen concludes, Gershwin "soon came upon DuBose Heyward's *Porgy*."

49. Ronald Sanders, "The American Popular Song," in Douglas Villiers, ed., *Next Year in Jerusalem: Portraits of the Jew in the Twentieth Century* (New York: Viking, 1976), 202. Irving Howe instead argues for the importance of the Old World–New World breach: to Howe, the Jews in America were good at pastiche because they did not care at all about American ideals of art and so on. Howe, *World of Our Fathers*, 561.

50. Berndt Ostendorf, "The Musical World of Doctorow's *Ragtime*," *American Quarterly* 43.4 (1991): 586. See similarly Laurence Bergreen, *As Thousands Cheer: The Life of Irving Berlin* (New York: Viking, 1990), 47.

51. Edward Berlin, "Ragtime Songs," in John Edward Hasse, ed., *Ragtime: Its History, Composers, and Music* (New York: Schirmer, 1985), 75–76.

52. The long-running show *Abie's Irish Rose* typified the "ethnicity as one happy gag" approach. See James Dormon, "American Popular Culture and the New Immigration Ethnics: The Vaudeville Stage and the Process of Ethnic Ascription," *Amerikastudien* 36.2 (1991): 179–193.

53. Irving Berlin, *The Songs of Irving Berlin*, vol. 3 (Miami Lakes, Fla.: Masters Music, n.d.), 3–7.

54. Irving Berlin, *The Songs of Irving Berlin*, vol. 1 (Miami Lakes, Fla.: Masters Music, n.d.), 15–17; see also Kenneth Kanter, *The Jews on Tin Pan Alley: The Jewish Contribution to American Popular Music, 1830–1940* (New York: Ktav/Cincinnati: American Jewish Archives, 1982), 137.

55. Goldberg, *George Gershwin*, 275.

56. Samuel Charters and Leonard Kunstadt, *Jazz: A History of the New York Scene* (1962; New York: Da Capo, 1981), 276; Paul Oliver, Max Harrison, and William Bolcom, ed., *The New Grove Gospel, Blues, and Jazz with Spirituals and Ragtime* (New York: Norton, 1986), 256–257.

57. In Klein, *Foreigners*, 110.

58. Jablonski, *Gershwin*, 136–137; Deena Rosenberg, *Fascinating Rhythm: The Collaboration of George and Ira Gershwin* (New York: Dutton, 1991), 127.

59. This Irving Berlin quotation is from a 1915 *Green Book Magazine* interview quoted in Berlin, "Ragtime Songs," 77.

60. This is from a 1920 interview in *American Magazine* quoted in Ian

Whitcomb, *Irving Berlin and Ragtime America* (New York: Limelight Editions, 1988), 15.

61. Quoted in Gerald Bordman, *Jerome Kern: His Life and Music* (New York: Oxford UP, 1980), 343.

62. Edmund Wilson, *I Thought of Daisy* (New York: Scribner's, 1929), 289.

63. Quoted in Philip Furia, *The Poets of Tin Pan Alley: A History of America's Great Lyricists* (New York: Oxford UP, 1990), 155.

64. Thomas Gossett, *Race: The History of an Idea in America* (1965; New York: Schocken, 1971), 404–408; John Higham, *Strangers in the Land: Patterns of American Nativism, 1860–1925* (1955; New York: Atheneum, 1977), 324.

65. Robert Singerman, "The Jew as Racial Alien: The Genetic Component of American Anti-Semitism," in David Gerber, ed., *Anti-Semitism in American History* (Chicago: U of Illinois P, 1987), 120.

66. Rabbi Joel Blau succinctly described Jews in 1922 as "out of the Ghetto, but . . . nowhere in particular," in "The Modern Pharisee," *Atlantic Monthly* 129 (January 1922): 10. This article deserves attention as a full, focused expression of religious anti-assimilationism. Daringly taking on the immigration restrictionists, Blau reminds his readers that as a minority people, Jews are "more mongrelized than mongrelizing" (9).

67. Gabriel Miller, Introduction, in Samuel Ornitz, *Allrightniks Row (Haunch Paunch and Jowl: The Making of a Professional Jew)* (1923; New York: Markus Wiener, 1985), xix–xx. The original edition was *Haunch Paunch and Jowl: An Anonymous Autobiography* (New York: Boni and Liveright, 1923). All references to this source will be made parenthetically in the text.

68. This information was supplied in telephone conversations with Gabriel Miller, 5 December 1991, and Markus Wiener, 13 December 1991.

69. Quoted in Miller, Introduction, xii, xix.

70. Eileen Southern, *The Music of Black Americans: A History* (1971; New York: Norton, 1983), 329.

71. On boundary formation as a key component of ethnic development, see Frederik Barth, Introduction, in *Ethnic Groups and Boundaries: The Social Organization of Cultural Difference* (Boston: Little, Brown, 1969), 9–38.

72. Allen Guttmann, *The Jewish Writer in America: Assimilation and the Crisis of Identity* (New York: Oxford UP, 1971), 35.

73. Miller, Introduction, xiii; Louis Harap, *Creative Awakening: The Jewish Presence in Twentieth-Century American Literature* (Westport, Conn.: Greenwood, in cooperation with the American Jewish Archives, 1987), 50–52.

74. For a still valuable account of the Yiddish theater, see Hutchins Hapgood, *The Spirit of the Ghetto*, ed. Moses Rischin (1902; Cambridge, Mass.: Belknap/Harvard UP, 1967), 124–176; for the influence of Yiddish theater on Gershwin, see Schwartz, *Gershwin*, 24–27.

75. Howard Eilberg-Schwartz, *The Savage in Judaism: An Anthropology of Israelite Religion and Ancient Judaism* (Bloomington: Indiana UP, 1990), 130–132.

76. Ibid., 131.

77. For a much different reading of Ornitz, see Rachel Rubin, "Reading, Writing, and the Rackets: Jewish Gangsters in Interwar Russian and American Narrative" (Ph.D. diss., Yale University, 1995).

78. Sophie Tucker, with Dorothy Giles, *Some of These Days: The Autobiography of Sophie Tucker* (Garden City, N.Y.: Doubleday, Doran, 1943), 82; Mark Slobin, *Tenement Songs: The Popular Music of the Jewish Immigrants* (Chicago: U of Illinois P, 1982), 49–63; on the "coon" song craze in general, see James Dormon, "Shaping the Popular Image of Post-Reconstruction American Blacks: The 'Coon Song' Phenomenon of the Gilded Age," *American Quarterly* 40.4 (1988): 450–471.

79. Tucker, *Some of These Days*, 90. As I have noted, Berndt Ostendorf explains that for a while ragtime was simply incorporated into minstrelsy, in "Musical World of Doctorow's *Ragtime*," 591.

80. William Schafer and Johannes Riedel argue that the adoption of the "coon" song format by African American composers was a strategically defensive move rather than the expression of self-hate others have taken it for. Nonetheless they admit that even in these songs African American men are generally portrayed as lazy, stupid, helpless, sly, and murderous, while African American women are shown to be desirable, malicious, and promiscuous. See William Schafer and Johannes Riedel, *The Art of Ragtime: Form and Meaning of an Original Black American Art* (Baton Rouge: Louisiana State UP, 1973), 17, 25.

81. Luc Sante, *Low Life: Lures and Snares of Old New York* (New York: Vintage, 1991), 207.

82. The demonstration of Irish-Jewish sympathy would have had an enormous resonance when Ornitz's book came out in 1923: one year earlier, *Abie's Irish Rose*, with its Jewish-Irish intermarriage plot, had opened in New York to huge success. Isaac Goldberg was perhaps the only contemporary commentator who attempted to draw connections between Jews, Irish, and African Americans: "Between Negro and Irishman, between Irishman and Jew, between Jew and Negro, stretch subtle bonds of sympathy that unite them under the surface tension of racial . . . antipa-

thies." Isaac Goldberg, *Tin Pan Alley: A Chronicle of the American Popular Music Racket* (New York: John Day, 1930), 34.

83. Bergreen, *As Thousands Cheer*, 21–29.

84. Sidney Finkelstein, *Jazz: A People's Music* (1948; New York: International, 1988).

85. Maxim Gorky, "Fat Men's Music," in *Articles and Pamphlets* (1928; Moscow: Foreign Language Publishing House, 1951), 161–162; Theodor Adorno, "On the Fetish Character in Music and the Regression of Listening," in Andrew Arato and Eike Gebhardt, eds., *The Essential Frankfurt School Reader* (New York: Continuum, 1988), 271.

86. Max Horkheimer and Theodor Adorno, "The Culture Industry: Enlightenment as Mass Deception," in *Dialectic of Enlightenment*, trans. John Cumming (1944; New York: Continuum, 1989), 127.

87. Michael Kater, *Different Drummers: Jazz in the Culture of Nazi Germany* (New York: Oxford UP, 1992), 20, 33.

88. With this episode it seems possible that Ornitz was thinking about the popular ragtime song "When Rag-time Rosie Ragged the Rosary." For a mention of this number, see Mark Sullivan, *Our Times: The United States, 1900–1925*, vol. 4 (New York: Scribner's, 1932), 250.

89. It is interesting to note here that just as Irish stage performers provided Jews with an example of how Blackness might be manipulated for gain, so too (according to Ornitz) did Irish civic leaders give Jews a lesson in urban politics.

90. Rubin, "Reading, Writing, and the Rackets."

91. On the various diseases assigned to Jews down through the ages, see Sander Gilman's work, especially *Difference and Pathology: Stereotypes of Sexuality, Race, and Madness* (Ithaca: Cornell UP, 1985), and *The Jew's Body*.

92. Sol Liptzin, *The Jew in American Literature* (New York: Bloch, 1966), 132.

3. "Swanee Ripples"

1. Deborah Dash Moore, *At Home in America: Second Generation New York Jews* (New York: Columbia UP, 1981), 7.

2. Ishmael Reed, *Reckless Eyeballing* (1986; New York: Atheneum, 1988), 67.

3. David Roediger, *Towards the Abolition of Whiteness: Essays on Race, Politics, and Working Class History* (New York: Verso, 1994), 191.

4. Sander Gilman, *The Jew's Body* (New York: Routledge, 1991), 172–174.

5. Michael Gold, *Jews without Money* (1930; New York: Carroll and Graf, 1984), esp. 36–37.

6. Ibid., 42.

7. "Eight Ball, the boys called him, or Nigger or Coke or Dope Schmug-guggle, because of his odd gait, his squat bulk, the unnatural heaviness of his features." See Daniel Fuchs, *Low Company*, in *Three Novels* (New York: Basic Books, 1961), 253.

8. Jenna Weissman Joselit, *Our Gang: Jewish Crime and the New York Jewish Community, 1900–1940* (Bloomington: Indiana UP, 1983), 39, 52.

9. Albert Fried, *The Rise and Fall of the Jewish Gangster in America* (New York: Holt, Rinehart and Winston, 1980), 35, 116; Willie the Lion Smith, with George Hoefer, *Music on My Mind: The Memoirs of an American Pianist* (1964; New York: Da Capo, 1978), 21.

10. Fried, *Rise and Fall of the Jewish Gangster*, 195.

11. See, for instance, Gilman, *Jew's Body*, 99–101. James Axtell, "The White Indians of Colonial America," *William and Mary Quarterly* 32.1 (1975): 88. With a few minor adjustments, Axtell's description of "white Indians" could apply to the twentieth-century practice of white Negroism: "They stayed because they found Indian life to possess a strong sense of community, abundant love, and uncommon integrity."

12. David Roediger, *The Wages of Whiteness: Race and the Making of the American Working Class* (New York: Verso, 1991), esp. 144–150.

13. Robert Orsi, "The Religious Boundaries of an Inbetween People: Street *Feste* and the Problem of the Dark-Skinned Other in Italian Harlem, 1920–1990," *American Quarterly* 44.3 (1992): 315–318; see also Arnold Shankman, *Ambivalent Friends: Afro-Americans View the Immigrant* (Westport, Conn.: Greenwood, 1982), 83–110.

14. Leslie Fiedler, "Negro and Jew: Encounter in America," in *No! In Thunder: Essays on Myth and Literature* (Boston: Beacon, 1960), 248.

15. I should note here that I have encountered only one example where the nickname "Nigger" seems to have been self-chosen. The Yiddish critic Samuel Charney wrote under the pen name "Nigger." Although his last name is the Russian word for "black," Charney was obviously making a comment, with his choice of pseudonym, on the affiliations of Russian Jews and African Americans. I am indebted to Rachel Rubin for calling my attention to this example, and for explaining the significance of the translation from Russian.

16. George Devereux and Edwin Loeb, "Antagonistic Acculturation," *American Sociological Review* 8.2 (April 1943): 133–147.

17. Thanks to Ruth Feldstein for her help on this issue.

18. Alexander Woollcott, *The Story of Irving Berlin* (New York: G. P. Putnam's Sons, 1925), 40, 61. Ian Whitcomb also discusses Salter's physiognomy, adding the racist tidbit that it was not only his face but his "simian" build too which earned him this nickname. Ian Whitcomb, *Irving Berlin and Ragtime America* (New York: Limelight Editions, 1988), 27.

19. Isaac Goldberg, *Tin Pan Alley: A Chronicle of the American Popular Music Racket* (New York: John Day, 1930), 293.

20. The "Blackness" of the Jew sometimes appeared in less highly-charged exchanges. Max Kaminsky relates bringing Billie Holiday home to meet his mother, who immediately said to the great singer, "Why, you look just like my Betty!" In Max Kaminsky, with V.E. Hughes, *My Life in Jazz* (New York: Harper and Row, 1963), 105.

21. Samson Raphaelson, *The Jazz Singer* (New York: Brentano's, 1925), 9.

22. Robert Snyder makes the suggestion, which I have not seen elsewhere, that part of the costume of the comic stage Jew was yellow greasepaint. According to Snyder, Irish figures would don red paint, and Sicilians used an olive color. Robert Snyder, *Voice of the City: Vaudeville and Popular Culture in New York* (New York: Oxford UP, 1989), 111.

23. Michael Rogin, *Blackface, White Noise: Jewish Immigrants in the Hollywood Melting Pot* (Berkeley: U of California P, 1996), 73–120. Here, Rogin argues that *The Jazz Singer* was the swan song of Jews on-screen for years.

24. Robert Carringer, ed., Introduction, in *The Jazz Singer* (Madison: U of Wisconsin P, 1979), 14. That such a number could be arrived at tells us something about the visibility—whether in physiognomy or consumer habits—of Jews at this moment.

25. Clippings from the *Sun* (New York), 15 September 1925, and *Herald Tribune* (New York), 16 September 1925, both found in the Harvard University Theatre Collection file on *The Jazz Singer*.

26. A 1927 revival of the play evidently drew a more mixed audience, a large portion of whom tended to "giggle at every manifestation of East Side Yiddish idiom." Clippings from the *Boston Transcript*, 7 September 1926 and 15 November 1927, in the Harvard University Theatre Collection file on *The Jazz Singer*.

27. Henry Jenkins has carefully demonstrated that movie studios had some difficulty marketing Broadway entertainments and performers because they were so obviously marked with New York ethnic affect. See Henry Jenkins, *What Made Pistachio Nuts? Early Sound Comedy and the Vaudeville Aesthetic* (New York: Columbia UP, 1992), 153–184.

28. Carl Wittke, writing in 1930, suggested that blackface minstrelsy's end could be dated to 1924 with the death of Lew Dockstader, "star and sole proprietor of Lew Dockstader's Minstrels." Carl Wittke, *Tambo and Bones: A History of the American Minstrel Stage* (Durham: Duke UP, 1930), 111.

29. Eric Lott, *Love and Theft: Blackface Minstrelsy and the American Working Class* (New York: Oxford UP, 1993), 38–62; Ella Shohat, "Ethnicities-in-Relation: Toward a Multicultural Reading of American Cinema," in Lester Friedman, ed., *Unspeakable Images: Ethnicity and the American Cinema* (Chicago: U of Illinois P, 1991), 229.

30. Raphaelson, *Jazz Singer*, 9–10.

31. Ludwig Lewisohn, *Up Stream: An American Chronicle* (New York: Boni and Liveright, 1922), 237–239. Here Lewisohn bemoans the fate of the immigrant son who reads the yellow press and loves Irving Berlin.

32. See also Gold, *Jews without Money*, 112.

33. The action I am most concerned with here can be found in Raphaelson, *Jazz Singer*, 63–68.

34. See, for instance, Stuart Berg Flexner, *I Hear America Talking: An Illustrated Treasury of American Words and Phrases* (New York: Van Nostrand Reinhold, 1976), 57.

35. Raphaelson, *Jazz Singer*, 152–153.

36. Perhaps the most important effect was as a training ground for classic blues performers such as W. C. Handy and Ma Rainey.

37. On Brice, see Barbara Grossman, *Funny Woman: The Life and Times of Fanny Brice* (Bloomington: Indiana UP, 1991), 46. For the quotation from the *Telegraph*, see James Dormon "American Popular Culture and the New Immigration Ethnics: The Vaudeville Stage and the Process of Ethnic Ascription," *Amerikastudien* 36.2 (1991): 183. Dormon also provides much excellent analysis of the stage Jew more generally.

38. Brice's visible Jewishness became a major media issue in 1923, when she had a nose job. In its coverage of the event, the *New York Times* remarked that after her rhinoplasty Brice now had a "normal" nose. But speculation soon developed that Brice, having lost her easiest sight gag, would never be as funny as she had been before the nose job. See Grossman, *Funny Woman*, 147–150.

39. In this guise Jewish blackface performers, as Michael Rogin argues in *Blackface, White Noise* (esp. 12–13, 112), certainly were using the mask of blackness as part of a claim for their own whiteness, which was predicated on erasing or persecuting African Americans.

40. Rogin, "Blackface, White Noise: The Jewish Jazz Singer Finds His Voice," *Critical Inquiry* 18.3 (1992): 430.

41. Ibid., 441.

42. The Leo Frank case of 1913–1915 was a prime example of the contested status of the Jew's whiteness. See my 1994 Harvard University dissertation, "Ancestors and Relatives: The Uncanny Relationship of African Americans and Jews." It was certainly common through at least the 1930s to make distinctions betweens Jews and other whites.

43. Lott, *Love and Theft*, esp. 111–135.

44. *Jewish Tribune and Hebrew Standard*, 30 September 1927: 3. Herbert Goldman, *Jolson: The Legend Comes to Life* (New York: Oxford UP, 1988), 36. According to Goldman, Jolson's career did not really take off until he put on blackface.

45. Sophie Tucker, with Dorothy Giles, *Some of These Days: The Autobiography of Sophie Tucker* (Garden City, N.Y.: Doubleday, Doran, 1943), 33.

46. Eddie Cantor, as told to David Freedman, *My Life Is in Your Hands* (New York: Harper, 1928), 114. Rogin, "Blackface, White Noise," called my attention to this source.

47. Cantor, *My Life Is in Your Hands*, 122, 159; Goldman, *Jolson*, 61; Tucker, *Some of These Days*; Irving Howe, with the assistance of Kenneth Libo, *World of Our Fathers* (New York: Touchstone/Simon and Schuster, 1976), 562. Edward Marks commented on actual gay men in the profession in 1934, noting with revulsion that in "show business today the flowery name of 'pansy' makes the 'fairy' acceptable. His presence is tolerated and his antics and follies are regarded as highly amusing. In the old days that class of performer was not welcomed." Edward Marks, as told to Abbott Liebling, *They All Sang: From Tony Pastor to Rudy Vallee* (New York: Viking, 1934), 56. Along the same lines was a song written by Billy Rose in 1930 called "When a Pansy Was a Flower." Cited in Gerald Bordman, *American Musical Theater: A Chronicle* (New York: Oxford UP, 1978), 465. On the "pansy craze," see George Chauncey, *Gay New York: Gender, Urban Culture, and the Making of the Gay Male World, 1890–1940* (New York: Basic Books, 1994), 300–329.

48. Cantor, *My Life Is in Your Hands*, 159 and picture between 50 and 51.

49. Chauncey, *Gay New York*, 310.

50. Tucker, *Some of These Days*, 61–63.

51. Cantor, *My Life Is in Your Hands*, 144.

52. Ibid., 186–187.

53. Robert Dawidoff, "Some of Those Days," *Western Humanities Review* 41.3 (1987): 263–286.

54. We might say that this move out of blackface parallels, or prefigures, the relocation of the center of America's entertainment industry from Jewish New York to Christian Los Angeles. See Lenny Bruce, *The Essential Lenny Bruce*, ed. John Cohen (New York: Ballantine, 1967), 41; and Neal Gabler, *An Empire of Their Own: How the Jews Invented Hollywood* (New York: Crown, 1981).

55. This quotation, from the *New York Times* in 1930, is cited in Jenkins, *What Made Pistachio Nuts?* 153.

56. Ibid., 182; see similarly Charles Musser, "Ethnicity, Role-playing, and American Film Comedy: From *Chinese Laundry Scene* to *Whoopee* (1894–1930)," in Friedman, *Unspeakable Images*, 70.

57. Goldman, *Jolson*, 48; Howe, *World of Our Fathers*, 563. Both of these accounts come from testimony by the performers themselves and should be taken not as "false" but as important components of their public self-making.

58. Goldman, *Jolson*, 115.

59. Tucker, *Some of These Days*, 275. Did Jean Paul Sartre think Sophie Tucker was an African American? In *Nausea* the narrator recounts listening to "Some of These Days" and having his disquiet momentarily eased by the voice of "the Negress." There were other recorded versions of the song he could be referring to, but Tucker's was the most famous. In Sartre's work Roquentin imagines that the song he hears is sung by a "Negress" but written by a Jew "with coal-black eyebrows." Jean-Paul Sartre, *Nausea* (1938), trans. Robert Baldrick (New York: Penguin, 1986), 38, 250. On this issue, see Dawidoff, "Some of Those Days."

60. Laurence Bergreen, *As Thousands Cheer: The Life of Irving Berlin* (New York: Viking, 1990), 56–57.

61. I am grateful to Paul Franklin for helping me think about this issue.

62. Albert Lindemann, *The Jew Accused: Three Anti-Semitic Affairs (Dreyfus, Beilis, Frank), 1894–1915* (New York: Cambridge UP, 1991), 174–193. Beilis was ultimately cleared and finally emigrated to Palestine, and then to the United States.

63. Barbara Miller Solomon, *Ancestors and Immigrants: A Changing New England Tradition* (1956; Boston: Northeastern UP, 1989), 167–175.

64. Bergreen, *As Thousands Cheer*, 245–275. Mary Ellin Barrett, *Irving Berlin: A Daughter's Memoir* (New York: Simon and Schuster, 1994), 43.

65. Whitcomb, *Irving Berlin*, 81; Bergreen, *As Thousands Cheer*, 269–270.

66. Quoted from the April 1916 issue in Bergreen, *As Thousands Cheer*, 69.

67. Ibid., 70; Edward Berlin, *Reflections and Research on Ragtime* (Brooklyn: Institute for Studies in American Music, Brooklyn College of the City University of New York, 1987), 42.

68. Barry Singer, *Black and Blue: The Life and Lyrics of Andy Razaf* (New York: Schirmer, 1992), 334–337.

69. Max Wilk, *They're Playing Our Song: From Jerome Kern to Stephen Sondheim—The Stories behind the Words and Music of Two Generations* (New York: Atheneum, 1973), 272.

70. Singer, *Black and Blue*, 334–335.

71. Paul Franklin, "Homosexual Jew(el)ry: Homophobia and Anti-Semitism in the Prosecution of 'Babe' Leopold and 'Dickie' Loeb," paper delivered at the 1993 American Studies Association Conference, Boston; Marjorie Garber, *Vested Interests: Cross-Dressing and Cultural Anxiety* (New York: Routledge, 1992), 224–232; Gilman, *Jew's Body*, 53–55. This was not only an anti-Semitic line of attack on Jews; it was also of concern to certain Zionists (especially Max Nordau) who were trying to imagine a new, more physical Jewish man.

72. See, for instance, Michael Selzer, ed., *"Kike!"* (New York: Meridian/World, 1972), 30–31, 36–37.

73. Robert Dawidoff, "The Kind of Person You Have to Sound Like in Order to Sing 'Alexander's Ragtime Band,'" 13, manuscript in author's possession.

74. Seymour Krim, *Views of a Nearsighted Cannoneer* (New York: Excelsior, 1961), 40.

75. Norman Mailer, "The White Negro," originally published in 1957, is most easily found in *Advertisements for Myself* (New York: G. P. Putnam's, 1959), 315.

76. Andrew Ross, *No Respect: Intellectuals and Popular Culture* (New York: Routledge, 1989), 79, 82, and 65–101 more generally.

77. Krim, *Views of a Nearsighted Cannoneer*, 51.

78. Ioan Davies, in an interesting essay on Lenny Bruce, rightly argues that the label "white Negro" should really have been expanded to "Jewish White Male Negro." Ioan Davies, "Lenny Bruce: Hyperrealism and the Death of Jewish Tragic Humor," *Social Text* 22 (1989): 107.

79. Ross, *No Respect*, 96.

80. I am relying on memory here, and the exact wording might be slightly different than I have indicated. But if I do remember correctly, Charlie also wore a beret and bebop glasses (as he continues to on current-day

labels of the product), which would place him exactly in the cultural milieu which Mailer and others evoked.

81. Of course I intend to suggest here not that stage blackface depended solely on visual cues, but rather that this was an effective starting point for dramas of identification and distance. The most famous example is probably Milton "Mezz" Mezzrow, who appended a glossary of slang to his autobiography. See Milton "Mezz" Mezzrow and Bernard Wolfe, *Really the Blues* (1946; New York: Citadel Underground, 1990).

82. On Smith, see my essay "A Black Man in Jewface," in Josef Jarab and Jeffrey Melnick, eds., *Race and the Modernist Artist* (forthcoming, Oxford UP). Mezzrow and Smith knew and played music with each other.

83. Mezzrow and Wolfe, *Really the Blues*, 49. "Hamfat," incidentally, appears to have derived from minstrelsy. According to Isaac Goldberg, before the advent of greasepaint, ham fat was used by minstrels to coat their faces before applying burnt cork; in turn, all third-rate actors came to be known as "hamfats." Perhaps for Mezzrow this was another way of saying "not kosher." Goldberg, *Tin Pan Alley*, 38.

84. This letter, dated 15 June 1931 can be found in the Gershwin file at the Harvard University Theatre Collection.

85. Joan Peyser, *The Memory of All That: The Life of George Gershwin* (New York: Simon and Schuster, 1993), 237; Isaac Goldberg, *George Gershwin: A Study in American Music* (1931; New York: Frederick Ungar, 1958), 41.

86. Hollis Alpert, *The Life and Times of Porgy and Bess: The Story of an American Classic* (New York: Knopf, 1990) 71. As late as 1933 a columnist in the *New York Evening Post* wondered whether the musical version of Porgy would feature a Negro company "or a white mammy singer, such as Mr. Jolson." See clipping from 3 November 1933 in the Harvard University Theatre Collection file on *Porgy and Bess*. In 1932 Gershwin suggested to Heyward that it might be good for the playwright to get Jerome Kern and Oscar Hammerstein II to work on a musical version of his play (Alpert, 74).

87. DuBose Heyward, "Porgy and Bess Returns on Wings of a Song," *Stage Magazine*, October 1935. I have relied on a reprint in Merle Armitage, ed., *George Gershwin* (New York: Longmans, Green, 1938), 35. A few years earlier Gershwin had written to Heyward that he was planning to be in Charleston and hoped to hear some spirituals "and perhaps go to a colored cafe or two if there are any." Quoted in Alpert, *Porgy and Bess*, 79.

88. Lott, *Love and Theft*, 94. Other Jews were more willing to publicize the fact that African American materials were available in their own back-

yard; Fanny Brice, in the middle of an argument with a theater producer about how to sing a "coon" song, insisted that she knew better because she lived on 128th Street, which was "the edge of Harlem." The man in question was Abraham Lincoln Erlanger. Quoted in Grossman, *Funny Woman*, 41.

89. For Mailer's original pronouncements, see his "White Negro." For another important, if neglected, statement of Jewish white Negroism, see Krim, *Views of a Nearsighted Cannoneer*. Of course the fullest expression in practice is the life and work of Mezz Mezzrow, discussed later in this chapter. I should note, too, that the ritual of immersion in authentic "Blackness" is not limited to Jews, or even whites. The "descent" into the Black South is a familiar move in books as diverse as W. E. B. Du Bois's *The Souls of Black Folk*, James Weldon Johnson's *The Autobiography of an Ex-Colored Man*, and Jean Toomer's *Cane*.

90. I was helped substantially in thinking about what it means to "go native" by Marianna Torgovnick's *Gone Primitive: Savage Intellects, Modern Lives* (Chicago: U of Chicago P, 1990), 3–41.

91. Henry Botkin was the brother of Benjamin Botkin, the folklorist. Alpert, *Porgy and Bess*, 88; Charles Schwartz, *Gershwin: His Life and Music* (New York: Da Capo, 1973), 316n24.

92. As far as I can tell, there is virtually no discussion of Gershwin's sexuality in the extant literature—outside of some prurient giggling about his sexual immaturity, hypothetical affairs with "starlets" (Paulette Goddard for one), and penchant for prostitutes. Typical is Charles Schwartz: "Considering that he could have had all the free sex he wanted—probably more than he could possibly have handled—one must reasonably ask why he needed recourse to brothels." Schwartz, *Gershwin*, 52, and 47–51 in general. See also Robert Payne, *Gershwin* (London: Robert Hale, 1960), 63.

93. On this, see, for instance, Marcus Klein, *Foreigners: The Making of American Literature, 1900–1940* (Chicago: U of Chicago P, 1981), 130–181.

94. Robert Dorman, *Revolt of the Provinces: The Regionalist Movement in America, 1920–1945* (Chapel Hill: U of North Carolina P, 1993), 149–150; William Stott, *Documentary Expression and Thirties America* (1973; Chicago: U of Illinois P, 1986); Klein, *Foreigners*, 130–181.

95. Charles Hamm, *Putting Popular Music in Its Place* (New York: Cambridge UP, 1995), 313.

96. Kobena Mercer, *Welcome to the Jungle: New Positions in Black Cultural Studies* (New York: Routledge, 1994), 217.

97. Alpert, *Porgy and Bess*, 88; Edward Jablonski, *Gershwin: A Biography* (Boston: Northeastern UP, 1987), 272.

98. My attention was drawn to these articles by Jablonski, *Gershwin*, 273; Gilbreth wrote under the name Ashley Cooper; see *Charleston News and Courier*, 19 June 1934: 12.

99. *Charleston News and Courier*, 29 June 1934: 9A. When Gershwin came back through Charleston the next winter, the same paper made a point of noting that the composer was now several "shades lighter than when he left Charleston." *News and Courier*, 31 January 1935: 7.

100. Torgovnick, *Gone Primitive*, 228.

101. *Charleston News and Courier*, 29 June 1934: 9A.

102. DuBose Heyward in Armitage, *George Gershwin*, 39. The *New York Times* article is from 6 October 1935; I found it in the *Porgy and Bess* clipping file in the Harvard University Theatre Collection.

103. DuBose Heyward in Merle Armitage, *George Gershwin*, 39; see also Edward Jablonski, ed., *Gershwin Remembered* (Portland, Ore.: Amadeus, 1992), 99. The shout story received wide publication at the time (not to mention in the ensuing years); see, for instance, clippings from the *New York Times*, 6 October 1935 and 19 September 1976, in the Harvard University Theatre Collection file on *Porgy and Bess*.

104. Schwartz, *Gershwin*, 316n25. See also Ann Douglas, *Terrible Honesty: Mongrel Manhattan in the 1920s* (New York: Farrar, Straus, and Giroux, 1995), 102–103, for another account which takes Heyward at his word, and adds that no one should be surprised because Gershwin had written "I Got Rhythm" only a few years earlier.

105. Jablonski, *Gershwin*, 273–274; *Charleston News and Courier*, 19 June 1934.

106. Kay Halle in Jablonski, *Gershwin Remembered*, 100; *Charleston News and Courier*, 29 June 1934: 9A.

107. It should be noted that Gershwin did not choose randomly but—per Heyward's stage directions—inserted himself into the lives of Gullahs, widely thought to be "closer" to a root Africanness than any other African Americans. For a good account of the formation of Gullah life and culture, see Charles Joyner, *Down by the Riverside: A South Carolina Slave Community* (Chicago: U of Chicago P, 1984).

108. Armitage, *George Gershwin*, 43; David Ewen, *George Gershwin: His Journey to Greatness* (1956; New York: Ungar, 1980), 230.

109. Ella Shohat notes, for instance, that in the film *High Society* (1956) it is the singing of Bing Crosby which seems to inspire the trumpet playing of Louis Armstrong, and not vice versa. Mark Winokur calls attention to

a similar move made in a 1930 Fred Astaire recording, in which a crowd of African Americans is deeply impressed by Astaire's dance steps, which Astaire learned, of course, from African American dancers. See Mark Winokur, "Black Is White/White Is Black: 'Passing' as a Strategy of Racial Compatibility in Contemporary Hollywood Comedy," in Friedman, *Unspeakable Images*, 202; and Ella Shohat "Ethnicities-in-Relation: Toward a Multicultural Reading of American Cinema," also in Friedman (226).

110. Edward Jablonski, *Harold Arlen: Happy with the Blues* (1961; New York: Da Capo, 1985), 68. See also Ronald Sanders, "The American Popular Song," in Douglas Villiers, ed., *Next Year in Jerusalem: Portraits of the Jew in the Twentieth Century* (New York: Viking, 1976), 197.

111. Armitage, *George Gershwin*, 45. See also Peyser, *Memory of All That*, 44–45, where Peyser argues that it was inevitable that Gershwin sympathized with African Americans because "WASP society treated Jews the way white society treated blacks: in a cold and dismissive way."

112. Peyser, *Memory of All That*, 132; see also Wilfred Mellers, *Music in a New Found Land: Themes and Developments in the History of American Music* (1965; Boston: Faber and Faber, 1987), 392, 397.

113. The play was quite successful during its New York run in 1927; In *Black Manhattan* (1930; New York: Atheneum, 1969), James Weldon Johnson argued that this play "loomed high above every Negro drama that had ever been produced" (211). There was also an abridged radio version featuring Al Jolson which was broadcast in the late 1920s. Alpert, *Porgy and Bess*, 71.

114. Sam Dennison, *Scandalize My Name: Black Imagery in American Popular Music* (New York: Garland, 1982), 467. Michael Rogin has made the fascinating argument that in the 1928 movie *The Singing Fool*, Al Jolson uses blackface "to become mammy and to mourn the loss of his child." Michael Rogin, *Blackface, White Noise*, 144–150.

115. Armitage, *George Gershwin*, 71.

116. Dorothy Heyward and DuBose Heyward, *Porgy: A Play in Four Acts* (1927; New York: Doubleday, Doran, 1928), 7; Alpert, *Porgy and Bess*, 81. In his first interview with the *Charleston News and Courier*, Gershwin said that all "of the spirituals will be original—not that I don't admire the beauty and color of your spirituals—but I want the music to be homogenous." For quotation, see *News and Courier*, 19 June 1934: 12.

117. On Mamoulian, see the *Baltimore Afro-American*, 19 October 1935: 9. See also Alpert, *Porgy and Bess*, 68; and DuBose Heyward's introduction

to the play *Porgy*, xiv–xv. In the play Bess also refers to Crown as being like "a little chil' dat los' its ma" (96).

118. Samuel Floyd, Jr., *The Power of Black Music: Interpreting Its History from Africa to the United States* (New York: Oxford UP, 1995), 218.

119. Thanks are due to Gideon Pollach, who explained this in personal correspondence. Thanks also to Rachel Rubin, who clarified the musicological issues here.

120. Gershwin did, however, already have the necessary knowledge to write a few of the other set pieces—such as "It Ain't Necessarily So" and "There's a Boat Dat's Leavin' Soon"—which are meant to evoke a "jazzier," more urban sound. Interestingly, Ira Gershwin received sole credit on these latter lyrics, for which his brother had already written the music. Apparently Heyward was out of his depth when the lyrics were meant to evoke New York Black as opposed to southern Black. See Alpert, *Porgy and Bess*, 79, 91.

121. It is worth noting that "A Woman Is a Sometime Thing" follows close on the heels of "Summertime" in the opera.

122. James Weldon Johnson and J. Rosamond Johnson, *The Books of American Negro Spirituals* (New York: Viking, 1969), includes *The Book of American Negro Spirituals* (1925) and *The Second Book of Negro Spirituals* (1926) and is still an excellent source of arrangements of spirituals.

123. In an interesting twist on all this, Chicago jazz musician Eddie Condon recalls in his memoirs that during a Carnegie Hall concert in the early 1940s which featured Fats Waller's organ playing, the great keyboardist kept quoting Gershwin's "Summertime" when he was supposed to be playing spirituals. See Eddie Condon, with Thomas Sugrue, *We Called It Music: A Generation of Jazz* (New York: Henry Holt, 1947), 281.

124. It is immediately after the performance of this song that Julie's racial status is thrown into question. Julie, of course, ends up as a singer of "coon" songs after being forced to leave the showboat. For good summaries of the major stage and film productions of this work, see Miles Kreuger, *Show Boat: The Story of a Classic American Musical* (New York: Oxford UP, 1977).

125. Serena's husband has been killed off early on in the opera.

126. "Mother and Child Reunion" is the name of a Paul Simon song from 1970 which stands as another example of a New York Jew adapting a form associated with Black people, in this case reggae music. See Paul Simon's eponymous solo debut album (1972, Warner Brothers) for this song.

127. Cab Calloway and Bryant Rollins, *Of Minnie the Moocher and Me* (New York: Thomas Y. Crowell, 1976), 185. Calloway went on to play Sportin' Life in a revival of the opera in the 1950s.

128. Edward Jablonski and Lawrence Stewart, *The Gershwin Years* (1958; Garden City, N.Y.: Doubleday, 1973), 143.

129. Rogin, "Blackface, White Noise," 421, 431.

130. Artie Shaw, *The Trouble with Cinderella: An Outline of Identity* (1952; New York: Da Capo, 1979); Mezzrow and Wolfe, *Really the Blues*. Additional references to each of these will be made parenthetically in the text.

131. Burton Peretti, *The Creation of Jazz: Music, Race, and Culture in Urban America* (Chicago: U of Illinois P, 1992), 205–206.

132. Pops Foster, as told to Tom Stoddard, *The Autobiography of a New Orleans Jazzman* (Berkeley: U of California P, 1971), 167. See also Al Rose, *I Remember Jazz: Six Decades among the Great Jazzmen* (Baton Rouge: Louisiana State UP, 1987), 17–19; and Calloway and Rollins, *Of Minnie the Moocher and Me*, 258.

133. Peretti, *Creation of Jazz*, 89.

134. See Bernard Wolfe's afterword to Mezzrow and Wolfe, *Really the Blues*, 389–404.

135. Ross, *No Respect*, 79–82.

136. On Mezzrow, see William Kenney, *Chicago Jazz: A Cultural History, 1904–1930* (New York: Oxford UP, 1993), 95.

137. See also Louis Armstrong, *Swing That Music* (1936; New York: Da Capo, 1993), 5–10.

138. For "yomelkeh," see Mezzrow and Wolfe, *Really the Blues*, 201. Incidentally, Mezzrow and Willie the Lion Smith differ on the meaning of the word "hincty": Smith defines it as referring to "low-life" clubs, while Mezzrow defines it as "snobbish." Willie the Lion Smith, with George Hoefer, *Music on My Mind: The Memoirs of an American Pianist* (1964; New York: Da Capo, 1978), 94; Mezzrow and Wolfe, *Really the Blues*, 374.

139. This is in Wolfe's afterword, not the autobiography itself.

140. This takes place as Mezzrow speaks with two chorus girls who are trying to pass for white, but their hipster speech gives them away. They cannot believe Mezzrow is white, because he too can talk the talk.

141. For a more recent example of Jewish white Negroism, see Jerry Wexler's autobiography, *Rhythm and the Blues*, which is similarly full of leads for further study of the musical interactions of African Americans and Jews—and, I should add, also for the study of how "Jewishness" and "Blackness" have circulated in American culture. Jerry Wexler and

David Ritz, *Rhythm and the Blues: A Life in American Music* (New York: Knopf, 1993). See also my "Black and Jew Blues," *Transition* 62 (1993): 106–121.

4. "Lift Ev'ry Voice"

1. James Weldon Johnson and J. Rosamond Johnson, eds., *The Book of American Negro Spirituals,* in *The Books of American Negro Spirituals* (1925–26; New York: Viking, 1969), 28.
2. Quoted in William Kenney, *Chicago Jazz: A Cultural History, 1904–1930* (New York: Oxford UP, 1993), 123.
3. Eugene Genovese, *Roll, Jordan, Roll: The World the Slaves Made* (1972; New York: Vintage, 1976), xv.
4. Jeffrey Decker, "The State of Rap: Time and Place in Hip Hop Nationalism," *Social Text* 34 (1993): 53–84.
5. Houston Baker, Jr., *Modernism and the Harlem Renaissance* (Chicago: U of Chicago P, 1987), 71, 85.
6. Bernard Bell, *The Folk Roots of Contemporary Afro-American Poetry* (Detroit: Broadside, 1974); Arnold Rampersad, *The Art and Imagination of W. E. B. Du Bois* (1976; New York: Schocken, 1990), 74. For Eric Sundquist, see especially *To Wake the Nations: Race in the Making of American Literature* (Cambridge, Mass.: Harvard UP, 1993), 540–625.
7. Robert Hill with Barbara Bair, eds., *Marcus Garvey: Life and Lessons* (Berkeley: U of California P, 1987), xx, liii. As early as 1920 Garvey was making analogies to Zionism. For the need for a "strong nationalism," see the 1920 *New York World* interview with Michael Gold in Hill and Bair, lvi.
8. Alain Locke, ed., *The New Negro* (1925; New York: Atheneum, 1970), 14 (and see also 7–8); Sundquist, *To Wake the Nations,* 574–575.
9. H. Bruce Franklin, *Prison Literature in America: The Victim as Criminal and Artist* (1978; New York: Oxford UP, 1989); 73; Eric Lott, *Love and Theft: Blackface Minstrelsy and the American Working Class* (New York: Oxford UP, 1993), 89–107.
10. In Constance Rourke, *The Roots of American Culture and Other Essays,* ed. Van Wyck Brooks (New York: Harcourt, Brace, 1942), 272.
11. Sundquist, *To Wake the Nations,* 286–287; Burton Peretti, "Music, Race, and Culture in Urban America: The Creators of Jazz" (Ph.D. diss., University of California, Berkeley, 1989), 28.
12. W. E. B. Du Bois, *The Souls of Black Folk* (1903; New York: New American Library, 1969), 265; see similarly Locke, *New Negro,* 199.

13. James Dormon, "Shaping the Popular Image of Post-Reconstruction American Blacks: The 'Coon Song' Phenomenon of the Gilded Age," *American Quarterly* 40.4 (1988): 450–471.

14. Quoted ibid., 458.

15. Benedict Anderson, *Imagined Communities: Reflections on the Origin and Spread of Nationalism* (London: Verso, 1983), 129–140; Raymond Williams, *Keywords: A Vocabulary of Culture and Society* (1976; New York: Oxford UP, 1983), 213–214.

16. Quoted in Dormon, "Shaping the Popular Image," 469n34.

17. We should leave open the very real possibility that the "rags" Gershwin was writing of were those written by his Jewish colleagues. Ira Gershwin, *The Complete Lyrics of Ira Gershwin*, ed. Robert Kimball (New York: Knopf, 1993), 4–5.

18. Quoted in MacDonald Moore, *Yankee Blues: Musical Culture and American Identity* (Bloomington: Indiana UP, 1985), 144.

19. Gene Bluestein, *The Voice of the Folk: Folklore and American Literary Theory* (Amherst: U of Massachusetts P, 1972); see also William Austin, *"Susanna," "Jeanie," and "The Old Folks at Home": The Songs of Stephen C. Foster from His Time to Ours* (1975; Chicago: U of Illinois P, 1987), 42–45.

20. Bluestein, *Voice of the Folk*, 105. See also Bell, *Folk Roots of Contemporary Afro-American Poetry*; Sundquist, *To Wake the Nations*, 254. For a good overview of the "folk" question in American music, see Austin, *"Susanna," "Jeannie," and "The Old Folks at Home,"* 282–316.

21. Bell, *Folk Roots of Contemporary Afro-American Poetry*.

22. Alain Locke, *The Negro and His Music; Negro Art Past and Present* (1936; New York: Arno and the New York Times, 1969), 13.

23. Hasia Diner, *In the Almost Promised Land: American Jews and Blacks, 1915–1935* (Westport, Conn.: Greenwood, 1977), 61.

24. Michael Gold, "What a World," *Daily Worker*, 8 September 1933: 6; see also Charles Edward Smith, "Class Content of Jazz," *Daily Worker*, 21 October 1933: 6; and S. Frederick Starr, *Red and Hot: The Fate of Jazz in the Soviet Union, 1917–1980* (New York: Oxford UP, 1983), 96–99.

25. Gold, "What a World," *Daily Worker*, 8 September 1933: 6. See also Mark Naison, *Communists in Harlem during the Depression* (New York: Grove, 1984), 17–19. S. Frederick Starr criticizes the desire on the part of the Communist Party to see jazz as rural in his *Red and Hot*, 96–102, but the party thesis must be placed in the context of a widespread move to install "folk" materials as crucial to high art. See Marcus Klein, *Foreigners: The Making of American Literature, 1900–1940* (Chi-

cago: U of Chicago P, 1981), 142, 184; finally, see Michael Gold, "What a World," *Daily Worker*, 26 October 1933: 6, where, after discussing the "New Negro," Gold welcomes him as "Comrade John Henry." "What a World" was the name of Gold's regular editorial column.

26. Starr, *Red and Hot*, 99.

27. Charles Edward Smith, "Class Content of Jazz," *Daily Worker*, 21 October 1933: 6.

28. One wonders if he is referring here to the red clay of Manhattan or the Russia of Gershwin's parents. Michael Gold, "What a World," *Daily Worker*, 20 September 1933: 6.

29. Quoted in Edward Jablonski, ed., *Gershwin Remembered* (Portland, Ore.: Amadeus, 1992), 170.

30. Berndt Ostendorf, "Anthropology, Modernism, and Jazz," in Robert O'Meally, ed., *New Essays on Invisible Man* (New York: Cambridge UP, 1988), 100.

31. In Johnson's 1922 preface to *The Book of American Negro Poetry*, for instance, the concept quoted in this passage of text would appear more simply: "As for Ragtime, I go straight to the statement that it is the one artistic production by which America is known the world over. It has been all-conquering. Everywhere it is hailed as 'American music.'" See James Weldon Johnson, ed., *The Book of American Negro Poetry* (1922; New York: Harvest/HBJ, 1969), 11.

32. James Weldon Johnson, *Along This Way: The Autobiography of James Weldon Johnson* (1931; New York: Penguin, 1990), 328.

33. On ragtime and jazz as "national" see especially Lawrence Levine, "Jazz and American Culture," *Journal of American Folklore* 102.403 (1989): 6–22, and Moore, *Yankee Blues*, 73–108.

34. This certainly competes with John Alden Carpenter's famous pronouncement (originally in *Etude*, August 1924: 518) "that the musical historian of the year two thousand will find the birthday of American music and that of Irving Berlin to have been the same."

35. Johnson was also certainly cognizant of, and perhaps folding his work into, the "usable past" rhetoric then in critical vogue. For Van Wyck Brooks's original pronouncement, see *The Dial*, 11 April 1918: 337–41.

36. Moore, *Yankee Blues*, 73–74. See also Alan Howard Levy, *Musical Nationalism: American Composers' Search for Identity* (Westport, Conn.: Greenwood, 1983).

37. In Johnson and Johnson, *Book of American Negro Spirituals*, 38.

38. Paul Joseph Burgett, "Vindication as a Thematic Principle in Alain Locke's Writings on the Music of Black Americans," in Amritjit Singh, William Shiver, and Stanley Brodwin, eds., *The Harlem Renaissance: Revaluations* (New York: Garland, 1989), 139–157.

39. James Weldon Johnson, *Second Book of Negro Spirituals*, in *Books of American Negro Spirituals*, 16. This idea appeared in his preface to *Book of American Negro Poetry* (12–13) in similar form: "Some of these earliest songs were taken down by white men, the words slightly altered or changed, and published under the names of the arrangers."

40. Locke, *Negro and His Music*, 4.

41. Sterling Brown, *The Collected Poems of Sterling A. Brown*, ed. Michael Harper (Chicago: TriQuarterly, 1989), 171.

42. George Schuyler, *Black No More* (1931; Boston: Northeastern UP, 1989).

43. Ibid., 86, 146–148.

44. Herbert Goldman, *Jolson: The Legend Comes to Life* (New York: Oxford UP, 1988), 115.

45. Johnson, *Book of American Negro Poetry*, 11–12. Johnson's timeline seems appropriate. Irving Berlin's ascendancy, beginning with "Alexander's Ragtime Band" (1911), is one way to date the takeover by Jews of the songwriting marketplace.

46. Johnson, *Book of American Negro Poetry*, 20.

47. Langston Hughes, "The Blues I'm Playing," in *The Ways of White Folks* (1934; New York: Vintage, 1971), 110. Hughes's rejoinder is particularly effective because it does not deny the significance of the Jew for the African American artist but instead revalues the example negatively. In naming his character, Hughes might have been thinking of Osceola Blanks, who, according to Abbe Niles, played a significant part in popularizing W. C. Handy's "Memphis Blues." In W. C. Handy, ed., with text by Abbe Niles, *Blues: An Anthology* (1920; New York: Da Capo, 1990), 35.

48. Johnson, *Book of American Negro Poetry*, 16.

49. See, for instance, Clive Bell, "Plus de Jazz," *New Republic*, 21 September 1921: 92–96: "Niggers can be admired artists without any gift more singular than high spirits: so why drag in the intellect?" See also Berndt Ostendorf, *Black Literature in White America* (Totowa, N.J.: Barnes and Noble, 1982), 65–94; and Nathan Huggins, *Harlem Renaissance* (1971; New York: Oxford UP, 1973), 244–301.

50. Claude McKay, *The Negroes in America*, ed. Alan McLeod, (Port Washington, N.Y.: Kennikat, 1979), 62.

51. Diner, *In the Almost Promised Land*, 50–62.

52. Eugene Levy, *James Weldon Johnson: Black Leader, Black Voice* (Chicago: U of Chicago P, 1973), 141–142. This quotation from Johnson should be considered with some caution: it was written to Booker T. Washington, and the ever politic Johnson may not have been entirely averse to writing what might please his audience.

53. Ibid., 93.

54. Ibid., 90.

55. Johnson *Along This Way*, 335.

56. Valerie Smith, *Self-Discovery and Authority in Afro-American Narrative* (Cambridge, Mass.: Harvard UP, 1987); Robert Stepto, *From behind the Veil: A Study of Afro-American Narrative* (1979; Chicago: U of Illinois P, 1991), 3–31.

57. This quotation comes from the preface to the revised edition of *Book of American Negro Poetry*, 7. Johnson repeated the formula often; it can be found in almost exactly the same form in the *Second Book of Negro Spirituals* (22).

58. Johnson, *Second Book of Negro Spirituals*, 20–21.

59. Frantz Fanon develops this theme in his essay "Racism and Culture," in which he argues that "without oppression and without racism you have no blues. The end of racism would sound the knell of great Negro music." This 1956 essay can be found in *Toward the African Revolution* (New York: Grove, 1967), 37.

60. Johnson, *Along This Way*, 152.

61. Johnson, *Book of American Negro Poetry*, 16.

62. Levy, *James Weldon Johnson*, 302–308. Levy points particularly to a review in *The Liberator* written by Floyd Dell, as well as to the success of Ridgely Torrence's "negro play" *Granny Maumee*, as inspiring to Johnson.

63. Levy, *James Weldon Johnson*, 319.

64. Johnson, *Book of American Negro Poetry*, 17.

65. Joseph Skerrett, Jr., suggests that "the period of Johnson's theatrical work was fraught with race-based anxieties and discontent," in "Irony and Symbolic Action in James Weldon Johnson's *The Autobiography of an Ex-Coloured Man*," *American Quarterly* 32.5 (1980): 548.

66. Levy, *James Weldon Johnson*, 88, 93–94. Levy does admit (89) that there is an undeniable suggestion in Johnson's lyrics that "both blacks and whites experienced the same romantic emotions." This alone would make Johnson appear less cautious than Levy suggests.

67. Johnson, *Second Book of Negro Spirituals*, 22. Johnson had already taken

this stance in *Book of American Negro Poetry* (19–20), castigating "native composers" for ignoring the spirituals while rushing to employ "so-called Indian themes" in their work. See also Johnson's admiration of Harry Burleigh, who pointed Dvořák toward the implementation of "Swing Low, Sweet Chariot" in his *From the New World.* James Weldon Johnson, *Black Manhattan* (1930; New York: Atheneum, 1969), 116–117. In the same book (103) Johnson also applauded Will Marion Cook for being "the first competent composer to take what was then known as rag-time and work it out in a musicianly way." Du Bois also classed ragtime as a folk expression, categorizing it as expressive of "the musical soul of a race unleashed" from the bonds of church constrictions. W. E. B. Du Bois, *The Gift of Black Folk: The Negroes in the Making of America* (1924; New York: Washington Square, 1970), 156; and, finally, see Tom Lutz, "Curing the Blues: W. E. B. Du Bois, Fashionable Diseases, and Degraded Music," *Black Music Research Journal* 11.2 (Fall 1991): 137–156.

68. See Edward Berlin, *Reflections and Research on Ragtime* (Brooklyn: Institute for Studies in American Music, Brooklyn College of the City University of New York, 1987), 61. Berlin points out that for Johnson and for his colleagues centered at the Marshall Hotel, ragtime "was valued as an important and unique part of their racial heritage, but its position in the musical hierarchy was as a building block rather than as a finished art form, a basis on which a higher racial music might be erected."

69. Quoted in Levy, *James Weldon Johnson*, 88.

70. As noted earlier, "Under the Bamboo Tree" was a variation on the theme of "Nobody Knows de Trouble I See."

71. Benjamin Lawson, "Odysseus's Revenge: The Names on the Title Page of *The Autobiography of An Ex-Coloured Man*," *Southern Literary Journal* 21.2 (1989): 97n.

72. Johnson, *Book of American Negro Poetry*, 12; and James Weldon Johnson, *The Autobiography of an Ex-Colored Man*, (1912), in John Hope Franklin, ed., *Three Negro Classics* (New York: Avon, 1965), 447.

73. Johnson attended the World's Columbian Exposition of 1893, which is where his friendship with Paul Laurence Dunbar began. See Levy, *James Weldon Johnson*, 40.

74. Johnson, *Book of American Negro Poetry*, 12. Shades of Ishmael Reed!

75. Quoted in Henry Osgood, *So This Is Jazz* (Boston: Little, Brown, 1926), 144.

76. Johnson, *Book of American Negro Poetry*, 13.

77. Carl Van Vechten, Introduction, in *The Autobiography of an Ex-Coloured Man*, (1927; New York: Knopf, 1979), ix.

78. Johnson, *Along This Way*, 136.

79. Levine, "Jazz and American Culture," 10–11.

80. In *Stomping the Blues* (1976; New York: Vintage, 1982), 203, Albert Murray reminds us that "the assumption that folk expression is the unalloyed product of a direct stimulus/response interaction with natural environmental forces is fallacious."

81. Quoted in Jablonski, *Gershwin Remembered*, 169. Arnold Rampersad has written that Langston Hughes's approach to the blues in 1923 was very similar to Gershwin's attempt "the following year . . . to elevate American music." Arnold Rampersad, "Langston Hughes and Approaches to Modernism" in Singh, Shiver, and Brodwin, *Harlem Renaissance: Revaluation*, 65.

82. Gershwin, *Complete Lyrics*, 28–29. See also Deena Rosenberg, *Fascinating Rhythm: The Collaboration of George and Ira Gershwin* (New York: Dutton, 1991), 42.

83. Of course Ira Gershwin's brother was after "highbrow" recognition, but he never gave up writing show tunes either.

84. Murray, *Stomping the Blues*, 205.

85. Krin Gabbard, "The Quoter and His Culture," in Reginald Buckner and Steven Weiland, eds., *Jazz in Mind: Essays on the History and Meanings of Jazz* (Detroit: Wayne State UP, 1991), 102. As Gabbard puts it, bebop quotation may "provide the best example of how jazz artists have used the limited means at their disposal to question their culture's institutionalization of art." For a divergent view, see Gary Giddins, *Riding on a Blue Note: Jazz and American Pop* (New York: Oxford UP, 1981), 154. Instead of irony in bop quotation, Giddins hears mainly sympathy. Of course the most influential modern discussion of such revising comes not in musicology but in Henry Louis Gates, Jr., *The Signifying Monkey: A Theory of African-American Literary Criticism* (New York: Oxford UP, 1988). Although Gates rarely turns to music itself, he does argue that "jazz—and even its antecedents, the blues, the spirituals, and ragtime," are the source of "signifyin(g)," his "trope for black intertexuality in the Afro-American formal tradition" (64; see also 123–124). Also see James Snead, "Repetition as a Figure of Black Culture," in Henry Louis Gates, Jr., ed., *Black Literature and Literary Theory* (New York: Routledge, 1984), 59–79.

86. In J. D. Considine, "Don't Play Duke Ellington Like Haydn," *Baltimore Sun*, 11 April 1993: 5K. This playful declaration is especially effective because the dominant media image of Marsalis is as a dour classicist,

interested primarily in recapitulating the note-for-note content of the works of a few titans (from Miles Davis to Duke Ellington to Louis Armstrong).

5. "Melancholy Blues"

1. Lawrence Levine, *Highbrow/Lowbrow: The Emergence of Cultural Hierarchy in America* (Cambridge, Mass.: Harvard UP, 1988), 85–168. Levine argues that part of this process entailed deprecating popular musical forms. My contention is that the very terms of the "popular" were being reconsidered as part of the work of figuring out what was "high." For a good cautionary note on scholars' use of "sacralization," see Jean-Christophe Agnew, "Times Square: Secularization and Sacralization," in William Taylor, ed., *Inventing Times Square: Commerce and Culture at the Crossroads of the World* (New York: Russell Sage, 1991), 11.
2. Levine, *Highbrow/Lowbrow*, 140.
3. Eric Sundquist, *To Wake the Nations: Race in the Making of American Literature* (Cambridge, Mass.: Harvard UP, 1993), 5–6, 309–313.
4. Gary Giddins has wisely pointed out that even the "blue note," that defining sound of African American music, does not even exist per se, but is "appreciable only in relation to another note" of Western scales. Gary Giddins, *Riding on a Blue Note: Jazz and American Pop* (New York: Oxford UP, 1981), xiii. The exoticizing of African and African American music has always been based on the idea that it was at once simple yet out of reach: as early as 1819, a commentator on Ashanti music suggested that to "have attempted anything like arrangement, beyond what the annexed airs naturally possess, would have altered them, and destroyed the intention of making them known in their original character." See Eileen Southern, ed., *Readings in Black American Music* (New York: Norton, 1983), 15.
5. Lucy McKim Garrison, "Songs of the Port Royal 'Contrabands,'" in Bernard Katz, ed., *The Social Implications of Early Negro Music in the United States* (New York: Arno and the New York Times, 1969), 10; originally printed in *Dwight's Journal of Music*, 8 November 1862.
6. William Eleazer Barton, "Old Plantation Hymns," in Katz, *Social Implications of Early Negro Music*, 81; Sundquist, *To Wake the Nations*, 320; and *New Republic*, 3 February 1926: 292.
7. James Miller McKim, "Negro Songs," in *Dwight's Journal of Music*, 9 August 1862; reprinted in Katz, *Social Implications of Early Negro Music*, 2. Numerous African American musicians throughout the twentieth cen-

tury have recounted how the appearance of spontaneity was required of them whenever they performed. Eubie Blake, for instance, recalled that although he and his bandmates were competent readers, they would fake playing by ear. See Terry Waldo, *This Is Ragtime* (New York: Hawthorne, 1976), 33.

8. See Lawrence Levine, *Black Culture and Black Consciousness: Afro-American Folk Thought from Slavery to Freedom* (New York: Oxford UP, 1977), 17–18; Sundquist, *To Wake the Nations*, 529. Here Sundquist quotes Kelly Miller, who says white men cannot perform black music because they lack the "pathetic quality of voice."

9. Isaac Goldberg, *Tin Pan Alley: A Chronicle of the American Popular Music Racket* (New York: John Day, 1930), 139; Burton Peretti "Music, Race, and Culture in Urban America: The Creators of Jazz" (Ph.D. diss., University of California, Berkeley, 1989), 28; Sundquist, *To Wake the Nations*, 472.

10. In Phyl Garland, *The Sound of Soul* (Chicago: Henry Regnery, 1969), 186.

11. Laurence Bergreen, *As Thousands Cheer: The Life of Irving Berlin* (New York: Viking, 1990), 35. A "Salome" fad had exploded in the United States in 1907–8; by the end of the decade at least one state (Iowa) tried to ban this sexy dancing with an anti-Salome law. See Barbara Grossman, *Funny Woman: The Life and Times of Fanny Brice* (Bloomington: Indiana UP, 1991), 28–29.

12. Michael Rogin, *Blackface, White Noise: Jewish Immigrants in the Hollywood Melting Pot* (Berkeley: U of California P, 1996), 73–120. Of course the film *The Jazz Singer* itself can stand as a summary statement about the fears of second-generation declension. For a journalistic version of a similar story, see Ray Stannard Baker, "The Disintegration of the Jews: A Study of the Synagogues of New York City," in *The Spiritual Unrest* (New York: Frederick Stokes, 1910), 101–141.

13. Quoted in Samuel Charters and Leonard Kunstadt, *Jazz: A History of the New York Scene* (1962; New York: Da Capo, 1981), 79.

14. James Weldon Johnson, *The Book of American Negro Poetry* (1922; New York: Harvest/HBJ, 1969), 41: "The Negro in the United States has achieved or been placed in a certain artistic niche. When he is thought of artistically, it is as a happy-go-lucky, singing, shuffling, banjo-picking being or as a more or less pathetic figure. The picture of him is in a log cabin amid fields of cotton or along the levees. Negro dialect is naturally and by long association the exact instrument for voicing this phase of Negro life; and by that very exactness it is an instrument with but two

full stops, humor and pathos." For an interesting parallel, see Paul Rosenfeld's description of Aaron Copland in *An Hour with American Music* (Philadelphia: J. B. Lippincott, 1929), 136; here Rosenfeld describes Copland's two moods as "nostalgic" and "ironical."

15. I put "cantor" in quotation marks for a few reasons: first of all, it is an Americanization of the Hebrew/Yiddish *hazzan;* second, the popular image of Jewish cantors often confused the role of the cantor with that of the rabbi; and finally, the single word "cantor" cannot do justice to the different stations occupied by the fathers of these men. Whereas Arlen's father held stable, high-status jobs, Berlin's father was something of a journeyman failure. See Mark Slobin, *Chosen Voices: The Story of the American Cantorate* (Chicago: University of Illinois P, 1989); and his "Some Intersections of Jews, Music, and Theater," in Sara Blacher Cohen, ed., *From Hester Street to Hollywood: The Jewish-American Stage and Screen* (Bloomington: Indiana UP, 1983), 30. Others Jewish entertainers who were the sons of cantors include George Burns and the vaudevillian brothers Willie and Eugene Howard.

16. Michael Freedland, *So Let's Hear the Applause: The Story of the Jewish Entertainer* (Totowa, N.J.: Vallentine, Mitchell, 1984), 45, 123.

17. In *American Hebrew*, 27 November 1925: 59.

18. Slobin, *Chosen Voices*, 54, 22. For my understanding of the American cantorate I am indebted to this fine book. See also J. Hoberman, *Bridge of Light: Yiddish Film between Two Worlds* (New York: Museum of Modern Art and Schocken, 1991), 260; Hoberman reports that Cantor Yosele Rosenblatt was "forced to go on the vaudeville stage after he lost all his money in bad investments."

19. Slobin, *Chosen Voices*, 7, 5, 12; Eliyahu Schleifer, "Jewish Liturgical Music from the Bible to Hasidim," in Lawrence Hoffman and Janet Walton, eds., *Sacred Sound and Social Change: Liturgical Music in Jewish and Christian Experience* (Notre Dame: U of Notre Dame P, 1992), 42.

20. Hoberman, *Bridge of Light*, 115, 259; Eric Hobsbawm and Terence Ranger, *The Invention of Tradition* (1983; New York: Cambridge UP, 1993).

21. Mark Slobin, *Tenement Songs: The Popular Music of the Jewish Immigrants* (Chicago: U of Illinois P, 1982), 19–20.

22. Bergreen, *As Thousands Cheer*, 82.

23. *American Hebrew*, 14 October 1927; also quoted in Robert Carringer's introduction to the screenplay of *The Jazz Singer* (Madison: U of Wisconsin P, 1979), 11. Carringer recalls the date as 1917.

24. Sampson Raphaelson's short story "The Day of Atonement" originally

appeared in *Everybody's Magazine*, January 1922; reprinted in Carringer, *The Jazz Singer*, 147.

25. In Herbert Goldman, *Jolson: The Legend Comes to Life* (New York: Oxford UP, 1988), 302.

26. In *Jewish Tribune and Hebrew Standard*, 30 September 1927: 5. Jolson obviously consented to this interpretation of his career, as the evidence of *The Jolson Story*, the 1946 film of his life, attests. Here Jolson is originally formed as a singer when he first, serendipitously, comes upon jazz in New Orleans. He gets hooked on it, of course, and tries to convince his father that, in important respects, jazz is a variant of liturgical music. Young Al tells his father he wants to sing a music "nobody ever heard of before" and the cantor asks, "Is this music so peculiar?"
Al: You sing it all the time papa.
Cantor: You want to sing prayers?
Al: No, no, no, just the feeling in prayers. That what's in the people I'd got it from, and that what's in their music, even when it's fast and happy.

27. Alexander Woollcott, *The Story of Irving Berlin* (New York: G. P. Putnam's Sons, 1925), 13, 86.

28. Max Wilk, *They're Playing Our Song: From Jerome Kern to Stephen Sondheim—The Stories behind the Words and Music of Two Generations* (New York: Atheneum, 1973), 153. Arlen also recalls here that his father used to incorporate the Tin Pan Alley composer's songs into his services. Here, then, is the perfect antidote to *The Jazz Singer*, as the father explicitly gives his approval to the work of the secular son.

29. Raphaelson, "Day of Atonement," 79.

30. Edmund Wilson, *I Thought of Daisy* (New York: Scribner's, 1929), 290–292. As a novelist, Wilson was a mediocre essayist.

31. Ben Hecht, *A Jew in Love* (New York: Covici Friede, 1931), 217. One Hecht biographer claims that this passage makes reference to George Jessel; see William MacAdams, *Ben Hecht: The Man behind the Legend* (New York: Scribner's 1990), 139–140.

32. Constant Lambert, *Music Ho! A Study of Music in Decline* (1934; London: Faber and Faber, 1947), 149. For a similar sentiment from one of Lambert's countrymen, see the quotation from Aldous Huxley in Harry Geduld, *The Birth of the Talkies: From Edison to Jolson* (Bloomington: Indiana UP, 1975), 178. Huxley refers to jazz as dominated by "young Hebrews" playing "mournfully sagging, seasickishly undulating melodies."

33. Irving Howe, with the assistance of Kenneth Libo, *World of Our Fathers*

(New York: Touchstone/Simon and Schuster, 1976), 558; Giddins, *Riding on a Blue Note*, 154. Stephen Whitfield also repeats this mistake in *Voices of Jacob, Hands of Esau: Jews in American Life and Thought* (Hamden, Conn.: Archon, 1984), 161.

34. Deena Rosenberg, *Fascinating Rhythm: The Collaboration of George and Ira Gershwin* (New York: Dutton, 1991), 265–267; Robert Payne, *Gershwin* (London: Robert Hale, 1960), 21.

35. Merle Armitage, ed., *George Gershwin* (New York: Longmans, Green, 1938), 245.

36. Ibid., 55.

37. Mezzrow is thrilled when he adds "Negro inflections" to "Jewish or Hebrew religious music" and they jibe perfectly; and of course Ornitz's singers add "Semitic coloring" to "African rhythms." Mezz Mezzrow and Bernard Wolfe, *Really the Blues* (1946; New York: Citadel Underground, 1990), 316; Samuel Ornitz, *Haunch Paunch and Jowl: An Anonymous Autobiography* (New York: Boni and Liveright, 1923), 148.

38. This, for instance, is what the *Forward* critic had in mind when he wrote of *Green Pastures* that in it "the souls of two nations are woven together." See Hasia Diner, *In the Almost Promised Land: American Jews and Blacks, 1915–1935* (Westport, Conn.: Greenwood, 1977), 81. Zora Neale Hurston's *Moses: Man of the Mountain* (1939; Chicago: U of Illinois P, 1984) participates in similar cultural work.

39. In Abraham Cahan, *"Grandma Never Lived in America": The New Journalism of Abraham Cahan*, ed. Moses Rischin (Bloomington: Indiana UP, 1985), 419.

40. Strikingly and optimistically, Giddins does this in order to explain why jazz musicians have been so attracted to the material of "Gershwin, Arlen, and Berlin . . . as well as Kern, [Richard] Rodgers, Weill, and Johnny Green." Giddins, *Riding on a Blue Note*, 154; Rosenberg, *Fascinating Rhythm*, 46, 58, 298. Also see Isaac Goldberg, *George Gershwin: A Study in American Music* (1931; New York: Frederick Ungar, 1958), 40: "Perhaps our native theorists have over-philosophized the blue note of the Negro, for the most popular scale of the Khassid has a blue note that is quite as cerulean or indigo as the black man's blues maybe."

41. Goldberg, *George Gershwin*, 230; see also on "Funny Face": "It begins Yiddish and ends up black. Put them all together and they spell Al Jolson, who is the living symbol of the similarity" (41). Ben Sidran has released an attempt to combine jazz with Jewish musical forms on a work titled *Life's a Lesson* (Go Jazz, 1994). In a phone conversation (3 March 1994) Sidran—the author of *Black Talk*—told me that he has found broad

points of similarity between Jewish and African American culture, including uses of humor and a matrifocal orientation in the family. I thank Sidran for generously sharing his time and thoughts.

42. In Diner, *In the Almost Promised Land*, 68–69.

43. Samson Raphaelson, *The Jazz Singer* (New York: Brentano's, 1925), 51.

44. This encompasses scenes 180–187 in the film (as marked in the published screenplay). For easy reference, see the screenplay in Carringer, *The Jazz Singer*, 86–87.

45. Ibid., 76–77. In the movie Mary does utter a similar line to Jack, but the next cut is not to the cantor and Moey.

46. Michael Rogin focuses on revenge rather than return, reading *The Jazz Singer* as being mostly about parricide. See Rogin, *Blackface, White Noise*, 81–87. Interestingly, in discussing these second-generation Jews, Isaac Goldberg offered up an analogy which made it seem as if they were third-generation: "From the cantor grandfather to the grandson who yearns 'mammy' songs is no vaster a stride than from the Negro spiritual to the white 'blues.'" Goldberg, *Tin Pan Alley*, 293.

47. Cited in Hoberman, *Bridge of Light*, 121. Hoberman also notes that some "anti–*Jazz Singer*" Yiddish movies were made, in which the return to tradition is even more directly portrayed.

48. In Diner, *In the Almost Promised Land*, 68. No one elaborated on this attraction more fully than Willie the Lion Smith. See his memoir, written with George Hoefer, *Music on My Mind: The Memoirs of an American Pianist* (1964; New York: Da Capo, 1978).

49. In the *Jewish Tribune and Hebrew Standard*, 22 July 1927: 2.

50. Ethel Waters, with Charles Samuels, *His Eye Is on the Sparrow: An Autobiography* (Garden City, N.Y.: Doubleday, 1951), 168. A contemporary critic wrote that Waters "achieved greatness" when she sang "Eli, Eli." Quoted in Arnold Shaw, *The Jazz Age: Popular Music in the 1920's* (New York: Oxford UP, 1987), 64. The song was also incorporated in the all-Black musical *Rhapsody in Black* in 1931. See Gerald Bordman, *American Musical Theater: A Chronicle* (New York: Oxford UP, 1978), 468. Finally, in her 1976 memoir *Singin' and Swingin' and Gettin' Merry Like Christmas* (1976; New York: Bantam, 1981), 18, Maya Angelou recalls hearing "Eli, Eli" and thinking that "the beautiful high melodies and the low moaning sounded very close to the hymns of my youth."

51. Lynnette Geary, "Jules Bledsoe: The Original 'Ol' Man River,'" *Black Perspective in Music* 17.1, 2 (1984): 34.

52. J. P. Telotte, "The Movie Musical and What We 'Ain't Heard' Yet," *Genre* 14.4 (1981): 512; Robert Snyder, *The Voice of the City: Vaudeville and Popular Culture in New York* (New York: Oxford UP, 1989), 112.

53. Leslie Fiedler, "Negro and Jew: Encounter in America," in *No! In Thunder: Essays on Myth and Literature* (Boston: Beacon, 1960), 244. Diner, *In the Almost Promised Land*, 67–68: "Yiddish-speaking New York was enthralled by several black performers who sang Yiddish and Hebrew songs. Reb Tuviah, a black thespian, performed in all the Yiddish theaters, starred in a Yiddish play . . . and according to the *Forward* his rendition of 'Eli, Eli' conveyed more deeply and more movingly the Jewish sorrow, the Jewish martyrdom, the Jewish cry and plea to God, than . . . could have ever been imagined."

54. Hollis Alpert, *The Life and Times of Porgy and Bess: The Story of an American Classic* (New York: Knopf, 1990), 202.

55. MacDonald Moore, *Yankee Blues: Musical Culture and American Identity* (Bloomington: Indiana UP, 1985), 130–145; Cynthia Ozick, "Literary Blacks and Jews" (1972), in Paul Berman, ed., *Blacks and Jews: Alliances and Arguments* (New York: Delacorte, 1994), 93.

56. Further studies of "Black-Jewish relations" might consider other key terms which link the two groups, including "exodus," "diaspora," and "promised land." Paul Gilroy has started this project in the suggestive final chapter of *The Black Atlantic: Modernity and Double Consciousness* (Cambridge, Mass.: Harvard UP, 1993).

57. In Southern, *Readings in Black American Music*, 6.

58. Thomas Wentworth Higginson, *Army Life in a Black Regiment* (1869; Boston: Beacon, 1962), 202, 219–221.

59. Frederick Douglass, *Narrative of the Life of Frederick Douglass* (1845), ed. Benjamin Quarles (Cambridge, Mass.: Belknap/Harvard UP, 1960), 37–38.

60. W. E. B. Du Bois, *The Souls of Black Folk* (1903; New York: New American Library, 1969), 270, 273–274.

61. Albert Murray, *Stomping the Blues* (1976; New York: Vintage, 1982), 54, 87.

62. R. W. S. Mendl wrote this in 1927 in *The Appeal of Jazz*. The quotation is taken from David Meltzer, ed., *Reading Jazz* (San Francisco: Mercury House, 1993), 55.

63. Paul Whiteman and Mary Margaret McBride, *Jazz* (New York: J. H. Sears, 1926), 151.

64. Goldberg, *George Gershwin*, 18.

65. The critic in question, Hans Herman, is quoted in Magnus Hirschfeld, *Racism*, ed. Eden Paul and Cedar Paul (Port Washington, N.Y.: Kennikat, 1938), 70. He did not mean it as a compliment.

66. Lazare Saminsky, *Music of the Ghetto and the Bible* (New York: Bloch, 1934), 5–6.

67. Goldberg, *George Gershwin*, 18.

68. Woollcott, *Story of Irving Berlin*, 86.

69. Ibid., 6–7, 86–87. See also Joan Peyser, *The Memory of All That: The Life of George Gershwin* (New York: Simon and Schuster, 1993), 15; Payne, *Gershwin*, 26, 56. Otto Kahn, financier and patron of the Metropolitan Opera House (and George Gershwin), dissented from the dominant line on Gershwin. In a tribute to the composer written in 1929, Kahn wrote that missing from Gershwin was "the note that sounds a legacy of sorrow, a note that springs from the deepest stirrings of the soul of the race. The American nation has not known the suffering, the tragedies, the sacrifices, the privations, nor the mellow and deep-rooted romance, which are the age-old inheritance of the peoples of Europe." He then goes on to express the hope that Gershwin will have a brief experience of "that driving storm and stress of the emotions . . . which are the most effective ingredients for the deepening and mellowing and the complete development, energizing and revealment, of an artist's inner being and spiritual powers." Otto Kahn, "George Gershwin and American Youth: An Appreciation," offprint from *The Musical Courier*, 22 January 1929, 3–6.

70. Yip Harbug quoted in Wilk, *They're Playing Our Song*, 153. The novelist John O'Hara also noted the "melancholy beauty" in Arlen's work; see Edward Jablonski, *Harold Arlen: Happy with the Blues* (1961; New York: Da Capo, 1985), 145. Gilbert Seldes, writing in 1925, wondered why the "Hebraic strain, the song of exile, the lament of the dispossessed" was so cherished by Americans. *New Republic*, 5 August 1925: 293–294.

71. Raphaelson, "Day of Atonement," 151.

72. As Robert Burton, the "anatomist" of melancholy, put it: "I writ of melancholy, by being busy to avoid melancholy." Quoted in Wolf Lepenies, *Melancholy and Society* (1969; Cambridge, Mass.: Harvard UP, 1992), 13.

73. Raphaelson, "Day of Atonement," 151. See also the play version of *The Jazz Singer*, 48.

74. See Whiteman and McBride, *Jazz*, 295; the 1903 quotation is cited in Tom Lutz, "Curing the Blues: W. E. B. Du Bois, Fashionable Diseases, and Degraded Music," *Black Music Research Journal* 11.2 (Fall 1991): 151.

75. Fred Davis, *Yearning for Yesterday: A Sociology of Nostalgia* (New York: Free Press, 1979), 31.

76. Goldman, *Jolson*, 231.

77. Davis, *Yearning for Yesterday*, 83.

78. Renato Rosaldo, *Culture and Truth: The Remaking of Social Analysis* (Boston: Beacon, 1989), 70.

79. Rogin, *Blackface, White Noise*, esp. 177.

80. Constant Lambert, racist and anti-Semite that he was, captured this movement succinctly in his screed on contemporary music: "The nostalgia of the negro who wants to go home has given place to the infinitely more weary nostalgia of the cosmopolitan Jew who has no home to go home to." Lambert, *Music Ho!* 148.

81. Lepenies, *Melancholy and Society*, 46, 66.

82. Juliana Schiesari, *The Gendering of Melancholia: Feminism, Psychoanalysis, and the Symbolics of Loss in Renaissance Literature* (Ithaca, N.Y.: Cornell UP, 1992), 5–8, 11–12, 15–16.

83. Janice Doane and Devon Hodges, *Nostalgia and Sexual Difference: The Resistance to Contemporary Feminism* (New York: Methuen, 1987), xii, 3.

84. Goldman, *Jolson*, 199. See Chapter 3 for information on Berlin and Gershwin. See also Paul Franklin, "Homosexual Jew(el)ry: Homophobia and Anti-Semitism in the Prosecution of 'Babe' Leopold and 'Dickie' Loeb," paper delivered at the 1993 American Studies Association Conference, Boston.

85. Schiesari, *Gendering of Melancholia*, 32, 112, 94.

86. Ibid., 32.

87. For an interesting triumphalist text, see the eulogy delivered by George Jessel at Jolson's funeral in 1950. Jessel said that Jolson had been an inspiration to those Jewish immigrants early in the century who "sang with lament in their hearts and their voices, always as if they were pleading for help from above." Then Jolson "came on the scene a young man, vibrantly pulsing with life and courage who marched on the stage, head held high with the authority of a Roman emperor, with a gaiety that was militant, uninhibited and unafraid, and told the world that the Jew in America did not have to sing in sorrow but could shout happily about Dixie." Indeed. Quoted in Goldman, *Jolson*, 301–302.

88. Butterfield's line, from 1931, is quoted in Peter Novick, *That Noble Dream: The "Objectivity Question" and the American Historical Profession* (New York: Cambridge UP, 1988), 13.

89. Nicholas Tawa, *A Sound of Strangers: Musical Culture, Acculturation, and*

the Post–Civil War Ethnic American (Metuchen, N.J.: Scarecrow, 1982), 154.

90. David Ewen, *George Gershwin: His Journey to Greatness* (1956; New York: Ungar, 1980), 229–230.

91. Quoted from Burton Peretti, *The Creation of Jazz: Music, Race, and Culture in Urban America* (Chicago: U of Illinois P, 1992), 189 (ellipsis and lack of quotation marks around "Eli, Eli" in original).

92. Quoted in Wilk, *They're Playing Our Song*, 152–153.

93. Raphaelson, "Day of Atonement," 151; Max Kaminsky, with V. E. Hughes, *My Life in Jazz* (New York: Harper and Row, 1963), 193; Telotte, "Movie Musical," 512.

94. Allen Ginsberg, "Howl" (1955–56), in *Howl and Other Poems* (San Francisco: City Lights, 1959), 16; Jerome Weidman, *The Enemy Camp* (New York: Random House, 1958), 523–524. Thanks are due to Rachel Rubin for alerting me to the Weidman book.

95. Stephen Sherill, "Don Byron," *New York Times Magazine*, 16 January 1994: 20.

96. Robert Bone, *Down Home: Origins of the Afro-American Short Story* (1975; New York: Columbia UP, 1988), 222.

97. Jean Toomer, *Cane* (1923; New York: Liveright, 1975), 14. All further references to "Fern" will be made parenthetically in the text.

98. Sander Gilman, *The Jew's Body* (New York: Routledge, 1991), 169–193.

99. Emily Miller Budick, in a personal communication, has suggested to me that the focus on Fern's evocative eyes might also be considered as part of the tradition of "dark-eyed Rebeccas" familiar to readers of nineteenth-century American and British literature.

100. It is not necessarily true that Fern is the child of a Jewish father and an African American mother. We do not know, as some critics have suggested, where Fern got her last name, and we certainly do not know that she was the direct result of a mixed relationship. Without stepping too far into a currently raging debate, one can say that the assumption that Fern's Jewish last name can only have entered her family line in a recent generation erases the possibility that people named Rosen might once have owned slaves and hence passed the family name on in that way. The African American writer Chester Himes, for instance, claimed that his last name came from a Jewish slave owner named Chaim—hence "Chaim's." See John A. Williams, "My Man Himes: An Interview with Chester Himes," in John A. Williams and Charles Harris, eds., *Amistad 1* (New York: Vintage, 1970), 82. Rachel Rubin has suggested in personal correspondence that the nail on Fern's porch which seems to keep her

locked in place—added with the evidence of her last name, which implies resurrection—underlines her connection to Jesus Christ, another Jew.

101. Barbara Johnson, citing Paul de Man, reminds us that metaphor, with its illusion of necessity, has throughout literary history been privileged over metonymy, in which the relationship of contiguity is often seen as resting on mere chance. See Barbara Johnson, "Metaphor, Metonymy, and Voice in *Their Eyes Were Watching God*," in Henry Louis Gates, Jr., ed., *Black Literature and Literary Theory* (New York: Routledge, 1984), 208

102. David Roediger, *The Wages of Whiteness: Race and the Making of the American Working Class* (New York: Verso, 1991), 180.

103. See ibid., 11–13; and W. E. B. Du Bois, *Black Reconstruction in America, 1860–1880* (1935; New York, Atheneum, 1969), 700.

104. On Hollywood moguls and their meanings, see Neal Gabler, *An Empire of Their Own: How the Jews Invented Hollywood* (New York: Crown, 1981); Andrew Heinze, *Adapting to Abundance: Jewish Immigrants, Mass Consumption, and the Search for American Identity* (New York: Columbia UP, 1990), 203–218.

105. My understanding of the importance of the category of "producer" is derived in large part from Michael Denning, *Mechanic Accents: Dime Novels and Working-Class America* (New York: Verso, 1987), esp. chaps. 7 and 9.

Epilogue

1. Glenn Loury, "The End of an Illusion," in *One by One from the Inside Out: Essays and Reviews on Race and Responsibility in America* (New York: Free Press, 1995), 13; Paul Berman, "The Other and the Almost the Same," *New Yorker*, 28 February 1994: 71. Leslie Fiedler predicted this turn of affairs in 1966, when he ended his essay "Negro and Jew" with the fear that optimism about the implications of romantic relationships between Jewish women and African American men—his own sense of hope included—was bound to lead to a hefty share of disillusion. See his "Negro and Jew" in vol. 2 of *The Collected Essays of Leslie Fiedler* (New York: Stein and Day 1971), 174. I should also note here that a familiar argument in the literature on leftist movements in America is that Jewish women were particularly likely to become romantically involved with African American men. A nice summary of this belief can be found in Barbara Probst Solomon's novel *Smart Hearts in the City* (New York: Harcourt Brace Jovanovich, 1992), esp. 147.

2. Berman, "The Other and the Almost the Same," esp. 66, 68. See, for a less hopeful vision, Henry Louis Gates, Jr., "Black Demagogues and Pseudo-Scholars," *New York Times*, 20 July 1992: A13, where Gates laments that these "are times that try the spirit of liberal outreach."

3. Alfred Uhry, *Driving Miss Daisy* (1986; New York: Theatre Communications Group, 1988), 20–24.

4. Ibid., 38.

5. It is interesting to note, at least in passing, that *actual* relationships between Jews and African Americans have resulted in *real* children who are *both* Black and Jewish. It will continue to be fascinating to see how such dual identities will be worn and received. The jacket copy on Laurence Thomas's recent comparative philosophical inquiry into the Holocaust and African American slavery (*Vessels of Evil*) provides one example: according to this blurb, Thomas is uniquely "qualified to write this book as an African American and a Jew." See Laurence Mordekhai Thomas, *Vessels of Evil: American Slavery and the Holocaust* (Philadelphia: Temple UP, 1993).

6. Eve Kosofsky Sedgwick uses the phrase in a number of places in *Epistemology of the Closet* (Berkeley: U of California P, 1990), 20–21.

7. In Henry Louis Gates, Jr., "Thirteen Ways of Looking at a Black Man," *New Yorker*, 23 October 1995: 59.

8. Michael Lerner and Cornel West, *Jews and Blacks: A Dialogue on Race, Religion, and Culture in America* (New York: Plume, 1995). On this general impulse, see also Michael Rogin, *Blackface, White Noise: Jewish Immigrants in the Hollywood Melting Pot* (Berkeley: U of California P, 1996), 73–120.

9. Maya Angelou, *Gather Together in My Name* (1974; New York: Bantam, 1990), 2. This, too, is one of the morals of the 1992 documentary *The Liberators* (directed by William Miles and Nina Rosenblum). This film focuses on the African American 761st Tank Battalion, which played a role in liberating concentration camps (although their exact involvement is still a matter of dispute). *The Liberators* is an important work which visibly moved many in the audience I saw it with at Harvard University, and I have no desire to be cynical about it. But in some respects it seemed a too-perfect antidote for the increasingly popular fear developing at this time that Black-Jewish relations was really the story of Jews controlling African Americans. What better way to refute this than with powerful images of African Americans literally carrying emaciated Jews to safety? Whereas the rhetoric of Black-Jewish relations has frequently implied a situation whereby Jews show African Americans how to become full-

fledged American citizens, in *The Liberators* it is African Americans who are the Americans, and who appear almost by magic, to protect the remaining Jews of Europe.

10. Harper Lee, *To Kill a Mockingbird* (1960; New York: Warner, 1982), 244–245.

11. Ibid., 247.

12. Gary Giddins, *Rhythm-a-ning: Jazz Tradition and Innovation in the '80s* (New York: Oxford UP, 1985), 148. This overstates the case quite a bit, especially considering that Jewish producers still exerted a major influence on Black music in the 1950s.

13. Andrew Ross, *No Respect: Intellectuals and Popular Culture* (New York: Routledge, 1989), 97. Ross offers this conclusion during a discussion of 1960s soul music, a form that gave rise to few white starring performers.

14. See, for instance, Frank Rich's opinion piece in the *New York Times*, 6 February 1994: E17.

15. Gloria Naylor, *Bailey's Cafe* (1992; New York: Vintage, 1993), 220–221.

16. Ibid., 227.

17. It is also worth mentioning that even though this child—the son of a Black and Jewish mother who swears no man has ever touched her—will be put up for adoption, the most profound sense as the novel ends is that he is the surrogate son of Gabe and Bailey, brought together in one more chaste marriage with "separate beds." The child's birth mother was named Mariam, a possible combination of Mary and Miriam (who watched over the infant Moses); attached to the secular transcendence implied by "George," then, is the hint that this Black Jewish child is both Moses and Jesus.

18. Edward Jablonski, *Gershwin: A Biography* (Boston: Northeastern UP, 1987), 2–3.

Index